Strafford

The Posthumous Memoirs of Thomas Wentworth, First Earl of Strafford

Volume 1 of a Trilogy

In the Beginning

A Novel by

T. G. Stanton

Strafford

Part 1: In the Beginning

All Rights Reserved

© T.G.Stanton 2025

The right of T.G.Stanton to be identified as the author of this work has been asserted by him in accordance with the Copyright, Designs and Patents Act, 1988.

All rights reserved. No part of this publication may be reproduced, stored in a retrieval system, or transmitted, in any form or by any means (electronic, mechanical, photocopying, recording or otherwise) without the prior written permission of the publisher and author.

ISBN: 978-1-7638043-6-4

For information address tez_stanton@hotmail.com

Dramatis Personae.

Thomas Wentworth, later Earl of Strafford.

Sir William Wentworth, Baronet, Thomas's father.

Henry Clifford, later Earl of Cumberland, Thomas's school-friend, and brother-in-law.

Christopher Wandesford, Thomas's school-friend and colleague in Government.

Margaret Clifford, Henry Clifford's sister, and Thomas's first wife.

George Radcliffe, Thomas's friend and colleague in Government.

Sir Arthur Ingram, Thomas's close business acquaintance and entrepreneur.

Sir John Savile, one of Thomas's enemies, a Yorkshire magnate.

Lionel Cranfield, later the Earl of Middlesex, the Treasurer.

Richard Weston. Replaces Cranfield as Treasurer.

Sir Edward Osborne, a friend of Thomas's and his Vice-President on the Council of the North.

George Villiers, Duke of Buckingham, James I's 'favourite', and then Charles I's best friend.

Charles I, King of England from 1625.

Queen Henrietta Maria, Charles's wife.

Arabella Holles, daughter of Earl Clare, Thomas's second wife and mother of his son William and daughters Arabella and Anne (Nan).

William Laud, rising clergyman and ultimately Archbishop of Canterbury, Thomas's close colleague and friend.

John Pym, one-time Parliamentary colleague of Thomas, and later his bitter enemy.

Thomas

I wasn't a good man; I can see that now. Mind you, I thought I was pretty good at the time, trying to do what I thought was honourable, endeavouring to be honest. At least I didn't attribute all my deeds to God, like that hypocrite Oliver Cromwell. On the other hand, I don't think I was an entirely bad fellow, either, but I recognise that a lot of people perceived me, and still do, as always acting entirely in my own interests, which isn't entirely true. After all, the very last scene of my life could hardly be said to have been in my interests, yet it was a piece of theatre I had crafted completely, most wittingly, on my own. True enough, there were hundreds, if not thousands, of people who were very anxious indeed to have a part in that play, but if it hadn't been for what I wrote to the King at the end, they might have been deprived of the opportunity.

However, that all comes later, much later.

In preparing this account of my life, I have called upon a number of people I knew, some of them friends, some of them anything but, who are up here too. They have contributed, as best they can, in their own words, what happened; what they thought about me at the times of which they write.

Why am I writing this now? Many serious books have been written about me. The authors have either liked me or loathed me. I want to set the record straight. I want to show people the real me. I hope I can.

This is my story.

In The Beginning.

Thomas. 8th October, 1599. Rotherham, Yorkshire

I had never seen so many people milling about; the noise was tremendous.

"Who are all these people, Father? Where have they come from?"

Sir William Wentworth grasped my hand more tightly, dragged me along in his wake as fast as my six-year-old legs would carry me. "They are the people of Rotherham, and from the surrounding villages and farms and hamlets. When …."

"What is a hamlet, Father?"

"What are you on about, boy?" He sounded a bit crusty, but he was a loving Father, kind, gentle, but firm in his handling of me and the other children.

"Hamlet. Isn't it …."

"A hamlet is a very small collection of houses, maybe five, or ten."

Sir William stopped; looked at me affectionately. "Now Thomas, you have to stop asking questions all the time. People who do that are called lawyers, like your Grandfather Atkinson. And you don't want to become one of those, whatever you do! Now come along, or we shall be late." We started off again, picking our way carefully between the people, wicker crates of chickens stacked on the ground, cow-pats, horse droppings.

"Why have they all come here?"

"It's Rotherham market day. See that woman over there? She's selling bread, and that one's got a barrow full of turnips and vegetables. And there, behind those hurdles, the farmers have brought their cows and sheep to market to sell."

I stopped in my tracks; Sir William lost his grip, having to come back for me. "Why is that man sitting on the ground, Father? And what has happened to his legs? Why are they stuck through that plank?"

"Thomas, that is a very naughty man. He's a robber, a thief. He is in the stocks – that's the plank of wood. Actually it's two planks, and they trap his legs so that he can't get out. The Justices of the Peace have made him sit there for three days to teach him not to steal again, warning other people not to steal either."

"What is a justitches?"

"Will you please stop asking questions for a minute? I'll tell you about Justices when you are old enough to understand."

"That's what my sister always says – that I'm too little to understand."

"When did she say that?"

"When I asked her why she goes to wee-wee sitting down and I do it standing up."

"Quite right too. And a very bright answer considering she's only seven herself."

I did not give up. "But why has the man got apple squashed in his hair, and clods of mud on his face and clothes?"

"Because the local folk, especially the ones he robbed, throw things at him."

"That's not fair. He can't throw anything back. Look. His arms are in those other planks."

"I think you really will have to be a lawyer after all. Anyway he should have thought of that before he started stealing."

"Where are we going?"

"I told you. I'm taking you to see a friend of mine to play with his son whilst I go to the Quarter Sessions and …."

Suddenly a stentorian voice shouted out from across the other side of the street: "Wentworth!!" To our right a large man on a large black horse glared at Father, who immediately transferred me from his right to his left, as though to protect me from the newcomer. He took my hand again, so hard it hurt.

"Wentworth, I say!!" The man shouted again. He was a very big man indeed, bigger than Father, looking even more gigantic astride his horse. Until then I had always thought my Father the tallest man in the world. The man was dressed in burgundy coloured velvet with gold slashings in the sleeves, and a large earring. His broad hat was of the same hue as his knickerbockers suit, surmounted by two or three large feathers. He whipped his steed's neck with the reins and moved across the street towards us. The contrast between this magnificent if frightening personage and my father's rather puritanical black costume was startling.

"Have you nothing to say, Sir?" shouted the man.

"Should I have anything to say to you, Sir Thomas? Do you expect me to know what you think I might say? I'm no mind reader. You may be given to shouting loudly in the street, but I am not."

The man laughed, shouted again. "You always were a pusillanimous clod, Wentworth. And now you're interfering with my tenants, damn your hide."

Looking down at me, my Father must have seen that I was quite terrified. Determining to try to keep the peace, he replied gently: "I haven't the slightest idea what you're talk – yelling – about."

"That blaggard Holt. You've been lending him money."

"I don't deny it, but he's no blaggard. He's a good man, an excellent farmer, and a kind neighbour. Last year when my daughter Anne fell in the village pond, he dived in and rescued her."

"Good man be damned. He's a peasant. If you're lending money to scum like him you can't be much better."

Father smiled. "Sir Thomas, we are both Justices of the Peace, we are not setting a peaceful example, and we…."

"Peaceful example be buggered. I haven't finished with you. I'll see you on the Bench later." He spurred his horse away.

I trembled: "Who was that, Father?"

"Sir Thomas Reresby, one of our neighbours."

"No-one is ever going to talk like that to me, Daddy. I'll thrash the man who tries".

Father smiled again: "Well, son, you're a bit on the small side for that yet. Come on, I'll not leave you now. I'll take you to Court and you can sit at the back."

The Court seemed huge, was full of people of all sorts and shapes and sizes. Before the cases started my Father and the nasty man were up on the bench, and appeared to be talking angrily to each other; at least, Sir Thomas seemed angry. He shouted very loudly, "A turd in your teeth, Wentworth, you're a rascal, a villain; a coward who dares not draw a sword. I sent you a challenge a while ago, but you were too afraid to accept it."

My Father was rather quieter, but I could still hear him. "You're wrong, Sir Thomas. I am not afraid but we are …"

Suddenly Sir Thomas grabbed my Father's collar, hit him in the face and then pushed him off the Bench, holding onto his ears and pulling Father about by them. Papa tried to pull him off, but as the man had so firm a grip this just made his pain worse and he cried out. Their retainers leaped forward to join in the quarrel, daggers drawn and clearly ready for use. Two other justices seized Reresby, pulling him away as three others came between the servants and commanded them to sheath their weapons.

Pandemonium ruled for a while, until the magistrates called the watch and the constables. At last calm prevailed, but in the most frigid atmosphere. Father got up. He was shaken, but did not retaliate. I was even more determined that no-one would ever treat me like that.

Father was in no fit state to hear any cases; he came to the back of the Court and took me home. He was bleeding from the ears; the skin was torn where the lobes join the jaw-line. He told me nothing more then about Sir Thomas Reresby. That day of violence was my earliest clear memory.

****

As we went home I asked Father what had happened, but I was too young to understand. Some years later he told me that Reresby and he had quarrelled a couple of years before about the ownership of some farm land. At least, Reresby was suggesting that by lending money to his tenant, Holt, my Father was pretending that he was the owner of the farm Holt rented in Sir Thomas's manor in part of Hooton Roberts. After the quarrel, Reresby sent his uncle to our house to ask Father if it were true that he had said he wanted to fight a duel with Reresby. Father sent the uncle back with a message that he had no intention of fighting, having said nothing of the sort. He bore Sir Thomas no malice; as far as he was concerned the quarrel was over and done with.

The two men did not see each other again until the Court Session. A prisoner had escaped; there was some difficulty about empanelling a jury, and Reresby made these problems an excuse for challenging Father to a duel. He declined to fight, and Reresby hit him. Papa was never a bold fighting type, but the two magistrates who rescued him were so appalled at what had happened that they reported it to the Star Chamber. This was a very strict and powerful Court which dealt particularly with the prosecution of rich, mighty people. Reresby was fined one thousand pounds. That was an enormous sum of money.

He was also removed from the Commission of the Peace so he could no longer sit as a magistrate.

When I was somewhat older and thought about this, I learned a lot from it. First, rich and powerful people can't do just what they like and get away with it (unless they are very rich and powerful indeed). Secondly, it is better to be peaceful and law-abiding (like Father), if you could.

Thirdly, if you use the law properly you can make other people do what you want, or stop them doing things you don't want. Father had said to me earlier that day that I shouldn't become a lawyer, but it was a bit of a joke, because Mum's Father was a lawyer; many young men of the landed classes went to the Inns of Court to learn about the law even if they didn't want to be advocates. So when I was fourteen, and sent off to the Inner Temple, I was very happy about it. If you think you can run two manors, manage a lot of farms and tenants without some knowledge of the law, let alone go into politics, you need to think again. I was not to be content with just two manors, or a lowly rung on the political ladder.

Around the time Father told me all about Reresby something else happened which taught me the value of knowing the law. Thomas Gargrave was my Uncle; he was married to Father's sister. He was arrested for murdering one of his servants. He must have done it because no-one in their right mind would do what he did otherwise. When the case came to Court, he refused to plead Guilty or Not Guilty. He wasn't tried for the crime after all. No. He was punished for refusing to plead. The Sheriff and the constables laid him out, slowly heaped heavy slabs of stone on top of him; he wasn't fed either. Gradually he starved, or was crushed, to death, or both. It took days. Most people gave up long before that and entered a plea. But not Uncle Thomas Gargrave. He stuck it out to his bitter end.

Why did he do that? He knew that if he were tried and found guilty he would hang, and if he was hanged, all his land, all his goods, and all his money would be forfeit to the King. But if he died under this punishment for not pleading, his fortune would be safe for his family.

Still, you might say he wasted his breath if he hadn't had it all squeezed out of him. He was in financial trouble when he was killed, and his land fell into the hands of a grasping swindler called Sir Arthur Ingram. You'll hear more of him later.

****

I was born in London on Good Friday, 13th April, 1593. It wasn't too bad. My mother had already had my older brother (but he died soon after I appeared), and my sister Anne, so she was getting quite good at it. She needed to be; she was going to have another eight babies in the next sixteen years - they all lived. I don't think she lost any in child-bed, as it used to be called.

My mother was an Atkinson, daughter of Sir Robert, a pretty wealthy chap with thousands of acres of land at Stowell in Gloucestershire, most of those acres packed with sheep, most of the sheep producing lots of wool to be spun and woven by the people (peasants, we called them), who lived in hovels and cottages in the hamlets and villages on those acres. Sir Robert's carts trundled the lanes round his acres collecting the wool and the cloth, taking it to the markets, sometimes to Bristol to be shipped to France, Spain, and later to the American colonies. Some of the ships were Sir Robert's too, and all the money from all those enterprises came back to him. So, yes, he was a pretty wealthy chap. He was also a barrister of Lincoln's Inn, with a house in Chancery Lane.

And he was my grandfather. Of course, I didn't know that then, when the midwife stuck me on my mother's lovely nipple for the first time. But my mother, Anne, was Sir Robert's only child, his heiress. I didn't know that either, but one day Sir Robert would die, and leave a generous slice of it to my mother. Then she'd leave me to manage it all for her, and I'd be good at it. When she died I'd give a proper share to my siblings, which I did, which shows, as I said at the start, that I wasn't all bad.

Good Friday is the day of the ultimate sacrifice. What sort of omen would my birth on the 13th of April 1593 prove to be for me?

I was christened Thomas Wentworth nine days later in London. St. Dunstan's in the West is a funny little London church in Fleet Street. Inside it is a very holy place; calm, peaceful, difficult to remember that a few yards away, just beyond the oak doors, hundreds of people, dozens of carts, wagons, and carriages, are shouting and milling about.

Everyone in Tudor England believed in God, and for many people the way you were supposed to worship Him and pray to Jesus was a passion. People had been dying for it in England for the best part of that century after King Henry parted company with the Pope. All this dying for faith or religion – well, for religion, anyway, since if the people had stopped to think about it they'd have seen that their faith is all the same – was a tragic waste of life and time.

Why did this happen in London, when our home was in Yorkshire, at Wentworth Woodhouse, where my father was lord of the manor? Well, as I say, my grandfather was a pretty wealthy chap, and he could afford a nice house in London, in Chancery Lane. We were staying there when my Mother realised I was on my way. We always went to St Dunstan's when we stayed at Grandfather's.

His was a tall and narrow house with a winding stair up the middle, built of dark grey bricks set between grey oak beams. London burns coal from Durham and Newcastle. The smoke from the coal fires was turning London black.

Thomas. September, 1601. Well, Yorkshire

He is fair haired, with a golden skin, an inch or two taller than me. He is quite different from me, since I am quite pale, my hair dark, almost black. He is the first person I see as I walked into the garden of the strange looking house. What is strange is that, although it is a Tudor house of black oak beams and white plaster, there seems to be an awful lot of black oak, only small spaces of white. It is the home of Dr John Higgins. He runs it as a small private school for sons of the gentry.

The boy walks along a path at the edge of the lawn. Like me he is dressed in grey clothes with a small lace collar. He is engrossed in a book, taking no heed of his surroundings. On the other side of the path lies a knot garden of low box hedge, the dark green leaves highlighted by the tiny red berries. It is odd I remembered that, because I'm not much interested in nature and plants and flowers. I can only put this impression down to the effect what happens next has on me.

As I watch him, two larger boys come running along the path behind him, and quite deliberately cannon into him as they pass. Knocked off his feet, he falls over the box hedge into the knot garden. His book drops on the path and one of these bullies stamps on it. They run on, laughing and shouting: "Swotty Wandy! Swotty Wandy!"

I look around. No-one else is in sight. I walk swiftly to the boy, step over the hedge, crouching down beside him. "Are you alright?"

He rolls over onto his back. "Alright, I think." He has a blob of mud on the end of his nose, and his hands and knees are muddy too. He wipes the mud from his nose with the back of his hand, so I take my handkerchief from my sleeve and offer it to him. Having wiped his nose and hands with it, he gives it back. "Thanks," he says.

"What was that all about?"

"What was what all about?"

"Them bowling you over like that!"

"Oh, that! Nothing really. Happens all the time. To me, anyway."

I remember old Reresby hitting my father, and how I had promised myself that I should never let anyone do anything like that to me. "And what was it they shouted at you? Sounded like 'Swotty Wandy'."

The boy laughs in an oddly sad sort of way. "That's it. They knock me about because I'm no good at sport. No, they call me Swotty because I'm always wandering about with my head in a book."

"I'm Thomas; Thomas Wentworth."

"And I'm Christopher Wandesford. You can call me Kit if you like. That's what my Father calls me." We shake hands. "Do you have any friends?"

"No. I only got here last night. You can call me Tom, if you like. No-one else does." I get up and cross the hedge to pick up his book. The spine is broken; some pages fell out. I pick them up, go back, and give him the sorry bundle. "Is that a school book?"

"No, it's mine, I'm glad to say. I can't think what the Head would do if it was his. I've been here three weeks. We've both got a friend now. That's if you want to be friends with me." He smiles shyly as he says this. I grab his hand again. "We'll always be friends! And I won't let those idiots bully you again!"

"Don't be silly. You're not as big as me, and they're even taller."

I let go of his hand, standing as tall as I can. "Well, I'm not afraid of them. I'm not afraid of anybody. Anyway, if we're friends we can beat them together."

"How?"

"I don't know. But I'll think of something." I look at him again. Why do small boys always want to know how old other small boys are? Well anyway, I asked him.

"I'm nine. How old are you?"

I had felt so ashamed that this boy is at least an inch, maybe two, taller than me, but now I know that I am his junior by a year! "I was eight in April. But I'm going to be taller soon!" Christopher laughs.

Christopher. 1601. Well, Yorkshire

Boys of eight make lots of rash statements and promises, but the promise of friendship from this Thomas - Tom - was one that was to last, and bring me enormous benefits. If I hadn't been sent to Dr Higgins' school I might never have met him, nor Henry, of whom more later. Well, maybe I'd have met Tom, because it turned out he only lived a few miles from us at Wentworth, and his Father and mine had known each other a long time.

Dr Higgins was the Dean of Ripon Cathedral, and an acquaintance of my Father's. The good Doctor accommodated a few boys for tuition at his home in Well, which was about fifteen miles away from Ripon. He was as unlike a priest or Dean as anyone could imagine – over six feet tall, with massive shoulders and a barrel of a body, he looked more like one of the wrestlers who toured the country taking on all comers at the fairs. Even so, he was a kindly man and Godly, but it was a foolish pupil – or adult, come to that – who got on the wrong side of him. He had an odd saying, too. When faced with a recalcitrant and guilty student who played the unlikely innocent he would shout: "Do you think I'm deaf, dumb, blind and silly?" All the boys knew this phrase by heart.

****

A few days after the incident in the knot garden Thomas and I were playing catch on the lawn. I was calling him Tom by then. Behind him the windows of the Headmaster's study overlooked the grass. Tom had taken it upon himself to try to get my limbs and muscles to coordinate, to see if I could develop an eye for a ball. That all sounds very altruistic, but as the years went by I found that much of what Tom stood for was altruistic, especially where an underdog – like me – was concerned. Actually, I wanted to be able to play the games my friend liked. I wasn't averse to sport; I just couldn't do it. We'd been playing for about ten minutes with quite a hard ball and I was beginning to get the hang of it – good thing as this was the third day in a row we'd been practising. Then I caught sight of the two boys who had knocked me down. I'd known them some time, and I'd told Tom that their names were Chesworth and Clifford. Chesworth looked strong, with ears that rather stuck out. He was taller than me, but not as tall as Clifford. They were coming our way and laughing. I was sure they had some little scheme to annoy us, or me, at any rate. Still, I pretended to take no notice.

I threw the ball to Tom. One of the boys – the one called Clifford, a tall, slim chap - leapt in between us, seized the ball, and threw it to Chesworth. I was surprised when Tom ran up to him and said: "It's our ball. Give it back."

"Say please!"

"Please give it back."

"Sod off." With that he pushed Tom hard in the chest and Tom fell flat.

I heard Clifford say: "You didn't have to do that, Chesworth. We were just going to nick their ball!"

The red mist came down. Where did my normal timidity go? I shouted out: "Chesworth. You're a flea-ridden bully." And I stuck my tongue out.

Chesworth threw the ball at me as hard as he could. I ducked. There was a crash of broken glass. Chesworth was running towards me. Suddenly I was afraid. I started to run but had hardly moved when the loudest voice I had ever heard shouted: "Chesworth! Come here at once!" Chesworth stopped, and I fell over. I looked round and up and there, looking through three small, broken, diamond-shaped panes in the latticed window was the face of Dr Higgins. "All of you, come to my study immediately!"

Two minutes later, Thomas and I, Chesworth and Clifford, were standing in the study. Higgins stood in front of us with his back to the fire. I could see his cane grasped in both hands behind his back. "What was that all about?"

Chesworth replied: "Just a bit of fun, Sir?"

"I do not find three broken pieces of my window fun, Chesworth."

Chesworth made his first mistake. "It was these two, Sir. They were playing with their ball."

"Do you think I'm deaf, dumb, blind and –"

" – Silly." Chesworth made his second mistake.

Dr Higgins roared again: "First you break my window, then you lie to me – yes lie, Chesworth – I saw you throw the ball; and then you dare to poke fun at my idiosyncrasies?"

Clifford said: "We're sorry about the window."

"You are part of this bullying enterprise, Clifford."

To my own amazement I stepped forward. "Excuse me, Sir, but Clifford only caught the ball. He didn't push Wentworth over or break the window."

Higgins looked at Tom. "Is that right, Wentworth?"

"Yes, Sir, and he didn't like it that Chesworth pushed me over. I heard him say so."

Chesworth, standing next to Tom, whispered: "I'll get you for this, runt."

Higgins told me, Tom, and Clifford to leave. He ordered Chesworth to remain for what he called a little gentle improvement session with the cane. As we walked off down the passage to the accompaniment of the swish of the cane and the squeals of Chesworth, Clifford grabbed me by the shoulder. I thought he was going to hit me, but Tom pushed him off, and snarled: "Leave him alone!"

Clifford was shocked. "Look," he said, "I was just going to thank him for sticking up for me like that. Specially after we've been so rotten to him in the past." He turned to me. "It was really decent of you."

I laughed. "Say no more. Anyway, I can't help it. I'm addicted to telling the truth."

Tom then introduced himself and me, and that is how we met Henry Clifford properly.

Thomas. The Same Day

Today Kit and I have some real fun when that chap Chesworth, who bullied me and Kit, and broke Dr Higgins' window, is caned. We also make friends with the other one, who's called Henry. He's a Lord! His father is the Earl of Cumberland.

Later, in the dining room, when I sit down to eat, Chesworth passes the back of my chair, and leans down to say: "Watch your back, Wentworth. I'll see to you."

I grasp his sleeve. "See if I care. You won't ever touch me." As he moved away I smacked him as hard as I could on the site of the gentle improvement. He cried aloud, tears springing from his eyes. He'll never touch me or Kit after that. I think that if I ever come across him again, it would be an interesting time.

Thomas. March, 1603. Well, Yorkshire

It was a beautiful early spring day; tiny buds were breaking out on the trees in the garden. I could see them from the classroom window where we took our lessons. Young Master Trenchard, a pole-like stooped figure, Dr Higgins' assistant, was trying, hopelessly in my case but with more success in Christopher's, to inculcate into us some semblance of Euclid's geometric genius. Suddenly, Dr Higgins burst into the room with an extremely uncharacteristic turn of speed.

He came to an abrupt halt by Trenchard's desk, and raised his hand for silence, a somewhat pointless exercise as you could have heard a pin drop; none of us had ever seen the Doctor move so fast or seem so disturbed. Or was he excited? Perhaps both.

"Master Trenchard; boys. I bear the gravest news. Please stand." We did so. "Queen Elizabeth is dead." Henry fainted. I caught him before he hit his head on the desk. Two of the boys sat down involuntarily. I was stunned. Gloriana, as the Queen was so widely known, had been on the throne longer than any of us could remember - nearly four times as long as I'd been alive. Come to think of it, she was on the throne when my father was born.

The headmaster went on: "There is good news too. King James VI of Scotland is now our King. There will be no war to establish the succession." I didn't know what he meant, but some of the boys cheered, and Higgins held up his hand again. "The Queen is dead. Long live the King." We all shouted that out too. He spoke again. "There will be church services all over the country. Some have already taken place in London and towns the news has already reached. I have to help organize a memorial tribute to the life of the late Queen, and our thanks to God for King James, at Ripon Cathedral. I shall close the school for two weeks from

Saturday. You must all send letters to your parents telling them that you will be home soon."

Class was dismissed. Henry recovered. He said he couldn't get a letter home in time. His father, the Earl, was away visiting some of his properties in Cumberland. I told him that Christopher and I would travel home together as we were neighbours, and he could come and stay with us at Wentworth Woodhouse. I'd never had a friend to stay at home before. I just hoped my parents would understand. I also hoped that one day Henry would take me home with him. I'd not met an Earl then.

"Sir!" I caught up with Dr Higgins in the corridor. "Yes, Wentworth, what is it?"

"Sir, what did you mean by 'there will be no war to establish the succession'?"

"Ah! We must have more history lessons. Learning Latin and Ancient Greek is all very well, but you young gentlemen need to understand how this country works. Why, you may be in the Queen's – I mean the King's – government one day. But, to answer your question: the Queen had no children. If she had, the eldest son would be King, or a daughter would be Queen if there were no boys. That is what usually happens. But as there is no child, the Queen had to choose her successor, and she chose James, who is the 6th King of that name in Scotland. Parliament is happy with her choice, and there is no other contender."

"Contender, Sir?"

"Yes, Wentworth. Contender. Someone who sets himself – or come to that, herself – up as a claimant to the Crown."

"Would a woman do that, Sir?'

"Not very likely, but fifty years ago some very powerful men put up a young lady – Lady Jane Grey - to be Queen instead of Queen Mary. Those men – and the unfortunate young woman – who probably had no choice in the matter – were beheaded for their pains."

"I bet it was painful, too, Sir."

Higgins laughed. "Not quite what I meant, boy."

"I hope you didn't mind me asking, Sir."

"Don't apologise, Wentworth. Nothing I like better than a question which shows someone has actually been listening to what I say." With that he whirled his gown about and strode away. I went in search of Henry and Christopher.

****

The three of us travelled to Wentworth Woodhouse by carriage, which we hired. At least, Henry hired it, and Kit and I gave him a coin or two towards it. Henry seemed to be much better off than we were; generous too. Spring was more advanced, and as we moved gradually from North to South Yorkshire, the weather improved by geometric progressions (I know what they are now). It had been unseasonably warm in Well and Ripon, but as we passed near Barnsley, temperatures soared.

Boys and girls sat on gates and styles as we clattered along chalky white roads from which dust rose under the wheels of our carriage. The horses drawing the vehicle were, for the most part, chestnut or darker, but frequently, by the time we reach a staging post, they looked more like dappled greys. We, inside the contrivance, were often little better, dust clogging our nostrils, hair and eyebrows. By the time we disembarked at a wayside inn to spend the night, even we, boys of ten in my case, and eleven in the case of Kit and

Henry, were glad to get out of our clothes, and wash ourselves down in the ewers and basins of water in our rooms.

The sun blazed down every day, and the next day we took it in turns to sit next to the coachman. Brambles grew in profusion by the roadside. I, for whom blackberries were a passion, could not wait for the end of summer to pick them.

Those were dangerous times, for the war in Ireland, fomented in large part by Philip the Spanish Beelzebub, was largely over. Discharged and unpaid soldiery hung about the lanes and byways of England, as well as footpads and highwaymen. We were unharmed, however, as Henry's Father, the Earl, always had Henry shepherded by two extremely violent retainers, carrying firearms, daggers and swords, far less threatening than the appearance of the men bearing them. As luck would have it, however, their martial skills were not called upon; they followed the carriage peaceably enough on their horses.

The only folk frequenting the highways were people going about their lawful business, or destitute beggars. These beggars were, of course, breaking the Poor Laws, but most of them were so pitiful that we gave them small coins. I was very moved by the sight of these people, especially those who had their wives and children with them. I resolved that, if ever I had the opportunity to do anything to alleviate the terrible sufferings of the really indigent, I should do so.

We took two uneventful days and a night to reach my Father's house, but for three quite young men who had never made such a journey without parents before, it seemed like an enormous adventure. It was the start of a superb holiday which laid the foundations of two of the most important friendships of my life.

Thomas. April, 1603. Wentworth Woodhouse

Henry was the same age as Kit, and an inch or two taller than me. Two years had passed since I arrived at the school in Well, and I had actually grown so that I was now two inches taller than Kit. Otherwise we looked much the same as before, but Henry was better looking than either of us, with all the arrogant charm of a young aristocrat. His bullying days were over. He was unfailingly polite, and when I say he had an easy, arrogant, charm I mean he had that air about him which, whilst being extremely pleasant, nevertheless meant that he did not expect, indeed could not imagine, that you would not do as he asked. I wanted to be like that.

He was dark-haired, but not as dark as me, and like me he was fit and athletic. He had started to write verse, and sing. Like Kit, he liked books for their own sake, whilst my interest in books was virtually non-existent; I read them only for the ideas and practical help they provided, and seldom for diversion. Henry was really good at mathematics, and my life at school would have been very miserable indeed if I had not had him and Kit to lean on when it came to numbers.

My parents welcomed Henry, thank goodness. In fact, I think they were delighted to have an Earl's son in the house. Mother would be the envy of the neighbours, and Father, who was quite ambitious, saw it as a definite step up the ladder to have a new connection with the nobility. I say new;

that's not really correct. This was his only connection with the nobility.

We had a wonderful holiday, riding over the country round about, walking, talking – frequently fantastical talk about what we would do and how rich and famous we should be one day – and learning new things. One day we were passing one of Papa's woods when we heard men felling trees. They were using big axes with long handles. I knew these men. They were some of our farm workers. Father was a good Master, the men were friendly to me and my brothers, so Henry and I stopped and asked them if we could learn to use their axes. They showed us how to hold and swing them. It was hard work, and soon we had large blisters on our palms, but I loved it. The men did not let us chop any trees down – we were too small – but they let us chop the trunks of smaller trees already felled into logs.

Thomas. Summer, 1604, Londesborough

Did I say that the holiday in 1603 was wonderful? Well, the summer vacation in 1604 was even better.

The Earl, Henry's Father, had some wonderful hunting country, and although I had often been hunting and hawking on my Father's lands, the riding and sport around the Londesborough Estates was in an altogether higher class. We hunted deer with hounds, and with bow and arrow, and went hawking for game birds. We even stalked stags with flint-locks, but that wasn't much fun. The guns were so inaccurate, and heavy, and the noise usually did us more harm than the shot did to the deer.

During this holiday hunting became my favourite recreation, especially hawking.

Henry was a wonderful host, and at his home I discovered just how cultured he was. He not only loved books and writing; he was even learning to play the lute. I liked music, and had no pretensions to musical skill, but Henry – he was a musician.

He also had something else: a sister. Margaret. She was as tall as me, and fair unlike Henry, and even an eleven year old me thought she was probably pretty. But a girl? No, we didn't play with her. I danced with her though. The Earl had a dancing master for his children; I was included in the dancing lessons too, that year and the one before. Just as well. The Earl said you could not succeed in society, and especially not in its upper levels which whirled around the King and Queen, if you couldn't dance. Even as a boy I was desperately ambitious.

Margaret. Summer, 1609, Londesborough

My brother, Henry, brought that Thomas Wentworth boy home again for the holidays. He seemed to stay with us nearly every year. Sometimes Henry went to his home in South Yorkshire. He is well-mannered, but clearly not a true aristocrat, like my Father. When he first came to stay with us, about 1609 I suppose, he had quite a thick Yorkshire accent, whereas Father had a Southern way of speaking. But then our family had been Earls since about 1250, and mixed with Royalty, or fought them, all those centuries. Later, when I met Thomas's Father he was obviously not a fighting type. He seemed somewhat timid compared with his wife.

Thomas talked about his Mother as though she was the strong one in their house.

My Father was the one with the power. Mother was much less forceful, but they were both lovely. Papa used to say he would have been even more powerful if we weren't so poor. That was hyperbole really. We had square miles of land and our huge house; more lands and another home in Cumberland; more land in other places, and a house in London. We had an army of servants, and farmers renting land from Papa, so the money rolled in. He was just too extravagant. He kept us 'poor', as he called it. He hoped to marry me off to someone rich one day. Someone who could help him back up the ladder to influence with the King and all the really rich men, like the Earl of Newcastle.

Thomas got on well with my parents, and he and Henry were great friends. They were both at university now. When they were not at college, they studied law in London, Thomas at the Inner Temple, I think. All this education at Cambridge and in London changed his accent. He was almost sounding like one of us. He wasn't really keen on books, but then he used to say: "If you want to be a great man, you need to know the law." Sometimes he spoke as though he was a great man already.

They - Henry and Thomas - rode together, hawking; sometimes they let me go with them, but that was not much fun for me. The boys were odd. Did they think that girls came from another planet? Did they ever wonder why their parents were together and did things together?

They were changing, though. I saw Henry looking – staring sometimes – at one of the really quite pretty maids, and other girls in the street if we went to York, or even in the village.

And Thomas, well, sometimes he just seemed to be unable to take his eyes off my chest. He didn't do that in past years, so he'd begun to take some notice of me. But then I only had very small bumps there the previous summer; this year they were not small at all. I rather liked them; I felt excited when he looks. My nipples were very sensitive. I stroked them in bed. Sometimes I thought it would be nice if Thomas did it for me. After all, he was quite good-looking in a dark sort of way. His hair was very black, and he had lovely long hands and sensitive looking fingers, just right for touching my even more sensitive buds. I wished I could just ask him.

****

Henry and Thomas were playing tennis on the grass today. It was a new game. Some people had indoor courts and hit the ball around the walls or something. Father said that was what the old King, Henry, used to do was about a hundred years ago!! Anyway, the boys were playing on the lawn at the back of the house, below the terrace, where I was sitting. Henry was very good at all games, and always beat Thomas. The amazing thing, though, was Thomas's determination. He really hated losing, and fought every inch of the way. You'd think he'd have been fed up with being beaten, but No! He came back for more every day.

Anyway, I was sitting there watching them run about and get all sweaty. Suddenly Henry hit a really wild ball which soared over the wall – well, sort of stone banisters really – along the front of the terrace. The ball bounced straight to me. I caught it, stood up and ran along the terrace and out of sight round the bushes at the end of the grass where Thomas was. He came running after me, shouting: "Margaret, don't be rotten. Give me the ball. I'm going to beat Henry this time."

Almost out of breath as I disappeared behind the bushes, I came to rest against a wall. "You can't beat him; he's too good," I panted.

Then Thomas rounded the corner, and I hid the ball behind my back. "Give it to me."

"If you don't say please, you'll have to take it."

"Right." And he put his arms round me feeling for the ball behind me. Then he stopped, and this really weird look came over his face, and he just looked at me. Slowly his face came towards me, kissed me, and pulled me by the waist towards him. I was out of breath from running, but it was not that which made me pant now. This kiss felt so different from any I'd ever had before. Why did we have to wear those stiff fronted dresses? The front of mine was like a board. My nipples pressed against it. I wished I could feel them pressing against Thomas. I want him to feel them doing it too.

"What's going on round there?" Henry was coming our way. I pushed Thomas away just as Henry appeared. "Come on, Margaret, give us the ball." I handed it to Thomas, ran my hand down his shoulder and arm as he turned away. I did not want him to think I wanted to push him off.

He understood. As he walked off with Henry he turned his head, smiling at me. His face and his expressions were quite stern and forbidding most of the time, but his smile transfigured him. It sounds silly now, but when it happened it made me think of the story in the Gospel. Jesus went up the mountain with St Peter and someone, and Moses and Elijah come to Jesus, whose face was shining blindingly. Not that I'm saying Thomas was like Jesus. He could be quite frightening when he wished, and he was far from perfect: he lost to Henry again.

Thomas. 1609. Londesborough

I was on holiday at Henry's home once more. It was a very large, sprawling place, three storeys with five large windows either side of the front door, and eleven above those. The floor above that were the servants' quarters. Joining either side of that edifice were two projecting wings, and each of those had three windows on each of the two floors. It had a yellow stone front, the back and sides brick. Henry said it was only twenty years old. Built in an H layout, surrounded by beautiful gardens, it was about five times the size of our manor house at Wentworth. Ours had a stone ground floor, and bricks above that.

I played tennis with Henry, and kissed Margaret behind some bushes in the middle of the game. She was growing really pretty. That kiss was on my mind most of the night and all next day. I'd been with a couple of whores in Cambridge, and another one when I'd been living down at the Temple – in fact I'd been with that one more than once – but I enjoyed kissing Margaret more just once than going all the way with those women. The other business was all so quick and somehow it didn't seem to me like something a fellow should be paying for. I was at St John's College and Kit at Clare College, so we met often in Cambridge. You weren't allowed to take women into your rooms. When I was at the Temple I stayed at Grandfather Richard's, and as I could hardly take girls back there either, harlots it had to be.

I wondered when I'd get the chance to kiss Margaret again. Just thinking about it caused a stiffness inside my codpiece. People kept on about sin, but I was sixteen now, and some chaps I knew were married and mating whenever they wanted. I really had to wrestle with my conscience over all this. It's enough to make you wonder what God's plan really was, when he gives a lad a cock, surrounds him with pretty girls, and then the priests say "you can't use it".

I had to think about something else. Like the law. I really enjoyed studying at the Inns of Court. All these fantastic lawyers I saw and heard! I had to learn to talk like them. I saw them in Westminster Hall. Many cases were small and boring, but when it was a murder, or a divorce in one of the big society families – they usually had to get an Act of Parliament – the way the barristers argued with each other, and with the judge, it was exciting. Best of all though, was when they questioned and cross-examined witnesses and caught them out lying. I would learn to do that. I wanted to have my own court one day – be a judge or something.

Kit and Henry studied law too. It was very fortunate for me that they were at Gray's Inn, and I was only half a mile away at the Inner Temple. We went to the eating houses and taverns together, dining with much merriment. We also went to the Hall at Gray's Inn. We all talked about it at dinner one night. It was a special dinner with the Earl of Cumberland because Henry had just heard that he had got his degree.

Henry was full of it. "Now that's behind me I expect to be called to the Bar next year."

I said: "If you want to be a great man, you need to know the law. That's why I'm studying it too." Everyone laughed and the Earl leaned towards me and said, kindly really, I hope: "That sounds a bit pompous, Thomas."

Margaret patted my hand under the table. "I'm sure Thomas will be a great man one day, won't you Thomas?"

The Earl laughed at us. A very amiable man, he could be curt. He was big, with a florid face from hunting and the amount of wine he drank at dinner. Margaret looked nothing like him. I had Margaret on the brain.

Talking of brains, I'd seen the Attorney General, Sir Francis Bacon, in action in the Courts. He was one of the cleverest men in the country; or even the world. He gave special lectures about law at the university too. He believed in the Divine Right of Kings, that the King should rule, Parliament should be obedient and do what he wanted: mainly to give him the money with which to govern. I wasn't sure I agreed with that. I felt that the King should listen to the advice Parliament gave him. That was what it was supposed to be there for; not just filling up the King's coffers. At least, that was what some of the other lecturers told us, and I agreed. But I was sure that in the end the King had to be in charge.

When dinner was over, we – I mean Henry, the Earl, and I – rose from the table to go and smoke a pipe or two. Well, the Earl smoked, and Henry tried to, but I didn't care for it. This tobacco leaf that Raleigh brought back from America had proved very popular. Anyway, as we got up from the table and the ladies went off to do some embroidery, Margaret pulled me aside: "Come to my room later." I couldn't think of anything to say. What did she mean by 'later'? Wouldn't her maid be sleeping in her room?

The following night I learned what she meant. After dinner tonight Henry and I went out for a stroll. Too much venison and trout made it essential to walk it off before bed. We played a few games of cards with the Earl when we returned, so it was about midnight when I walked as quietly as I could along the corridor to my room. Margaret's door opened. She saw it was me, pulled me into the room.

She was cross. "You didn't come to me when I asked you the other night."

"I couldn't; it was too late. What about your maid?"

"She's away. Her mother's ill. I told her to go home. So why didn't you come?"

"When they'd had a smoke the Earl wanted a few hands of cards, and then he challenged me to a game of draughts, so...."

Margaret was imperious. "I said later, didn't I? I didn't care how late."

"I didn't know what you wanted. I don't usually go into girl's bedrooms late at night."

"Oh, Thomas, don't be a dunce. You want to as much as I do."

I understood, and she was right. Now I knew that she wanted me to kiss her again, so I did. It was even better than the other day. This time Henry wasn't coming round the corner. I could feel her body through her nightgown, and she made me put my tongue in her mouth. How she made me do that I don't know, because I'd never done that before, but she opened her mouth under my lips; it just seemed like the right thing to do. We both gave a little moan.

She pushed my doublet off my shoulders and it dropped to the floor. Now there was only my shirt and her nightdress between my chest and hers, I could feel these small things pushing into my breast. I slid my hand up between us, clasping her breast; the thing that was pushing into me was a nipple getting harder.

Margaret moaned again, so I slid my other hand down her back and began bunching up the nightgown until I felt the skin of her thigh against the backs of my fingers. She then grabbed the hem and, breaking away from me, whipped it over her head.

There she was. Naked. I had thought she was pretty. Now I knew she was stunningly beautiful. I was pole-axed, like a bullock at the meat market. But she knew what to do. She came back, kissed me again, lifted my hands to her breasts, and I came back to life. Suddenly I realised that if I don't get my breeches and hose off I should burst; I pushed them off, as Margaret untied the fastenings on my shirt. We were naked together.

She took my hand, started to pull me to the bed, but then broke away once more to lock the door. I seized her hand pulling her onto the bed. I should have thought about God and my soul, but no; I didn't even think: "This is Henry's sister". I should; was I betraying him?

****

I was in paradise, but Margaret still moved beneath me. I felt I had let her down, but before I could say so, she said: "It's lovely Thomas, and it'll get better".

"When? Tomorrow?"

"No, silly. In about half an hour." And she was right. At the end she started making a loud noise, then bit down on my shoulder to keep herself quiet.

"Will there ever be another holiday like this one?" I wondered.

Margaret. 1609. Londesborough

I remember how I was thinking back then: I've never made love with anyone before. Now I'm doing it with Tom nearly every night, and as often each night as we can do it. I just can't get enough. I've no-one to compare him with, of course, but I am sure he is a very tender and affectionate lover. He seems to worry – well, perhaps not worry, but be concerned – that I am really enjoying our love-making. When we finish I just feel so fulfilled, satisfied, relaxed, overjoyed, and……. There just aren't enough words.

It's supposed to be wrong to enjoy sexual intercourse. They say it's wrong for girls, anyway. The Puritans are pretty miserable about it. I don't think it can be all that wrong; most of the ladies at Court seem to have new lovers all the time. And I hear strange stories about the King spending lots of time with handsome young men. Father says King James takes more notice of these youths than he does of the wise men on the Privy Council. Still, I know what Tom and I are doing is wrong because we're not married. I'm looking forward to being married. Then I won't have to worry about whether making love is wrong. Besides, how can anything to do with love be wrong? And the amount I like to do it means I'd be worried all the time I remain unwed. Nor would I be worried about getting pregnant!

It would be fantastic if I could marry Tom.

Henry Clifford. 1610. All Over the Place!

This has been the most incredible year. I was admitted to the Bar as a member of Gray's Inn in June – at the same time as Kit Wandesford - and on 25th July I was married to my lovely Frances. She is Robert Cecil's daughter, the Secretary of State, the most powerful political person in the Kingdom. We were married in Kensington, and soon afterwards we came to Paris, where we are living, and I am studying at a French academy. I'm a Lord because I'm an Earl's son, so Frances is a Lady, but she is also a Lady because her Father is an Earl too – the Earl of Salisbury.

This connection has given the family a leg up. If only we had some money! Thomas will be called to the Bar next year, and I think he will do well. He works really hard at making speeches. He studies all the arts of rhetoric, and his Yorkshire accent has almost gone, but he has this earthy country way of talking, and it mixes strangely with the things he's learned about Demosthenes, Cato, Cicero, all those old orators. Mind you, when Tom wants to make a point, he can be very forceful, persuasive, but he has a violent temper sometimes; then he doesn't even try to persuade people. He just tells them how things are. Not many can stand up to him when that happens.

Now how have I got onto all that? Ah yes, the family money. It made me think about Tom because his Father has money, and he's only a knight – Sir William Wentworth. So if Tom does well at the Bar or whatever he goes into he'll be really rich, I should think. I don't know if I'll ever be like that. Father always complains we – the Cliffords - are poor. I can't make a lot of money or get far in politics by playing the lute and writing poetry! And those are the things I care for.

I miss him, Thomas. He was my best friend at school and College, and I saw a lot of him in London. Mind you, sometimes, during the holidays he spent with us at home, I thought there might be something between him and Margaret. The way they looked at each other, often appearing to have just been whispering to each other even though you couldn't catch them doing so must mean something.

Thomas. October 1610. Inner Temple

I know this story happened in the past, but as my life is really moving forward now, I'm going to express most of the rest of it as if it's occurring now.

I've been back at Grandfather Atkinson's for a week; Bar lectures and dinners start next week. It's a funny old system, becoming a barrister. You qualify by eating a number of dinners each term, as though your appetite is what has to be tested, not your brain, let alone your knowledge of the law. But I'm working hard at the books, going to all the lectures, listening to as many cases as I can; I've even taken part in mock trials three times. I was prosecuting a murder (fiction, of course) once, and lost – the 'defendant' got off. Another time I was defending a farmer who was in debt with a mortgage. He hadn't been paying enough, but I showed that the lender had been calculating the interest wrongly, much too high, so the farmer had to pay half the so-called arrears, and could stay on his farm.

They set these test cases with all the facts in them. The lecturers and Judges who work out the facts don't tell you things like "the interest is wrong." You have to work that out for yourself, plan your legal arguments, and your questions. Great fun, but goodness gracious, was I nervous. When I was presenting my case I was on my feet for over an hour, and my legs were rigid with nerves. When I finished I couldn't sit down at first as my knees wouldn't bend. I hope I get over that sort of anxiety soon. As it is, I have visions of finishing an argument, bowing to the Judge, then toppling over sideways and disappearing between the benches.

Talking of getting over things, I had a letter from Margaret this morning. She tells me everything that's going on. Her parents were glad I was able to stay with them again during the Long Vacation, she enjoyed seeing me, and all that sort of thing. There is never a hint of what we get up to together. She tells me that her Mother looks at her letters before they are given to the post, but she occasionally manages to slip a little note in before the letter is sealed. She only does this when I'm at College, or here in London. We wouldn't want anyone at home finding out about us. I'm frightfully glad my Grandfather doesn't check my mail.

The note with today's letter said: "Darling Thomas, (or should I say Daring Thomas), We're in luck again. No babies this time!! Love and kisses (in those special places) from Margaret".

All this makes me happy, but every now and then the question of my soul and fornication comes into it; sometimes

I worry what my friend Henry thinks about us. Has he guessed?

Thomas. Christmas 1611. Paris

This has been an incredible year! And not just for me. The Prince of Wales has been causing quite a stir. I haven't met Henry Stuart, of course, but I caught sight of him once when I was near the Palace in Whitehall, and another time when I'd gone out of the Temple for a walk at lunch-time, he came riding up to the Tower. When he'd gone in, one of the guards (for a bribe, of course) told me that he goes there quite often to talk with Sir Walter Raleigh, who's been locked up there for years. Although to many Raleigh is a hero, and hardly anyone thinks he deserves to be a prisoner, no-one's making a fuss, but making him a victim is not helping to make King James popular; in fact, quite the contrary.

Prince Henry is so very different from his Father, and seems to have absorbed the mood of the people. I waited outside the Tower for him to emerge, and as he did so I heard him remark to his equerry: "No-one but my Father could have such a bird in such a cage." Since that weird Spaniard, Guido Fawkes, and his friends, tried to blow up the King and Parliament six years ago, any kind of talk that might be thought treason has virtually disappeared, but I suppose that if you're a Prince and don't say it too loudly, you can get away with it.

Prince Henry's tall and very good-looking, with reddish hair. They say he is very straight-forward and honourable. He must be pretty clever, too, to admire and be acceptable company for Raleigh. Apparently the King wanted him to marry a girl from the Spanish Royal Family, but he says he won't have a Catholic in his bed, and he's told the King he wants to marry a Protestant. And what about Henry's sister!! She's a blond beauty. How did old King James – pursy and fat old King James – as he called himself once, apparently – get such lovely children? Because he has a most beautiful wife, that's how. Queen Anne comes from Denmark and she is stunning. Nearly all the ladies at Court wear these low cut dresses, but few of them have the bosom to display that the Queen has. Did I say display? I mean flaunt. She takes no chances that you might not notice.

I have heard a rumour about Henry and Elizabeth – that's the daughter, the Princess – and it's this. They're not really James's children at all. People say that the Queen is rather indiscreet about her admirers (lovers would be nearer the mark), and there are several handsome men about Court who have been said to have done a lot of 'admiring' at one time or another. On the other hand Henry and Elizabeth's little brother, Charles, is certainly the King's son, if my opinion means anything. He's small, and neat, which the King probably was before he became 'fat and pursy' and old. They say he's shy, and not as bright as Henry, so it's just as well he's not going to be King when his Father dies. I don't think I believe the rumour anyway. Queens have their heads chopped off for adultery.

Mind you, if it is true that the Queen takes lovers, you can hardly blame her. The King is not at all lovely. He smells badly, as my nose tells me, looks dirty. He's often the worse for drink, and falls over, or falls off his horse. If he's not cuddling up to and stroking his handsome young companions, he goes out hunting (which is when he falls off), and pays the Queen hardly any attention at all. He has a particular favourite at present, a Scot called Carr – Robert Carr – who is not much more than a peasant really; it's said he can't read or write, yet the King apparently takes his advice, and a few months ago created him Viscount Rochester. If that doesn't show what the King's perve – I mean preferences – are, I can't imagine what does.

Yet on the other hand, almost at the same time as a Peasant became a Peer of the Realm, the King had the first Authorised Version of the Bible published. He'd commanded the Bishops and the Divines at the Universities to get together and perfect a translation of the Scriptures because there were too many home-made versions going around. It has become a very popular book already; no wonder. It is beautifully written, and most of it reads like poetry or Shakespeare, the language is so powerful. It is a supreme Protestant achievement. Even the Puritans are starting to use it. I wager some Catholics do too!

Which brings me back to Princess Elizabeth. She may be going to marry the Elector Palatine from Germany. He's a Calvinist, and leader of the Calvinist Princes of Germany, so he's opposed to Spain and the Emperor of Austria, and that will be a very popular wedding, if it happens.

That's why it is a good year for the country. Why has it been good for me? First, the whole family took a step up the social ladder early in the year. Not a very praiseworthy step, but a step up nevertheless. And this is why.

King James is hard up. King James is always hard up. In fact, according to Father, even Queen Elizabeth was hard up, and there was no money in the kitty when James came to the throne. It's a bit odd really, because as far as I can see, as I ride up and down from Yorkshire to Cambridge and London and back, most people in the country are doing very well. Now the war in Ireland is a fair way behind us there don't seem to be so many beggars and foot-pads about.

To get money, the King has created a new rank of the nobility. It's called a baronetcy. It's not as low as a Knight – Father was one of those already – and it's not as high as a Baron, let alone a Viscount or Earl. Anyway, you can buy a baronetcy direct from the King – well, his finance people – and Father bought one for five thousand pounds. He was one of the first men to apply for one. Now he is Sir William Wentworth, Bart. I'm his eldest son, so when he passes on, I'll be a Bart, too. It's a bit commercial – not like being made an Earl for winning a battle or doing some other heroic thing for the King – but it means the Wentworth family move in better – or perhaps I should say wealthier and more influential – circles than before.

It also means that he was able to take me to Court and present me to the King. That's when I saw the Queen. She must be about thirty-five or so, but she is still rather beautiful.

The baronetcy and going to Court have meant that at University and at The Inner Temple I get treated with a bit less contempt than I used to. So many of the law students are from the real upper classes – blue blooded aristocrats, even if they are often just the younger sons of the peerage – that even now they look upon me as some sort of country bumpkin. My Yorkshire accent doesn't help, but I have a feeling that one day my voice and my accent are going to be pretty important in this Kingdom. Being the son of a baronet made me feel a lot easier in all this exalted company when I was called to the bar, which happened half-way through the summer.

And this step up has led to something even better for me. I just couldn't believe it. About a month after becoming a fully qualified barrister, I arrived home for the holidays, and after dinner the first night, Father called me into the library, and gave me another glass of wine. When we sat down he opened the conversation. "As you know, Thomas, things are a bit different now that I've obtained this baronetcy."

"Yes, Father."

"And you are eighteen, and have a profession."

Where was this going? Why was he telling me things I already knew? "Yes Father."

"I have decided it is time you were married."

Dear God, what about Margaret? I didn't want to get married yet. My mouth had gone so dry I could drink a lake. I said nothing.

"I have therefore been to see a gentleman whose daughter, I think, would make you a very suitable wife, and at the same time take the family's social position considerably higher."

Oh God, Father, I thought, you're supposed to love me. How can you do this to me? I don't want to marry someone I've never even seen. I know what it's like to have sex with someone I really like – love even. And you know how you've brought me up. We're not exactly Puritans, but profligate promiscuity isn't what our family does after marriage. Don't sentence me to a life of fucking - or not fucking - someone I don't even like!

Unaware of my thoughts, Father continued: "The gentleman indicated that he approved, and has recently written to tell me he has informed his daughter, who appeared to be quite joyful at the prospect."

No, Father! No! She must be desperate, old, and ugly, with buck teeth, no hair, and a flat chest. I emitted a very slight groan, but Father seemed not to hear it, and went on:

"And the beauty of it is that we already know the family quite well and you know them very well. Lord Henry Clifford will be your brother-in-law, and I am sure the Earl of Cumberland will be a very good father-in-law. I think the young lady's name is …."

"Margaret!!" I leaped out of my chair rushing to embrace my Father. We were quite an affectionate family, but I excelled myself in kissing his old face.

****

What else did this incredible year do for me? Well, on 22nd October the entire Wentworth family and I went to Londesborough. Margaret and I were married in the Earl of Cumberland's private chapel by the Earl's private chaplain. Margaret's family were all there, except for Henry. He was already in Paris with his wife. Margaret looked stunning in a yellow velvet dress, very modest as to the neckline, and revealing little of the charms I knew it hid. My brother William stood with me in the chapel, and had custody of the ring. I was so nervous I dropped it when the priest handed it to me to put on Margaret's finger.

There was a banquet in the great hall which was far from full, as only the two families were there. Nevertheless, the Earl spared no expense with the food and the wine. Looking around at the opulence, the splendour, it was hard to imagine that he believed himself poor, which is what my darling told me he believed. There were twelve courses, and at least a glass of superb wine with each. The Household Steward acted as butler, and to help him there was a servant behind every chair to top up goblets, serve more food. My mother tried to restrain Father, but he ate as though he'd never had food before, and did not pretend to be impartial to the wine, either. However, he was not drunk, and no more the worse for wear than the Earl, brother William, and one of Margaret's aunts.

I noticed that Margaret, eating only small amounts from each plate, was sipping her wine. Once I even saw my gorgeous new wife empty her own glass into her tipsy aunt's as she distracted her. I decided to take it easy myself, fancying that one way or another I might have quite a heavy night ahead; there would be dancing after the dinner, before the heavy goings on. A very full stomach and bladder did not seem like a good idea.

I danced with Mama, and Margaret's Mother, her sister, my sisters, and, of course, Margaret. I was desperate to get to the bedroom, and when Margaret whispered: "holding your hand and dancing is just not good enough," I was nearly overcome. She looked so innocent, and had a sort of nervous seriousness outwardly that must have made her Mother think she was dreading what she'd find when I took my breeches off. What an actress!

Apart from that I hardly remember anything about the ceremony, even though I concentrated on it very intensely at the time. I cannot recall a great deal about the banquet afterwards, either.

Neither of our families felt the need to put us to bed, though my little brother George accompanied us to the bedroom door. How anyone ever put up with people ensuring that the marriage was consummated I'll never know. Unless you are a sexual athlete from a Roman orgy, nothing could be much more off-putting to someone who has no experience and does not know what he's doing, particularly if the lady were not his personal choice. It must be even worse for the girl, who is, at least in theory, a virgin, knowing nothing about 'marital relations', but anticipating being hurt.

Anyway, as I say, we were spared that. I don't think either of us could convincingly have acted innocent virginity and inexperience.

I may not remember a lot about the wedding and the banquet, but what followed I recall very vividly.

I was waiting for the dancing to end. And it did. Both families took us upstairs ….. and left us there. Was there a four poster bed with hangings? Curtains at the windows? I could feel a carpet on the floor. What colour it was is a mystery. I had eyes only for my wife. If any two people have ever got undressed faster than Margaret and I did then, their clocks must have been going backwards. It was two in the morning when the dancing ended and we closed the bedroom door. I was naked two seconds later, and so was Margaret.

Suddenly we were still. We stared at each other. "Father in Heaven, thank you," I thought. "Can anyone have ever been happier than I am now? Thank you."

A tear rolled down Margaret's cheek, but she was smiling; and incredibly beautiful. My organ was priapic. We both started to speak at once. "Margaret...." "Thomas ...." And we laughed. I started again. "Margaret." She waited. I moved a pace towards her, reached out and put an index finger on each nipple. She quivered, and put her hand on my cock.

I smiled. "You are so lovely, and I love you so."

She smiled, wickedly. "You are so handsome, ... and big. And I love you." And she stroked it. This was like the first time all over again. I thought I might come on the Turkish carpet.

"We can do this any time we like now."

"Yes. And as often. And anywhere we like."

I laughed. "But not in front of the servants. Nor your Mother."

"She isn't the prude you seem to think. As far as I can make out she likes these things" (giving it another stroke) "as much as I do."

Another stroke and I moaned loudly. Margaret took her hand from me and put both arms round my neck, leaped into the air, clasped her legs round my waist, and settled herself onto this thing of mine. "So make me happy Thomas."

I did. All night.

****

The year is still not over. Margaret and I have a seemingly inexhaustible appetite for each other. Sometimes I can barely stay awake during the day; if I go to the bedroom for a snooze, as often as not Margaret comes and finds me, sleep coming a poor second to a much more satisfying pastime, no matter how tired I am.

At the end of November Father dragged me off to Royston in Hertfordshire where King James was holding

Court. I don't know how it happened – maybe Father parted with more cash – but this time when I was presented to the King, he knighted me. 'Arise, Sir Thomas Wentworth." I liked it. Another little step up. Mind you, knights are fairly numerous, and I didn't perform any act of valour for it, as I should have had to if we had King Arthur on the throne. I was very nervous about being knighted, not least because the King's hand was very shaky; I feared he might stab or behead me by accident.

Maybe he was nervous too. Or just old. Or just drunk.

There was a ball, a masque – the Queen is mad on them, and they cost a fortune – no wonder the King has no money – and I went with Father. My Mother and Margaret were at home, so I was without my loved one for the dancing. We all had to wear masks, which made it more than rather intriguing. In most of the dances you lined up and danced with the lady opposite you, and kept changing partners at the end of each sequence of steps. There were pavanes and sarabandes, gavottes and country dances, and I was glad I had had lessons at Henry Clifford's.

****

"It is time your education was completed." Father was formal. We were in the library after dinner. It was not a large room, the walls lined with leather bound books, and the fire crackled in the hearth.

"How can it be, Father? You've always told me we never stop learning."

He smiled indulgently. "That may be true, Son, but there's a formal part of your training as a Gentleman still left undone."

I swallowed nervously. I'd been through school with Dr Higgins, I'd been to Cambridge and got a degree, and I'd qualified as Barrister. I'd learned to dance, ride, fence, and help Dad manage our estates. What else had I got to do?

"So I'm sending you on a tour of Europe, to learn French, foreign customs and ways, and see the remarkable achievements of civilizations even older than our own. Of course, many of them are Roman Catholics, and the fact that they aren't English is a disadvantage to them, but they have wonderful architecture, splendid works of art and music, and in the South, much tangible Roman history. You will enjoy it."

"Is that an order, Father, or a statement?"

He laughed. "It's my hope for you, Thomas. So many young men from good families make this tour nowadays, that with our improving financial and social position, it would be remiss of me not to insist that you have this experience."

"Henry – you know - Lord Clifford – he's staying in Paris with his wife. Margaret and I shall be able to stay with them for a while. Wonderful!"

"Yes, I was aware that your friend is there, and certainly you should be able to stay with him, but …. Well …"

"Well what?" I smelled a rat.

"Well, I have spoken with your Mother about this, and she … we feel that it would not be wise for Margaret to accompany you." Father was grave.

"How long will I be gone?"

"At least a year, maybe two or more. The reasons …."

"Damn it all, Father, I can't leave Margaret for that long. We've only been married six weeks. We love each other." I was furious.

"As I was saying, the reasons are that if she is with you, her presence will interfere with the studying I expect you to do ...."

"Studying?" I swore under my breath, but he heard it anyway.

"That's enough of that Thomas. Yes, studying. I have appointed a tutor to accompany you. He's Charles Greenwood of University College, Oxford, and ..."

"Look here Father, if I've got to go abroad without my wife, the last thing I want is to be ordered around by some old fart from Oxford!"

"Did I say he was old? He's only a few years your senior, and you will like him, of that I am sure. You're 18; he's about twenty-four, I think. And as for 'ordering you around', as you quaintly put it, if you can talk to me the way you have been for the last few minutes, young Master Greenwood doesn't stand a chance." Father was quiet but fierce.

I was ashamed. He was still my dear old Dad, and I had just been unforgivably rude. "Sorry Father. It's all a bit of a shock."

"I forgive you, Thomas. I should not have been happy when I was young, being torn from your Mother after so short a space." Probably not, I thought; after all, look how many babies you two have made. "Still, you will not be leaving until 20th December, so you have another three weeks to do your duty."

"What duty's that, Father?"

"Why, getting me a grandson, of course. And that's the other reason Margaret should not go with you. If you perform this duty …."

I interrupted with a laugh. "Trying for an heir is no duty."

He chuckled. "I rather thought not. But anyway, your Mother says that if you succeed, it would be quite wrong to have dear Margaret gallivanting about Europe if she is pregnant. And we hope she will be."

Even I could see the force of that. Come to think of it, why isn't she expecting already? It's not as though we haven't been trying, flashed into my mind "Maybe Mama is right. But it'll be really hard, leaving her behind."

A knowing smile lit Father's face. "I know, my boy. So you'd better make the best use of those three weeks before you get on the boat."

I ran from the library as fast as I can, looking for Margaret. She wouldn't want to waste a second.

****

"He wants you to do what?"

"He wants me to go to Europe for God knows how long. To complete my education!!"

"Listen Thomas, you're not going to defy your Father, are you? And I wouldn't want you to. He's a good man. You love him. I love him. He's kind to me. He treats me like a daughter." Margaret sat on the bed. "I'm not daft. I know he wanted you to marry me because I was a good catch dynastically, and I know he didn't know we were already in love. But some fathers in his position treat the daughter-in-law's dowry as just another addition to their property and estates, and care for her not at all."

"I know, darling, but even so, leaving you for a year or even more is …. Well, frustrating, to say the least. And that's not just the fornicating."

"How romantic!! You could say 'the lovemaking'." Margaret smiled to show she was joking. She was wonderful, holding out her hand. I took it. She pulled me to the bed. "Come on. We've got three weeks to banish frustration for a while. If we get it right, by the time you leave I'll be pregnant and you will be so worn out you won't feel frustrated for ages."

Margaret stood, starting to unfasten my shirt. "Thomas, if you're the hammer, I'm the tongs. Let's go to it."

****

So now it is the end of this fantastic year, and here I am, as I said before, staying with Henry in Paris. He has a beautiful stone house, with intricate carvings on the outside and quite stunning ornate moulded stucco work decorating the walls and ceilings inside. I miss Margaret badly, but Henry is good fun and company as always, and I like his wife, Frances. Theirs is a large house, which is just as well. They have about twenty servants - gardeners, an ostler, maids, chefs, cooks - and Father had me bring a small number of folk to look after me and Charles Greenwood.

He was right about Charles. He is very mild-mannered, almost shy; we get on very well. He won't have any nonsense from me, because he is authoritative in his quiet way. He has already started teaching me French, but in Henry's home I get little chance to practise it. We shall leave here in a few weeks and then, in the country, I should meet plenty of people who speak no English, so it'll be interesting to see how I cope. I've told Charles he mustn't nurse-maid me!

We go to the theatre together, but I don't understand the French dialogue much. The French also have this new art form; they call it the ballet. Non-stop music with dancing; and what dancing! It's not like ordinary dancing, with a partner or partners. It's all leaping about and twirling round and very intricate footwork. I don't know if it will catch on. Still, I like it, and really admire the skill of the dancers, and how fit they look. No fatties on their stage!

Sometimes Henry and Frances come with us. He is getting known in fashionable Parisian circles, and gets invited to dinners and balls, so I am now included. I just wish Margaret were with me. Some of the ladies are very beautiful, and, if I say it myself (and I shouldn't) some of them are clearly interested in me, but all their attentions do is make me yearn more for Margaret.

I find myself thinking about her a lot, wondering when I shall hear from her.

I write to her every couple of days, but it takes a courier at least two days to get to the coast, a day across the channel if the wind permits, longer if it doesn't, and then a day or two to get to London, if she's there, let alone Yorkshire. I've been here a week, so a letter from my love should arrive in a day or two.

I wonder if she's expecting a baby yet. She ought to be; we nearly wore the hammer and tongs out that last three weeks.

Margaret. March, 1612. Yorkshire

Dearest Thomas,

I am always so glad to get your letters. Today I had three!! As I did not get one for ten post days, and there are rarely any on Sundays, I had not seen one for twelve days. I was frantic and fed up, to put it mildly. It is good that you are happy, still, in Orleans, and that your French is coming along well. I shall have to try to learn some so that we can speak it at home and hardly anyone will know what we are saying.

This is the last time you need ask if I am expecting that baby. You have been gone three months now, I've just started a third course (what a curse). There is no chance I'm pregnant. We'll just have to start again when you come home. I can't wait for that. It's eighty-nine nights since you made love to me. Do you remember how to do it? More importantly, do you remember the way I like it?

Anyway, that's enough of that; if I go on about it I shall get either excited or depressed!

So you like the cathedral in Orleans better than Notre Dame. I must say from the sketches you have sent the Paris one looks extremely – well, heavy I suppose would be my word for it, but the Orleans one is light and airy looking. You are very lucky to be seeing all these places. I don't suppose I shall ever get to go abroad, especially if I do have that baby, or babies!! I've only ever been to my Father's houses in London and Yorkshire and Cumberland, your home (ours now) and your Grandfather's house in Chancery Lane.

By the way, I went down to London with your parents recently and we saw a new play by Shakespeare: 'The

Tempest'. It was really strange, all about a shipwrecked King and his daughter, and a deformed creature named Caliban. The King is called Prospero, and somehow he reminded me of your Father. Not that your Dad can do magic or anything like that, but he certainly knows how to Prosper. Sorry, that's a terrible jest, isn't it?

Anyway (sorry, I've used that word before), I noticed on the way back from London that your Father seemed rather tired. He bucked up when we got home. When I asked him if he was well, he laughed and said, in that jokey way he has of taking off the servants: "Eh oop, lass, there's nowt wrong o' me being back in Yorkshire won't see right." Even so, I'm still a bit worried about him. Your Mother is well, and doesn't seem worried for him. She is such a strong type you can't always tell what she's thinking.

How much longer are you going to be in Orleans, and where are you off to next? I hope you're being careful of all those Maids. They can't all be saints.
Remember I love you,
Your Margaret.

Thomas. 2nd April, 1612. Orleans

I've just read a letter from Margaret. She says she didn't get a letter for twelve days. Yet I write to her nearly every day. Letters from here to Yorkshire must be able to find their own way by now. It's the weather. Sometimes, when what I've written reaches the coast, it waits on a boat for a week for the wind to change so that the vessel can get out of the harbour. It's the same when she writes to me.

That letter upset me a lot. Little does Margaret know it but she really hit the nail on the head with what she wrote about the Maids of Orleans. She's not the only one who's been missing our love-making, and last night I went out on my own for dinner in a tavern. It was a clean and warm inn (auberge here), and a good bit better than some I've seen in France. It wasn't very different from an English Inn with a low beamed ceiling and smoky walls.

My French is really getting quite good (Charles Greenwood has been working me rather hard and getting me into lots of conversations with French people), so I was able to order a meal, and actually get what I thought I'd asked for, which was roast 'mouton avec legumes et pommes de terre'. Yes, potatoes!! I did not realise that those roots which Raleigh brought back from the Americas had reached France as well as England.

I had just started on my second glass of a really fine claret when a girl brought my dinner. She was slim, with blond hair and a superb bosom, and at first glance I thought she looked like Margaret. She was wearing a kind of local costume, with a black dress over a white shirt thing, which was very low cut, and as she put my dinner on the table she leant over in front of me I could examine her charms at very close quarters.

I have been a very good boy up to now, and had not strayed like a lost sheep, nor a randy ram, come to that, but the sight of this sensuous girl was more than I could bear. I might be nineteen soon, but I had never been in a situation like this before, and did not know what to do. From the way she smiled at me I thought – or at any rate hoped – that she liked the look of me as much as I liked the look of her. My

French deserted me for a moment and I asked her in English if she would like a glass of wine from my bottle. She smiled again and looked mystified.

I then managed to ask the same question in French. "Oui, monsieur," sounded like exquisite music when she said it. I was about to call to the patron for another glass when she pushed my hand down and said she would fetch it, which she did, and then came and sat with me. How she did not get into trouble I did not then know, but it turned out that the patron was her Father, and he was a very 'understanding' man.

What we talked about I cannot now say, but talk we did; she even helped herself to some of my dinner. Then she took my hand and led me out of the inn for what I thought was going to be a stroll, but after we had gone a couple of hundred yards she turned up an alley, turned again at the end of it, led me back to the rear of the tavern, and the back stairs to her bedroom. She was not shy, but she wasn't brazen either, and to say I would not have cared to make love to her would not be credible, but I could not bring myself to betray Margaret, so I put my arm around the girl's shoulder, and we went on down the alley, and out into the countryside to complete our walk.

I still felt guilty, and don't know if I shall have the strength to stay away from her for the rest of my sojourn in Orleans, nor how I shall cope with any other willing ladies I may meet in the rest of this tour. Since Margaret and I married I have done nothing I have not been able to tell her about. And I don't think I ever shall be able to. How would I feel if she told me of something like this lust for someone else? I don't even want to think about it.

Thomas. June, 1612. Saumur

My darling Margaret,

Today is our last in this lovely old town on the Loire. I wanted to stop here because it is the home of Philippe Duplessis-Mornay. Do you remember me talking about him at home? He is a Protestant, and was a great help to Henri IV, the last French King, who was stabbed to death eight years ago. Philippe drafted the Edict of Nantes, which was supposed to give religious toleration to the Huguenots, and he had supported Henri when he was the Protestant King of Navarre, but he was rather betrayed when Henri became a Catholic to get his hands on the French Crown.

Even so, Mornay is a well-respected elder statesman in France, and I wanted to meet him. Charles came with me. We found him to be a very sad and rather disillusioned man, and he's losing his sight. He had a huge library; we talked a lot about his books – he's written a great deal – and his religious and philosophical views. I had a feeling he was glad to have someone different to talk to, so I'd like to think we left him happier than we found him, but I probably flatter myself.

He let me buy some of his books, and I now have quite a collection of French works, including plays, not just Protestant religious tomes, but even some Catholic ones. You know me – wanting to see both sides of everything.

Heavens, don't I write serious letters? When I compare your funny, light-hearted outpourings with my diatribes and lectures, I can't help wondering what pleasure you can get out of reading this tripe at all.

But then you know what I'm like, and you tell me you love me, so I can't be all that bad. How could the most adorable wife in the world love a really bad man?

Next stops, La Rochelle and Bordeaux. Writing every day is not so easy now we are on the road, but I shall still write as frequently as I can. However, I may not be able to write from Bordeaux. After all, it is where the very best claret comes from, and I may be unable to see the paper. Let alone write on it.
All my love to my love,
Thomas.

Margaret. August, 1612. Yorkshire

Dearest darling Thomas,

I have just received your letter from Carcassonne. I love the sketch you sent me of the town and its fortifications. Your drawings are getting better and better, but then you are getting quite a lot of practice. It surprised me that you said that the countryside round there "does much resemble Yorkshire." I thought it was really hot down there, not far from the Pyrenees, and all rocky. Still, you've seen it; I haven't, so you must know what you're talking about.

And you're going on to Avignon and Arles!! How I wish I were with you!! I'd love to see all those Roman ruins and Roman pillars. I'd quite like to see your Roman column again, too. What do I mean by "quite"? I'm desperate to see it, let alone ..... It's been nine months now. Can I wait much longer? It's driving me mad.

Who's a clever boy then? Not only speaking fluent French; you can write Spanish, too. I showed that Spanish page of your last letter to a lady from Spain; she is one of my Mother's maids at the moment. She said it was almost perfect, and very easy to understand. Can you speak Italian too? You'll have to become a diplomat.

On second thoughts, you're the last person who could be a successful diplomat. You say exactly what you think. When you tell a fib, it is written all over your face that "I am not telling the truth." I think that's one of the things I love about you. It will also make it rather difficult for you to go into politics, which is what your Father wants. He's always talking at dinner about how he hopes to get you a seat in Parliament.

Must put the quill down now. Your Mother is calling me. We're off soon in the carriage to go to York for a few days. Your Father is going to see his Doctor. He still seems to be tired much of the time, and looks a bit grey in the face.

I don't think it's anything serious, but I just hope the treatment is not more blood-letting. I don't see how having all your blood let out can make you well. Still, what do I know?
I Love You With All My Heart.
Your Margaret.

Thomas. Avignon. September, 1612

Dearest darling Margaret,

Charles and I arrived here two days ago. It is a very old town; some of the streets are even narrower and more winding than those in York. Here they don't have the half-timbered houses we have. You know how they lean towards each other and it looks as though you could reach across the street and eat the breakfast off the plate of the man in the house opposite? Not here. The houses are close, but go up more vertically.

You can still see the neighbours getting dressed, though, if they don't pull the shutters, and only if you look. Of course, being a good husband I never would look. So how do I know what I might see if I did look? Charles tells me, of course. He's still a bachelor, and not averse to pretty women. He's not so keen when the neighbour is a fat old man, but when choosing a place to stay you can hardly knock at the house opposite and ask what sights are to be seen through the bedroom window.

Back to the real sights of Avignon. There is a narrow stone bridge across the river, and seven years ago three of its arches were swept away by huge floods. There's a little chapel on what's left of the bridge, the chapel of St Benezite, who was allegedly told in a dream by an angel about 500 years ago that he had to get the bridge built. Some of the bridge has been washed away before, and rebuilt. I suppose they'll try to mend it again one day.

It's been a very religious city in the past. There's a huge palace which nine Popes lived in for a hundred years or so when Rome wasn't safe for them. The town I like best near here is Orange. It is a fantastically old place, and has an amphitheatre from Roman times which is in remarkably good condition. Charles and I stayed there for a few days, had a very interesting day exploring.

We went into the amphitheatre and sat on the terraced seating – all stone. Then I went down onto the stage area, leaving Charles back at the top. I waved to catch his eye, and then I said, in an ordinary voice, not a stage voice: "Can you hear what I'm saying?" He answered;

"*Perfectly.*" *What amazing architects and builders those Romans were!! Some of their roads you can still see here and in England are much better than the muddy tracks we dignify with the name of The King's Highway.*

We get invited to dinner by some noble or other worthy in nearly every town we stay in. Tonight we will eat with the Bishop of Avignon, even if he is a Catholic. Catholic food tastes every bit as good as Protestant fare, I'm glad to say. Now that I can speak the language so much better I enjoy myself, but not as much as if you were here.

How are my parents? I wrote to them yesterday, but please give them my love anyway.
All my love,
Thomas.

Thomas. November, 1612. Lyons.

Darling Margaret,
Why did we come to Lyons? Charles and I had such a wonderful stay in Provence, and a beautiful journey up the Rhone. The weather was kind, but cooling as the autumn came on, and then it deteriorated drastically. It seems to rain nearly all the time. This is a big city, but somehow dull, without the charm of all the small towns and cities we have stayed in, nor the excitement and culture of Paris.

Even so, the cuisine is wonderful, and the wine. We think they send good vintages to us in England, but I'm sure they keep the best wine here in France. And of course, it is so much cheaper than at home, because here we are not paying tunnage and poundage on the imported barrels. Trying hard not to become a drunken sot gets harder with every glass!

Strafford

I know I say it in nearly every letter, but I do miss you dreadfully, and wish you were with me. Charles is good company, and we've met many interesting, amusing and challenging people, but none of them is a soul mate for me as you are.

We shall be in Lyons and exploring round about for another few weeks, and then we plan a trip down the Rhine, so I'll have to try out some German.

I am glad to read that you and Mother and all my brothers and sisters are well, but it's a great shame Dad seems to be no better.

We wrote about castles and fortresses in recent letters, do you remember? Well, we have visited nearly every castle and fortification wherever we have been, and in chess parlance I am just about castled out. If I'm not a world expert on towers and redoubts and salients I must be very close to it!! I could bore a portcullis to death.

I am going hunting in an hour or so with our host and his son. Frankly I can think of better things to do in this rain, but you are not here to participate. With the ground being so muddy, riding may be risky, but I can only appear churlish by refusing to go. Wish me luck!!

Write soon.
All my love,
Thomas.

Margaret. Yorkshire, November, 1612

Dear Thomas,
I have only just opened your letter from Lyons. It took three weeks to get here – one end of the month to the other!!

Strafford

This is only a quick note to tell you that your Father is not at all well. He will not take to his bed, but falls asleep in the drawing room, in the garden if he sits down, and last night he even fell asleep at the dinner table. Fortunately we had no guests, but your poor Mother was – is – so worried. I am doing all I can to help her.

I don't know how to tell you all that without worrying you, but I could not bear to upset you by not telling you, either. Fortunately some of your brothers and sisters are too young to realise there is anything wrong, but William and John – you know how sensitive they both are – are not taking it very well. I try to cheer them up, but it is a struggle.

I hope you enjoyed hunting in the rain!! And that you did not fall off your horse.

There is another very shocking piece of news. Henry, the Prince of Wales, has died!! Princess Elizabeth was supposed to be getting married to the Elector Palatine from Germany just then – the beginning of this month – and the wedding had to be put off. The whole country is in serious mourning. Henry was so popular. Your Father was down in the dumps for days and I don't think the shock helped his health at all.

Write soon!! Sorry this isn't one of my normal silly chatty missives.
All my love, dearest Thomas.
Margaret.

Thomas. Lyons. 10th December, 1612

My Darling Margaret,

The news about my Father is dreadful, and that about Prince Henry is devastating, but I cannot do anything at the moment. I did not fall off my horse while hunting, but I got completely drenched, there was a cold wind riding back to the Chateau, and by the time I got indoors I was chilled to the bone. I was stupid. Instead of getting into a warm bed, I changed and went down to dinner.

In the night, I was sick and going at the other end too and shivering, and I've been ill ever since. I can get up now for a few hours at a time, but am still off my food and only fancy broth and hot drinks. The weather is worse, and the Mistral – it's a terrible wind which whistles down the country at this time of year – has come early, so it is really freezing here now. If only it would warm up a bit I might be feeling better sooner.

As it is, Charles and I have decided to cancel the journey on the Rhine, and I shall come home as soon as possible to see Dad – and you of course. Please give him a hug and a kiss from me – you'll do it so much better – and Mother and all the little pests too. I am so glad you are being good to her and Will and John.

I love you and am dying to hold you close and kiss you over and over – and all over.
I am yours, through and through.
Thomas.

Margaret. 15th March, 1613. Wentworth Woodhouse

Thomas has been home a fortnight, and it has been heaven. I think we have made love more times than we did even in the week after our wedding. I have missed him so much, and it was so obvious how much he missed me. If I don't get pregnant now, then I never shall.

And we are doing some different and exciting things. All because of a book! A few weeks ago I was in my Father's library at Londesborough, where I'd gone for a family visit for three weeks. I was looking for something to read, and wandering along the shelves behind his writing table. The drawers in this desk have always been locked. I had never been able to open them when I was little. Once Papa told me very sternly when he spotted me trying one: "If you open that drawer, you'll never go to Heaven." He didn't smack me; he wasn't that kind of Father.

As I passed behind the desk this time, I did what I always did: put out a hand idly and tugged at the drawer-handle; the same drawer Papa had seen me try to open years ago. To my astonishment the drawer opened. I saw it contained some books. I could see two were in French, one in Italian. One looked as though it might be from China.

As I picked up the Chinese one I glanced down the room to check that the door was quite shut. It was. I then opened the book, roughly in the middle. Astonishment turned instantly to shock. I was looking at hand-painted pictures of a young woman on her knees and a man standing in front of her. She was doing something to him with her mouth!!

I shut the book with a slap, worried if anyone had heard. I slipped the book back in the drawer. I left the library fast.

A little later I realised I had found nothing to read, and might have another chance to look at this naughty book. Nobody was in the library; the drawer was still unlocked. I stared at the pictures for a good quarter of an hour. I turned the pages. There was one of the same girl lying on a bed with the man crouching on top of her, facing towards her feet, doing something with his head between her legs, whilst she had hers between his. Many pictures showed them in different positions. My heart was hammering away all the while. I then recalled what I was there for, put the book back, found a play by Marlowe, and took that away. Despite daily library visits I never found the drawer open again.

I couldn't wait to try out what I had learned on Thomas, though I was worried about what he might think.

Thomas, 16th March, 1613

This has been a marvellously happy period. When I got home the family were so pleased to see me, and I them, that there was a real party atmosphere. I gave them all small presents I had acquired for them – small but not necessarily inexpensive. The amethyst and diamond earrings and necklace I bought Margaret cost me a small fortune, as did the tiny devotional Italian oil painting of Jesus with John at the Jordan which I gave my Mother. It is supposed to be over two hundred years old, by a man called Della Francesca.

The blot on the landscape was Dad's health, or lack of it. My Father was up, and gave me a hug, and I was disturbed his formerly strong, quite muscular arms had become so thin and weak; he could not even stand for very long. He was almost hanging himself on me, like a sash. Tears ran down both our faces. In fact tears were running down all our faces, except little brother Matthew, who always seems to have a different way of behaving from the rest of us. He actually poked his tongue out at me.

I gave out the presents, and there were more tears, except from Matthew, but even he liked his present, a model of a French Castle with a drawbridge and portcullis that work, and a moat you could fill up.

I had a present for Smeaton, the steward, and summoned him to receive it. He is a tall, slim, almost gaunt, figure, with straight long grey hair. He is fiercely loyal, and devoted to the family. I gave him a set of French wine-glasses. Tears rolled down his face too. Then he announced that dinner was served. Brother William helped me assist Dad into the dining hall, and as I moved around the table to my chair, Smeaton took my arm, and said, very quietly, "The household and the estate staff would like to greet you on the terrace in the morning, Sir Thomas."

"How nice. Make it half-past eight, Smeaton." I had a gold French coin for each of them.

Margaret was very gay, and so was I. Soon all tears were forgotten, and happy chatter and laughter reigned.

We all retired to the music room and Mother played the spinet, and we sang for a while until my Father announced that he was done for, and had to go to bed. Margaret rose quickly, saying she was tired too, and would help Mother see Father up to his bed, and then go to bed herself. She gave me a sly wink as she went. My brother William went with them, and a few minutes later William returned. Margaret did not.

My sister Anne then played a few more tunes, and by this time I felt the need to join Margaret in the bedroom. I kissed everyone and left. I have never run up the stairs so fast, tired though I was.

****

Looking back, I can hardly describe how difficult I found the next few weeks after that last letter from France to Margaret. First, I was still unwell, couldn't even make a start for home for another week. Secondly, I was, obviously, rather worried about my Father. Thirdly, because of that, I wanted to get home as quickly as possible.

I had a choice between going on a horse, or in a carriage (slower), or by ship, which could be a bit faster or much slower than the other two, depending on the weather. If the wind keeps blowing you back into harbour it can take ages; when you get out to sea it can blow you in the opposite direction to the one in which you wish to go. Or send you down into the depths.

Charles Greenwood and I could have taken a boat from Lyons down to Marseilles, then a ship from there, westwards through the Mediterranean, round Spain and Portugal, through the dreaded Bay of Biscay, round Brittany, and at last (and with God on our side) into whichever English port the wind then favoured. On a ship you don't have to keep on looking for a bed for the night; with luck the vessel keeps on going through the night, but sea voyages are a lot more risky than land journeys. Your chances of ending up in Heaven instead of Hampshire are greatly increased.

We decided to go by horse and coach as fast as we could. Bearing in mind it was winter, the roads were appalling, most of them were deep mud; we were anything but fast most of the way. Our train of servants with all the baggage – greatly swollen during this Grand Tour by all the books, statues, pictures and other things I had bought – had to follow at an even more leisurely pace. Then the wind imprisoned us in Honfleur Harbour for a week, delaying our departure.

We eventually reached Wentworth Woodhouse at the start of this month, soon after the delayed wedding of Princess Elizabeth to the Elector Frederick had been celebrated.

I was shocked at the state in which I found my Father. He was a pale shadow of the man I had left fourteen months before. He had never been a fat man, but, rather, somewhat stocky; now he was very thin and fairly exhausted nearly all day, every day. It was the saddest part of my life up to that moment, and I cannot write about it as if I were back in that time. Here was a man I loved dearly, and he was fading away before my eyes. Even so, he had not lost all his old fire, and had a real rant about the tremendous expense of the Royal Wedding and the masques and parties that followed it, saying that when the King did not have two groats to rub together, he should have kept things simple.

Father was a died-in-the-wool Monarchist, so this tirade came as a bit of a shock to me, but the cost of the marriage certainly figured large in what people talked about all winter – much larger than the supposed advantages of an alliance with a small Protestant German state.

This topic livened him up for a little while, but then he lapsed back into lethargy. I got so miserable about it that one day I did something which seemed unforgiveable at the time; still is, really, although it had a temporarily good effect. I said to him: "Father, when you are so ill, how do you go on? Wouldn't you rather be with Jesus?"

He was silent for a little. "No, son. I don't want to die." He began to fight back. He began to get up more, walk about the estate a bit, talk to us (that was a great thing), and eat a little more.

Thomas. March, 1614. Yorkshire

And so Margaret and I went on for another year, thoroughly enjoying each other, sad that we were not yet parents, yet happy that pregnancy did not interfere with our love-making.

Yesterday I rode into the village blacksmith's to get my hunter shod. I got back at noon, handed the horse over to the groom, and went round to the terrace. I was delighted to see Father walking on the lawn. I vaulted the balustrade and ran down to meet him.

I smiled. He looked at me very seriously. "A messenger came from York. The King has called Parliament. I want you to stand as a Knight of the Shire. Do you good to get into politics."

"Why didn't you tell me before?"

"I had to take some soundings; send letters to some friends and neighbours; see what they thought."

"Couldn't you have asked me first?"

"Not a chance, lad. You and Margaret are inseparable – and I'm very glad about that – lovely woman, just lovely – but if I'd asked you you'd have said no, and you know me; I've never been the sort of parent to force you to do anything you didn't want to do."

I was livid. "You made me go on that tour. How do you know I won't say no anyway?"

He smiled now. "Because I know you, son. You love me and you're too considerate to hurt me by refusing when I've set it all up for you. You know how proud I am of you, and I'll tell you something else: you'll love it. There's a powerful streak in you, and once you've seen real power being exercised you'll want a share."

My anger faded fast in the face of this seductive flattery. He was right. I just knew it. I smiled back, rather sheepishly. He spoke before I could.

"You don't need to leave that lovely wife behind either. You can stay at the Earl's place in London. You'll be able to see Henry and Frances, won't you?"

"Yes. Henry's been back from Paris for some months. You've really thought all this out, haven't you?"

"I have. You've got a pretty good chance of being elected, as everyone I spoke to was keen. They know I'm not fit to stand. It's time a Wentworth made a mark in Yorkshire."

"Very well, Father. I'm a marked man. I shall do my damndest to hit the bulls-eye."

Margaret. 15th March, 1614. Yorkshire

This week ends on a slightly less than happy note, in a sense. At lunch Thomas tells me his Father wants him to go into politics! So now it's serious.

We are all sitting down to lunch in the dining room. It is a fine day and the sun is shining in the windows. There are daffodils on the lawn. There is not a lot of talking as everyone seems to be hungry - even my father-in-law, who has been out walking in the garden. Suddenly Thomas gets up from the table. He goes to the side-board, and brings back a couple of bottles of wine. They are already uncorked. He pours wine into everyone's goblet – even the smaller children's, but not very much in their case. Still standing, he proposes a toast to the new Knight of the Shire for Yorkshire.

One of the boys asks what a Knight of the Shire is, and another asks who it is. Sir William laughs, and so does Lady Wentworth. Thomas is majestic. Being married to him I am somewhat biased, but I have to say that he can – does – look very imposing when he wishes. "A Knight of the Shire, Philip, is a Member of Parliament, and the new one, Matthew, is – me!!"

There is uproar. Everybody talks or shouts at once, but eventually young William says; "But you haven't been elected yet."

Old William laughs again. "Don't you worry about that, Will. Your big brother will be the next MP. I've made sure of that."

Before I could utter a word, Thomas turns to me and kisses me. "The election is next week, and we shall be off to London the following week."

"But I'm not going to be an MP, Thomas. I'm not sure I want you to be one either."

"I've decided I'm going to be the greatest in the land, and with you at my side, I can do it." He says this with a smile, but then I can see that he was only half joking. With that, I want it for him, and for me.

I'm thinking our lives will change forever. Will they, though? If they do, will it be for better, or for worse? That's why I'm not entirely happy about it.

Henry Clifford. 14th April, 1614. Cumberland House, London

Thomas and Margaret have been here a week. Margaret and Frances get on so well. Thomas and I are very lucky fellows. Mind you, I'm luckier than Thomas at the moment for two reasons. First, Frances and I have a daughter now, whereas Margaret has had no babies yet.

Secondly, I am with both these lovely ladies a great deal, whilst Thomas is off to Westminster nearly all the time; I'm sure I'm having more fun, dining with the girls, taking them to the theatre, walks in the parks and fields around London, boat-trips on the river. Then Thomas comes home in the evening – that's pretty late – absolutely full of politics and what's going on in Parliament.

Mind you – goodness, I really should stop using that expression – so boring to keep repeating oneself – I'm not sure he really understands what is supposed to be going on. From what he tells us at dinner – repeats to me in the study afterwards, but with more detail – I get the impression that no-one in the House of Commons agrees with anybody else about anything.

Thomas says: "How can they do any government business like that? The King doesn't seem to have any kind of gathering of like-minded MPs to support him; even the MPs who oppose him aren't organized; they just obstruct."

All this shows me a Thomas I haven't seen before. He's always been quite a serious type of chap, but never really had any sort of focus. I knew he wanted to look after the underdog, like that time he helped sort me and that bully Chesworth out at school, but it was all ... well, rather woolly, I suppose. Now I can see that he is forming ideas about how politicians ought to act, to combine if they want to get anywhere. I'm not sure he sees it like that, but the other night, after dinner and over a glass or two of cognac, he was chundering on about the chaos in the Commons, with nothing getting done, and how he would do it.

I just couldn't help ribbing him about it. "Thomas, go on like this and you'll be running the country one day." And I laughed.

Thomas stared back for a moment. "You know, Henry, if the King gave me the chance, I think I'd like that."

Margaret. 22nd April, 1614. Cumberland House, London

Thomas and I have been here with Frances and Henry for over two weeks now. The time has gone very quickly. Henry is a marvellous host, and takes me and Frances to every sort of entertainment he can think of. I'm impressed with her, too. She has a very good housekeeper, and an even better cook. She oversees everything with such flair, and she is so polite to the servants. She doesn't command them imperiously, or rudely, ever. She always says "Please would you do this" and "Please do that". She almost always thanks them afterwards.

I've noticed, though, that she has a manner about her that makes her requests seem like commands. It wouldn't occur to anyone to say "no." When Thomas and I have a house of our own, I'm going to try to run it the same way. All the staff here seem happy and willing. I'm sure it's the way they are treated. Thomas's Mother works in much the same way, but she's not quite as kind, and does not take the interest in the servants' welfare Frances does. Frances knows if their children are ill, visits their rooms, and even their homes if they live out.

There's another thing that amazed me at first. Most people give their servants Sundays off to go to Church as long as there are enough of them about to do the basic tasks for the day, and an afternoon off every couple of weeks, and a week or weekend once a year. But Frances and Henry give most of their staff an afternoon off every week, as well as Sundays and opportunities to go home. No wonder they're happy! And they never seem to leave. But then why would any of them want to go and work anywhere else?

All this is quite different from the way my Papa behaves. He doesn't ask the servants anything. He just tells them: "Fetch this," or "Do that'. He's not rude. It's almost as though he doesn't know that the servants are people. You don't say to a chair "Please may I sit down?" The chair is there to sit on, so you sit on it. Father is the same with the servants. They're there; he pays them and houses them; he uses them as he wishes. I don't think he knows whether they have feelings or not.

There's something else here at Henry's that makes me want to laugh or cry by turns. That's Frances's baby. She is such a sweet little thing called Alice. And Frances loves her so much! She even feeds her herself, instead of getting in a wet-nurse. I don't think I know of any other woman in society who does it. It is so lovely and peaceful to watch. I know Henry sees her do it, but of course Thomas doesn't; it's not the sort of thing you do in public. Well, our sort doesn't, but I have seen the farm labourers' wives working and feeding their babies in the fields at home. The wife of one of our tenants even had her baby in a field last harvest time. Anyway, those baby things are what make me laugh and feel so gay. So what is it about Alice that makes me want to cry?

Well, Frances has this nasty habit (it seems unkind to me, but I'm sure she doesn't realise the effect it has on me) of keeping on saying things like: "It's such a shame you don't have a baby yet:" or: "I expect you'll have your own lovely little Alice person soon." I'm beginning to wonder if I ever will. It's not as though Thomas and I don't try. We love trying, and wear ourselves to a frazzle trying nearly every night, and nothing is happening.

Thomas is usually out at Westminster watching the parliamentary proceedings – he says he hasn't made a speech yet. He comes home late, and then sits up late telling Henry about it. But he still wants to make love to me when he comes to bed, and I'm usually dying for him to as well, even if he has to wake me up. And if he doesn't one or other of us makes the first move when we wake up in the morning. They say ladies ought to take it easy in the day if they want it to work. I don't rush about, and none of the trips Henry arranges for us are too energetic, so it can't be that – you know – too much violent exercise. That's enough of that. Let's think about Thomas. He's changed a bit since we came here and he went into Parliament.

He seems more thoughtful a lot of the time. He says some very provoking things about other MPs and the way the Commons does its business – or fails to. What really seems to get to him is the waste of time.

Last night at dinner he was furious. "The King called this parliament because he needs money to run the country.

Most of the Members are cross because they say he's not running it, won't listen to their 'grievances', as they call them, so they won't vote for any taxes or loans to help him run the country. Then the people who support the King say he can't do anything about their grievances or running the country until he gets the money. No-one gives an inch, and meanwhile the country goes to the dogs."

Henry laughed: "Thomas, go on like this and, as I told you the other night, you'll be running the country one day." And we laughed.

All except Thomas. He looked around at the three of us with an expression I've never seen on his face before. "And as I told you when you said it, Henry, if the King gave me the chance, I'd do it."

He is definitely not joking now. The trouble is I can't really see him as a politician. He's just too truthful about things. He is very clever – well, I'm bound to say that, I suppose. He might get on well to start with, but I'm sure he'd end up upsetting too many people. It might all end badly.

Thomas. 23rd May, 1614, Cumberland House

This Parliament is likely to drive me mad. It's like a bear pit, with the noise and oral warfare. Real battles may have been less bloodthirsty. It's been going on for two months, we haven't passed a single Bill, King James has been down here three times to make speeches which don't help at all, and we haven't voted him any taxes, loans, or subsidies. I've heard him called The Wisest Fool in Christendom, but no-one, wise or foolish, can run a kingdom without money.

How is the King foolish? Well, for a start he took steps to keep out of their seats men who, he knew, oppose him. They aren't unreasonable men; they know how things work. Instead all those seats have been filled with hot-heads; there have been interminable debates about unfair elections as a result, which take the King's business nowhere.

As far as I can make out, he wants to do everything in accordance with the law, just as Queen Elizabeth did, but hasn't taken the trouble to marshal anyone on his side. She used to get some of her Privy Counsellors into the Commons so they could guide debate and organize voting, but James just comes to the House to lecture us in his fine academic style and Scottish accent. He says things such as; "Never King was in all his time more careful to have his laws duly observed and himself to govern thereafter than I," and – and this was incredible – "The evidence of a King is chiefly seen in the selection of his officers, and in filling places, not to choose those whom he favours most, but to have every one according to his abilities".

What makes that so incredible is that he has cloth-head Carr – now Earl of Somerset, would you believe! – as his right-hand man. It's as though the King can't avoid saying one thing but doing exactly the opposite. They say Somerset sits in on all the Privy Council Meetings, saying nothing; no decisions are taken. He then goes off privately with the King for a while; they come back to announce their policy. If Somerset ever has his head cut off, it'll be hard to find a brain inside it.

I've must do something, but what? I'm definitely not a republican – as some of the wilder sort say they are. I'd die for the King if it would help, but this way of carrying on makes me feel more sympathetic to the opposition. I've met some MPs who are of a like mind. Two of them are particularly impressive, having very high principles, even if theirs are not quite the same as mine. One is John Eliot, and the other is John Pym. They are not leaders – or not yet, anyway. The bigwig in the House is Sir Edwin Sandys. He's a major merchant in the City, so he's quite different from me and the other two; we're all country landowners.

Sandys may be taking the lead, but he hardly sees things straight. He said the other day that the King was out to make us bondmen or slaves, which is just ridiculous. The King doesn't even have an army. He's in no position to force anybody to do anything, let alone enslave the people. The Judges certainly do not take orders from him.

I've been in Court listening to how cases are conducted, and at the Royal Court picking up hints and gossip from the usual sycophants. It was there I heard the Lord Chief Justice, Sir Edward Coke (far from a sycophant), state his view of the Law, which is that the King is subject to it just like everyone else. "The King is under the Law" is what he said. The boldness of it! Courageously he said it to the King: face to face. If anyone else had said it they'd be in the Tower by now. You can get away with a lot in a Court of Law, it seems to me, especially if you're the Judge, but talking like that to the King himself in one of his own palaces seems foolhardy. Henry VIII would have had Coke's head off in a trice. I suppose there'll be some kind of confrontation between the King and his lawyers on one side and the opposition lawyers on the other side soon, if this sort of argument goes on.

This Parliament will be dissolved before long: I can feel it. It's not called the Addled Parliament for nothing, since it is certain nothing can hatch out of it. Heaven knows when we shall have another, but if I get in again I'll be more vocal than this time. I haven't said a thing so far, but I don't think I shall endear myself to the monarch, even though I only want to help him. Criticism - even if it's constructive - doesn't seem to go down well with people in power.

Talking of which, try as I might, and as much as I like trying, I just don't seem to have the power to make Margaret pregnant; it clearly worries her. Disturbs me greatly. I'm even beginning to think that maybe my musket fires the wrong sort of balls. How many men want to think it might be their fault? This is doing neither of us any good. At least we're on the same side and don't fight with or blame each other over it.

Thomas. 1st June, 1614. London

Today I have a letter from Father.
My Dear Thomas,

I do enjoy your letters. It is very good of you to write me such interesting reports of the House. It is not so good to read that you and Margaret are still having no luck in the off-spring stakes. These things can take time. Look at Genesis and the story of Abraham, and think of Luke's account of Zechariah and Elizabeth, and continue to say your prayers, as your Mother and I pray for you.

I am not at all sure that what is being said about the decline in West Country trade is entirely accurate. As far as I can make out, merchants all over the country are doing well, and much wool is being shipped from Yorkshire to the markets in Europe, so I cannot see why the excellent broadcloth being woven in Devon, Cornwall, and Somerset, should not be selling just as well. Frankly, I fear it may be some kind of deceit on the part of men like Pym. I know you think highly of him, and I have never met him, but what I read in the pamphlets and some of the cartoons and lampoons that circulate make me suspicious of him and his motives.

He and his kind are against taxes for the King, and what better way than to say that they just don't have the money to pay tax down in Calne or wherever it is he sits for? I know you think the King shouldn't have the revenue if he doesn't redress grievances and has advisers like Carr, but you are not against the King in principle. I fear that may not be the case with Pym. You need to be wary of him.

And talking of being wary, I have heard that Arthur Ingram is MP for Romney. Now he is a Londoner of a sort, but he has quite a bit of property up here in Yorkshire, and he has a rather unsavoury reputation, so keep clear of him.

I have also heard a rumour that a young fellow called Villiers has appeared at Court, and seems to be vying with Carr, Earl of Somerset, for the King's affections. I suppose I'm getting old and intolerant in my dotage, but when I think back to the King's peculiar tastes I marvel. There was that fellow James Hay who came down from Scotland with him; he wasn't odd, as far as I know, but what did he do to deserve being made a Viscount? Still, I understand he is doing very well as a diplomat, but when you think of that sodomite Philip Herbert being made Earl of Montgomery, and Carr being made Viscount Rochester and now Earl of Somerset, it makes you wonder.

I believe Carr's only claim to fame was to fall off his horse and break his leg when jousting at a Royal Tournament, right in front of the King, who was so fascinated by his good looks that he arranged for his treatment by his own physicians. Gossip has it that the sure route to Royal favour these days is a predilection for sodomy.

It is all beyond me. If that sodomy business is true, why on earth was there all that fuss about Carr stealing the Earl of Essex's wife, and the rest of that scandal? I suppose these men are just like weather-vanes (I nearly wrote cocks, but that seems too near the mark in this context), so they turn to the front or the back according to the direction from which the best offers come.

I am glad to hear that Parliament has been dissolved and that you will be home soon. Your Mother and I are looking forward to seeing you and Margaret again. Mother is well, and you could say 'mothering' me. I am still not too fit myself, and I can see it worries her a lot. Most days I have very little energy, and the physician doesn't seem to do me any good. Much love from your Mother, a kiss for Margaret, and of course from me, your loving
Father.

****

What Father says in that letter about James's favourites is important. I must try to remember, when I get into power (as I shall), that having favourites is no way to run a government: ability and state-craft are what count. I shall also be sure to avoid turning my back in certain circles, no matter what preferment may be on offer.

Thomas. 24th September, 1614. London

We are staying at grandfather Atkinson's house in Chancery Lane. Margaret and I travelled down to London in early September so that I could undertake some cases in the Courts during Michaelmas Term, for which I had been briefed in York. Trying cases in Westminster Hall is, well, trying, to say the least. The crowds mill about at the back, and voices can be heard from the cases going on in the Courts on each side of the partitions. This means you have to raise your voice, which just adds to the din, and almost everyone ends up shouting. If the judge is hard of hearing – and some are – it is either tragic, or extremely amusing when he doesn't understand what is going on.

Some of the judges can be rather witty.

Juryman. My Lord, can I be excused from the jury in this case?

Judge. Why?

Juryman. Because the Missus is conceiving a baby today, and there's no-one else at home.

Judge. Don't you mean she is *having* a baby today? Well, whichever it is, I think perhaps you ought to be there.

I have taken Margaret out to the theatre a number of times, and we saw some bear baiting in a park on the other side of the Thames in Southwark, but Margaret thought it was disgusting; we stayed only a few minutes. I'm not too keen on that sort of thing myself. At least with hunting the stag or fox has a chance of escape, often does, but the bear is chained up, as many as six dogs torment him at once. I have to say I was very glad when the bear picked up one dog by the back legs, used it like a club to beat a couple of others away, and dispatched all three of them. We did not wait to see what happened in the end.

I had three briefs from Yorkshire, picking up another couple from London attorneys. Four went to trial, of which I won three, another settled on very good terms for my client. His ten acre field had been squatted on by a neighbour. We got the field back, 30 pounds in damages, and the neighbour had to agree to pay all my client's legal costs. These results were very promising; another two London solicitors said they would instruct me in future battles.

In fact today one of those attorneys is talking to me outside the Courts about another brief, when I see Margaret hurrying towards me followed by a man I recognise as one of my Father's servants from home. I excuse myself from the legal discussion, asking the solicitor to contact my clerk soon. I nod to the servant, taking Margaret's hands which are held out towards me as she runs.

"Oh Thomas, I ..." Margaret is breathless.

"What is it, my darling? And what is Isaac doing here?"

"I could not let him come to find you on his own." Margaret is terribly distressed, but not tearful, despite looking as though she has been. I put my arm around her, turn to Isaac.

"What is it, Isaac? What brings you to London?"

Isaac is a groom, an excellent horseman. I see that he is filthy with dust. He was obviously sent here for speed, rather than one of the usual messengers from home. I begin to apprehend something dreadful.

Isaac removes his cap, turns it in his hands. "Sir Thomas, Lady Wentworth – yer Mother - sent me. It's yer Father, Sir; Sir William is …. is dead. Ah'm sorry, Sir."

Margaret starts to weep. "Dear Thomas, I am so sorry too. Isaac arrived at Chancery Lane only two hours ago. The cook gave him a drink and a bite to eat, and then we came straight here." She puts her arms about me.

I am stunned. My Father is dead. Can I take this in? When Margaret and I left for London he seemed rather fitter than he had been for some time. We even walked in the parkland and fields of his estate a few times only four weeks ago. How can he be dead? He was not a bold man, but he was wise, and loved us all so. I know I shouldn't say it, but he loved me especially because I was his eldest son. He didn't love the others less, but there was a deep bond between us. We used to talk for hours about the estate, the tenants, local politics, national politics, religion and faith – so many things. I am going to miss him; in fact I'm missing him already. Who will give me wise counsel now?

Margaret puts both hands to my face gently and strokes my cheeks, and I realise I have been in a trance for a minute or more. I still have my arm around my wife, poor Isaac standing there like an earthenware statue, he is covered in so much dust.

Margaret is solicitous. "Let us go home, Thomas. Isaac and I came in the carriage. We can be home soon, and we can talk about it all."

I have tears rolling down my face. I see that Isaac now has tears coursing down his face too, making channels in the dirt. Neither of us is sobbing, but Margaret is, and we are attracting some attention from people going in and out of Court. We walk to the carriage, and make for Chancery Lane. On the way Isaac sits with us inside at my insistence, rather than with the coachman, as servants usually do. He tells me it took him three days to ride from Yorkshire, using eight horses, riding as hard as he could. Indeed, one of the horses actually died under him, a mile or two outside Nottingham, where he stayed one of the nights.

Margaret is rather concerned about him, has the housemaids prepare a bath and the cook a meal for him, after which she sends him to bed.

Thomas. 29th September, 1614. Yorkshire

Isaac and I reached Wentworth Woodhouse yesterday, having left London the day after he arrived. The journey took us five days. I'm not up to Isaac's feats of long-distance riding, even though I am no bad horseman myself. He was tired anyway from his previous ride, and slept for nearly twenty hours. I had told him to stay in London and travel up with Margaret and the other servants when he was rested. He would not hear of it.

"Ah doan't lark Lun'on, Sir, an' be best Ah ride with ye, Sir, to mek sure t'horses is well cared fur." Isaac's Yorkshire accent is broad and strong. I shan't try to write it again. Perhaps it can be imagined!

My Mother is strong, doing remarkably well. She always was stronger than Father, but they were devoted, and I'm worried she will fragment soon. Her usually serene face looks care-worn, and she has more grey hair. She tells me about him.

"He seemed to grow worse as soon as you and Margaret left for London, Thomas. I don't think he wanted to say anything; he wanted you to get on with your life, but he must have known the end was near. Two days after you went he didn't get up in the morning and stayed in bed until the end."

"What about the others?"

"Your brothers and sisters have all been very good, and done as much to help and comfort me as they can. Except Matthew, of course, as usual."

"I'll have a stern word with him, Mother."

"I don't think there's any need for that. I said 'as usual' because Matthew is the one who's normally naughty and a nuisance, as you know well, but this time he hasn't been naughty. Just the opposite. He's stayed in his room, barely says a word, and rarely comes down to meals. He's been so quiet and upset by losing his Father, yet I never knew he was so fond of him. It's as though all the rebelliousness has gone out of him."

"So he hasn't been much comfort to you, then?"

"No, but then I haven't been much help to him either. If you have a word with him, it had better be a kind one. Try to find a way to bring him back into the family, if you can."

"Do you know what killed Dad? Did the Doctor say?"

"Oh dear, you know how vague they can be! It seems your Father had a cancer on his liver. It grew very slowly, and that is why he's been ill for so long. There was nothing the physician could do. In the end William died very peacefully, in his sleep. Then I sent Isaac to find you."

Now it is Mum's turn to cry, silently, and with great dignity, like everything she does. I hold her close, and kiss her hair through her bonnet.

"And how is brother William doing?"

"You saw him at dinner last night."

"I know I did, but he's even quieter than you and gives little away."

"Well, we've left the running of the estate to Smeaton the last few weeks, so William hasn't had to do much there. He's been dealing with Peter, sorting out papers and legal things until you got home. As you know, William has his own home now, but comes to see me as often as he can."

Peter Man is the family solicitor. "I shall have to go into York to see Peter. I need to see him anyway, to tell him the results of the cases he sent me to London with. I'll take William with me." I start into one of my trances again, but snap myself out of it. "How did Smeaton manage, then? He must have found it hard with Father lying in bed. He never did anything without his agreement."

"That's the trouble, dear. He relied on Father for orders, and now he's gone it's clear Smeaton really doesn't have the skills or personality to manage the estate, or even to decide how it should be done, let alone do it. He needs help."

It suddenly hits me: I have to do all this from now on. Smeaton will look to me for instructions. My word will be the one that runs the parks, the farms, the tenants, labourers and other servants from now on, though Mother will continue to supervise the household. Margaret will have to take a bigger role in that. How much of this work is there for me? I need to see Peter Man sooner than I thought. Am I going to panic?

No. Panic is not going to help; it's not what I feel. What I feel is the need to get on with things: quickly. Mum must be able to hear the wheels and cogs and ratchets whirring and grinding in my head. I'm sure I can.

"I'll need to get a new steward."

Mother bristles. "You are not going to get rid of Smeaton, I hope; not after all these years. That is not how we do things here, Thomas."

"I know that, Mother. I have no intention of abandoning Father's kind ways - nor Smeaton, come to that. We shall have to find him a special project, and put him in charge. I shouldn't want him fighting with the new steward over territory."

"I have the very thing. You remember how your Father talked last year, before he became really ill, of creating a new lake by damming the stream below the south pasture, and stocking it with fish? Well, he was telling Smeaton about it again only a month ago."

"And if there's one thing Smeaton knows about, it's fish and fishing. I'll ask Peter about finding a new steward."

Then Mother drops another burden on my shoulders. "Whilst you were away we had another tragedy, I'm afraid. Anne's husband died three weeks ago. He was just lying in bed, cold and still, when she woke up in the morning next to him."

"Christ help us. She must have been really shocked. Had he been ill?"

"She was in a dreadful state. No-one knew he might be ill. His heart must have given up. He was only thirty-four."

Anne is my elder sister. She's five years older than me, and has two lovely young boys, my nephews, George and William. William is named after his Father, Sir William Savile. Anne is only twenty-six, and little George is six, and William four. Then this one hits me too: I'm head of the family, so these boys are my wards; in addition to being their guardian, I'm also pater familias to eight of my siblings who are still under twenty, and now I have to take care of Anne. Thank heavens brother William is old enough to be off my hands, and that Dad gave him his own estate a while ago.

Before we can say anything further a small personage with a mass of fair curls cannons into my legs, clasping me firmly round the thighs, and shouting "Fly me! Fly me!!" It is another George. This one is my youngest brother. There are too many Williams and Georges in this family, or there were until my Father and my brother-in-law passed away, but there are still two of each.

"Fly me! Fly me!" So I pick him up by left wrist and ankle and whirl him round until he is flying through the air at my waist height, his arms and legs stretched out. He is whooping with glee. He is five years old. I love him dearly, and Mother tells me he worships the ground I walk on. How am I going to deal with all this? I'm only twenty-one myself. Tomorrow I shall be burying my Father. Meanwhile George is shouting: "I'm an eagle; look, Mummy, I'm an eagle."

Margaret. 11th October, 1614. Wentworth, Yorkshire

We buried Sir William nearly two weeks ago. It was a quiet day, although neighbours, family and friends came from far and wide. Holy Trinity Church was full. The sun shone too. Lady Wentworth was very dignified, and no longer shedding tears. Much childbirth and the worry of her husband being ill for a long time and then dying have taken their toll. Her face is thinner, and her hair is quite grey now, but she is still a fine looking woman, and was clearly something of a beauty when young.

Thomas was stern, as he so often is in public. In the Church he stood for a long time gazing at the tomb of his grandparents, which his Father had had built. It's one of those sarcophagi with prone statues of the departed lying on the top; very mediaeval. He spoke to me afterwards about getting one done for his Father, and eventually his Mother, but I pointed out that the Church is quite small and you need to leave some room for a congregation.

He smiled at that. He hasn't done too much smiling for the last fortnight. Even our lovemaking had taken on a different character. Instead of the usual passion we engender, he seems to be using it more as a source of comfort. He's so gentle and slow. I think I love him more.

This makes me think of his parents, too, some of the time. They had twelve off-spring! Twelve!! How do you do that? I still haven't got one, and there's no sign of any either. And they were - they still are - all so healthy. Only one child died. Many of the women I know lose about one in two of their babies. It can be even worse for the lower classes; they live in such squalid conditions, some of them.

And Thomas is so good with these children. Someone has to keep them in order; he's rather strict and commanding, but he's also kind and makes time for them. He plays with the little ones. I think he has a favourite. It's George, who is rather a sweetie, with a face like a cherub, and masses of honey coloured curls.

John is dark and very quiet. He always was, and hardly ever seems to come out of the library except to eat or go to bed. We don't see a lot of William either, as he lives on his estate most of the time. He comes over at least once a week to see Lady Wentworth, and to talk business with Thomas.

They are off to York tomorrow to see Peter Man, the lawyer. I haven't met him yet, but Thomas thinks highly of him. He must think quite well of Thomas too, if he's prepared to brief him to handle cases in London and here at the Assizes.

I was writing about the children, the boys and girls.

I have to say that Matthew can be a little beast. He really seems to resent the fact that Thomas is now head of the family and in a position to tell him what to do. In his case, even more, what not to do. He can be so naughty and defiant. For the first few days after I got home, he hardly emerged from his room. I know Lady Wentworth worries about him. Thomas tries everything to get him to join the family at meals and cheer up, but I think he misses the point here. He's not always very good at working out how others think and feel. He was going on the basis that Matthew was sad about losing his Father.

But I had noticed how Matthew reserved his real rudeness and sullen attitude for Thomas. I had this idea that he was just very cross about Thomas being in charge. Whatever he suggested, to Matthew it was an order to be flouted. I knew he liked riding. I'd heard Thomas tell him to go with him when they were going for a canter or a hunt more than once, but the boy always said "No." Then a week ago I asked him, and he was down the stairs dressed in his riding clothes in a few minutes. He's been a lot better since that ride, which was fun.

Thomas. 12th October, 1614. York

William and I rode into York this morning; we're sitting in Peter Man's study. He practises from his rather lovely town house, which is in a row of Tudor buildings with overhanging upper storeys. The study is panelled in oak, with a few oil paintings, furnished with the latest dark oak furniture, which is very heavy, with quite a lot of carving. He has four clerks in an adjoining room who do all his copying and engrossing of documents and deeds.

He's about forty, I think, tall, academic looking, with dark hair, rather short, swept straight back from his forehead. His dress is sombre, plain, black, with white collar and modest lace cuffs. He wears a fairly thick gold chain round his neck, with a jewel, a dark yellow citrine, suspended from it on his chest. Apart from this sole item of decoration, his appearance is rather puritanical, but it is obvious that his whole outfit is expensive, beautifully made in an unostentatious way.

He is not a puritan, however. His simple elegance goes with the elegance of his mind. He's a fine lawyer, my Father trusted him implicitly, which is an excellent recommendation. The meticulous preparation of the briefs I have had from him reinforces that. William has also reported to me favourably on Peter's services whilst I was away in London.

We start with my giving Peter an account of the cases I did for him at Westminster Hall, and then we get down to the real business of the day; Father's Estate. Peter does not beat about the bush.

"Apart from the two original family Manors at Gawthorpe and Woodhouse, there's the one at Harewood, and another –Thornton Risborough - which Sir William acquired about the time he purch – um – I should say ….."

I laugh. "'Purchased' will do well, Peter. After all, that is the truth of how he came to be a baronet. Let's start as we mean to go on. I shall always tell you the truth and I expect you to give me the best advice bluntly and fearlessly."

"Thank you, Sir Thomas. I am far from inexpensive, as you will find out, but I hope you will always find the fees reflect the quality of the advice I give, and of the work I do."

"No false modesty there, then Peter." And we all laugh.

"So, there are now four manors, all in Yorkshire, as well as some farms elsewhere, and a large tract of sheep grazing in Gloucestershire, which I think came through your Mother. All these lands are let to good tenants, apart from the home farms at Woodhouse and Gawthorpe, which are kept in hand. The rents are substantial. What is more, they are always paid. Your Father was a fair landlord, his rents were not extortionate, and he chose good farmers, who recognise that if they fail to pay, their chances of getting equally good land from equally fair men were, let us say, somewhat remote."

"I intend to continue with Dad's policies. I can never understand why some landowners would rather try to maximise their rents even if it means land remains untenanted for months." I pause. "Is there any money?"

William leans forward. "There's about three hundred pounds in coin in the treasure chest in the library, and I think Mother has some cash with which she supplies the housekeeper."

Peter produces a ledger from the corner of his desk, and flicks to some recent entries. "I hold about a thousand pounds of your Father's, and here I keep an account of the money he has out on mortgages. There are fourteen of those, for a total of 68,000 pounds. One is in default at present, and we are endeavouring to foreclose, but the rest are paying the interest regularly." He looks at William, and then turns to me. "Currently, Sir Thomas, the income from your Father's Estate is six thousand, one hundred and thirty pounds per annum. You are a wealthy man. On the other hand, you have your Mother to care for, and extensive family responsibilities."

I cannot help smiling. "You know, Peter, we have a shepherd at Woodhouse, and two farm-workers at Gawthorpe, each of whom have eight children and an ancient parent living with them, and all they have is their rent-free cottage, a small vegetable plot, a small paddock for a cow or pig or two, and a few chickens, and we pay them about twenty-five pounds a year. As you say, I am a wealthy man. I shall never forget that I owe it to my Father, though."

William is sad. "And all that is after he set me up in some style."

"We are very lucky to have had such a Father." I actually have to dry my eyes with my kerchief.

Peter changes the subject. "I've been thinking about your letter asking if I could help find a new steward." He hands me a piece of paper. "That is the address of Richard Marris. I have met him and he comes highly recommended. He is looking for a new position because his last employer decided, a couple of months ago, to take a bigger role in running his own estates. You, I think, are too ambitious and will be too busy, to want to do that."

How right he is.

****

Wealthy man!! I should say so. Just think. If the cottage and vegetable garden and paddock are worth five pounds a year, those working men are on about thirty pounds a year, probably not as much as that. They are, of course, just above the lower rungs of the economic ladder, beggars and tramps being beneath even their feet. If the such men are worth thirty pounds a year, my income is two hundred times what theirs is, without thinking what the house I live in would command in rent from a tenant. I'm glad I don't have to pay rent for it!

Yes, I am a wealthy man. I'm ambitious, too, as Father was, but he was cautious, timid, whereas I feel bold, determined to get what I want. What couldn't I do, where couldn't I rise to, if I put my mind to it?

Should I be worried about the family finances, particularly having to find "portions" for my three young sisters of two thousand pounds each? No, I don't think so, for that will only be when they are adults or married. That doesn't worry me, then. Dad took me into his confidence early on, and even discussed how his estate should be disposed of when he died. Does anyone suppose he didn't talk to me about his daughters, my sisters? Of course he did. He recommended that at the right time I should assign to them one or more of the mortgages, or set aside money from the rents and keep it for them.

A bold man - a man like me - sees every difficulty as an obstacle to overcome, not to be cowed by, each problem an opportunity, and that is exactly how I see things. One of the problems occupying my mind is how to increase my wealth, become a bigger landowner than I am already. The best way to do that in Jacobean England is to get into government.

Well, let's face it, it always has been; probably always will be. The Ministers of His or Her Majesty's Government never stay poor. Power and wealth will enable me to help the poor, as well as myself, my family; I think about the working men again.

I do have one worry, though. Margaret still isn't expecting.

Thomas. 10th November, 1615. Westminster

Back in June last year I mentioned a letter from my Father about Robert Carr, Earl of Somerset, saying what a clot he was. Things have moved on a lot since then. This is the story.

Father's letter refers to James Hay, from Scotland. As Father said, Hay had been made Lord Doncaster. I'd met him in Parliament; he, of course is in the House of Lords, unlike me, in the Commons. He's a very nice chap, red-haired, tall, good looking, and very kind and helpful to me. I've even been to dinner at his house in London. Although he seemed to be a favourite of the King's when he got down to London, he clearly wasn't 'the one', certainly isn't now. The King was surrounded by the English in London; Hay did not want the Scots to be backed into a corner, or swept out of Court altogether. His plan was to find another Scot to whom the King might take a fancy, and Hay could then make sure that Scottish influence did not die out. That was where Robert Carr, who was a friend of Hay's, came in.

As Dad said, Carr was thrown by his horse (or the other fellow's lance) jousting in the lists. His leg was broken, but not irreparably. The King, taken with his good looks, actually went down from the stands to see the injured man. Being even more impressed close up, he ordered his own doctors to care for this young Adonis, visiting him every day, giving him everything he wanted. By the time he was up and about, Carr had become a friend of the King's bosom in more ways than one.

Carr was, and remains, as thick as the oak timbers of a man o' war, but the King, even so, tried to teach him Latin and politics. That was a wasted effort, because dear Robert's brain never did improve! But he was now the favourite, and somehow indispensible to every decision the King had to make.

But the King's gifts to his Robert were not just of the intellectual kind. No. Carr received money, and rings, a large house, an estate with the rents on various properties and farms. The worst thing was when some kind of fraud was perpetrated, and poor old Raleigh, still pining away in the Tower, had his castle and land at Sherborne in Dorset taken away; they were virtually given to Carr.

'Dear Robert', already a Gentleman of the Bedchamber, was also made Viscount Rochester, giving him more land in Kent. Being Gentleman of the Bedchamber was not inappropriate, perhaps, as most of the King's business was being transacted there.

So dear Robert became a Privy Councillor, and that really meant something. He was appointed Keeper of the Signet, a really glorified private secretary, which must have urinated from a great height over the Earl of Salisbury, the Secretary of State, and other very talented, reasonably upright men like him. Not that I'm saying Salisbury and his ilk were perfect and incorruptible, but they generally had the

King's and the country's good at heart. That was not the case with a favourite whose position – I use the word in both senses – is itself a form of corruption. It leads too easily to the giving and receiving of bribes and 'rewards'.

In 1612, Salisbury died anyway, leaving Robert Carr in undisputed control of the King, and therefore of the country. Perhaps that is a trifle unfair. The King was in charge, but because he procrastinated, relying so much on bad advice, he had effectively delegated control to Carr.

Carr wasn't too dangerous for a while, as he had an assistant named Overbury. Thomas Overbury was clever, worldly, experienced in diplomacy, could keep Carr from real disasters. Until, that is, they fell out. Fell out seriously. Indirectly the cause of their quarrel was a woman. Frances Howard was the daughter of the Earl of Suffolk, married to Robert Devereux, Earl of Essex. Essex is a good, intelligent man, so it is difficult to understand what it was that Frances found so attractive about dear Robert Carr, apart from his looks, his only good point. But find him attractive she did. Whatever Robert may have been up to in the bedchamber with the King, he clearly wanted to get up to something else with Frances.

And they probably got up to it, because the next thing was that Robert Carr and Frances wanted to get married. Of course, that meant she had to get a rather trumped up divorce from her husband, who was not happy about it, but the King's favourite could get anything he wanted. The trumped up nature of the 'divorce' was extremely shameful.

By some means the King forced Essex to agree that he was impotent. Essex was not a lucky chap. He was only a couple of years or so older than me, and at twenty-four he was compelled to admit that he couldn't rise to the occasion. I can't think of anything more humiliating, especially if it weren't true. I was worried about the possibility I might be sterile as Margaret was not getting pregnant; at least we kept that between ourselves. But impotent!! No, I didn't have to worry about that.

I can see the King's reasoning, and why Carr and his Frances would want it to be impotence, because a divorce pure and simple would not have allowed these illicit lovers to be married in the eyes of the Church. But impotence meant that Essex could not have consummated the marriage, which meant it was void, and could be annulled. Hey Presto! Frances had never been wed, thus a Church wedding with Robert was on, if the Commission appointed by the King pronounced the annulment.

Not only was Essex unlucky in losing his wife to another Robert. When he was about 12 his Dad, yet another Robert, had his head removed at the request of Queen Elizabeth for treason. Mind you, he deserved it, having marched into London with a small army to try to take over her Kingdom.

Now, as I say, Sir Thomas Overbury was clever. He realised that if Robert married Frances, he would fall into the powerful clutches of the Howards, and Overbury's lucrative career as Robert's eminence gris would be over. Gossip said Overbury governed Carr, whilst Carr governed the King; not a situation many men would be happy to lose. Robert quarrelled with Overbury about Easter time 1613, and Overbury vengefully promised to let the cat out of the bag about Robert and Frances if he lost his perquisites, which would put the annulment out of their reach.

Some say Thomas Overbury then did something to defy the King, but he was probably framed by Carr or Frances's uncles. He ended up in the Tower of London for it. He died in the Tower rather quickly, so the annulment went ahead, and the lovers married. Frances even turned up dressed as a virgin to marry the man she'd been rutting with for a year or so. This sort of behaviour is totally against God and the Bible. God plays a serious part in most people's lives, so having adultery the topic of common gossip in the streets and markets does a King and his reign no good at all.

That is why I shall strive to ensure that none of that sort of tittle-tattle arises about me.

The Howard clan then owned Carr, taking over and pursuing government policy. This policy was to give the Howards the important offices of State, and even more money than they already had.

The annulment case was heard by eight Bishops, including Archbishop Abbott; he and three others thought dear Frances was lying. It would have been a draw, but the King ordered the Bishops to give a verdict favourable to Frances and Carr, appointed two more compliant Bishops to make sure they did, and told Abbott he was to keep all the details secret. But that isn't how these things work out.

The King gave it his seal of approval! Having been married to the Earl of Essex, Frances was a Countess. The King couldn't let his favourite marry her when he was only a Viscount, now could he? That is how dear Robert became Earl of Somerset. It was all corrupt. But it was not the end of the story.

This vile saga affected my thinking – particularly about power and the way to govern. You have to keep your nose as clean as possible.

Thomas. 14th December, 1615. Yorkshire

Nearly the shortest day!! And another twelve months of making love to Margaret and her gorgeous body, and she still isn't pregnant. I have to say I am really quite depressed about it. I am already rich, and intend to get richer, but I have no heir of my loins. True, I have a gaggle of brothers, to any one of whom I could leave everything, but it will probably go to William, as he is the next eldest.

I expect he would be quietly capable, but I'd really like to give it all to George, except that he is still only a child. John is clever and studious, but I don't think he would put himself out to look after the family fortune, nor the family, come to that. He'd rather sit in the library and read. The others are all too young, just like George.

Ah well!! I'll just have to keep plugging away, as one might say. Not that it's a hardship. Goodness knows how many times Margaret and I have made love, but it always seems like the first time, apart from the fact it gets better and better.

Another thing getting better is the management of my estates. Richard Marris is making great progress. He's the new steward Peter Man recommended. He started here at the beginning of February. He is authoritative but fair to the tenants and the labourers, and has demonstrated a deep knowledge of the land, soil, cattle, sheep, and crops. He is also interested in trees and the forests, and tells me we should be ready to exploit any rise in the demand for timber for the navy. I hope I am going to be able to rely on him. Already we don't seem to be just Master and Servant. I must introduce him to Christopher Wandesford soon, see what Kit makes of him.

I'm going to need good men like them about me. I had a worrying visitor a few days ago: Sir John Savile. (Yes, he is related to sister Anne's deceased husband, after a fashion). That he came to see me was odd in itself. Men in his position don't usually call on men younger and not as wealthy. They send for us. So what is his position?

Well, he's rich; very rich. His interests in the wool trade hereabouts are vast. His sheep on the moors and elsewhere are almost as thick and numerous as the snow-flakes in winter. So he makes money from sheep, from their wool, from their mutton. He sends about half the wool to markets where yarn and cloth manufacturers buy it, he sends some of the sheep and lambs to the livestock markets where the butchers, other farmers and landowners buy them. He rakes in the coinage.

When the sheep have been shorn, the moiety of fleeces Sir John has not sold goes to the homes of the shepherds, his other labourers and farm workers where their wives and daughters spin the wool into yarn. This yarn goes into the cottages of his own weavers, and the houses and hovels of those who live in Leeds where he has a huge labour force. He sells the cloth in the markets, exports it to France and Spain, puts some of it into tailoring shops in Leeds which he owns. And he rakes in more coinage.

Then he takes this money to land agents and lawyers acting for deceased folks' estates; he buys those estates. He puts more of his sheep on those estates, raking in more money, and buys or builds more of Leeds. And then gathers in even more coinage. He also grows a lot of wheat and other crops, and makes money from that, as well as from rents on the properties he owns.

Do I dislike him for this? Not at all. I can learn from him. He has made his way in the world, as I intend to. He is wily, and shrewd. Do I like him at all? No. I can't say I do. My Father did not care for his company, and was rather wary of him, so I suppose that has influenced me. Sir John comes from a spur of the great aristocratic Savile family, but it is a spur with a spike to it. Two generations back one of the noble Saviles – Sir Henry - took a fancy to one of the maids. Not just an ordinary fancy, either; not the sort where the Lord of the Manor, feeling horny, takes a tumble in the hay with a farm girl. This Savile was besotted.

He installed the maid in a cottage, apparently treating her like a lady, except in one respect. He would have married a lady. But then he was married already, and besides, he could not marry a maid so far beneath his station in society. Married or not, the maid presented him with a fine son, of whom Sir Henry was very fond. When he grew up, having been christened a Savile, his Father gave him an estate, and bought him a knighthood to go with it. That knight was Sir John Savile's Father.

That is how this branch sinister of the Savile clan came into existence. Being a legitimate scion of the illegitimate branch, even a generation later, has embittered Sir John. This makes him sinister in both senses of the word. He felt he could look down on my Dad, who was not as rich, nor as well connected. Believe me, being bastard aristocracy like

Sir John is better than being mere landed gentry, like Father. Or me, come to that. For example, when that oaf Reresby hit Father and challenged him to a duel, Savile was one of Reresby's supporters, and when Reresby was punished in Star Chamber, Savile went about Yorkshire spreading the most awful slander about Dad bribing the judges. A lot of people believed him. I'd have sued him for defamation, but my Father wasn't that sort. Maybe keeping out of the Courts and the hands of lawyers is sensible, but as I said before, Dad was timid.

Father got his own back, though, even if he didn't intend to. He did it by marrying my sister Anne to another Savile; one of the real old untainted Saviles. Then Dad capped it all by marrying me to Margaret, the Earl of Cumberland's daughter. Her brother Lord Henry is one of my best friends; now Sir John has to look up to me, or at any rate to be respectful to my wife, treat me with some care.

On the other hand I have to be careful how I treat him. He's not just rich; he is very powerful politically in the West Riding, because so many people are dependent upon him for their farm, their job, their shop, or in other ways in which their livelihood means they cannot do without him. He controls votes at elections, power amongst the Justices of the Peace, and influence with many local lawyers. If he says to his cronies and friends "Don't buy from so-and-so," or "that man should be an outcast," the victim may well be doomed.

Savile is about sixty, and I am twenty-two. He has a good head of white hair, with a beard cropped short. He's about the same height as me, slim for the most part, but has a protuberant pot belly. They say this is due to his fondness for ale, an odd taste for a gentleman, since it is the mead of the labourer, but it takes all sorts. Myself, I prefer wine – good wine at that – but I take little of it. By contrast Sir Arthur Ingram is a vintage wine connoisseur. Unlike me, Sir Arthur drinks two bottles at a sitting, and frequently more.

I do not know him well. I first came across him in Parliament last year. He was MP for Romney. I find him very pleasant and helpful. Cynical friends like Henry tell me that is because I am gentry, and Arthur would like to be gentry too. He hopes to rise in the ranks by getting to know and help people such as me, thereby gaining entry to higher circles that way. Not that I am in the highest circles, of course, but Arthur is rich, getting richer, aiming for power and influence. He is great friends with the Howard family - well, that is what he says – which includes the Earls of Northampton and of Suffolk, but I doubt that they would say he is their friend, more likely an acquaintance with whom they do business. Suffolk is the Lord Treasurer, but that doesn't stop him spending more than his income, as so many of these really rich, powerful people do. As a result he borrows heavily from Sir Arthur.

There is nothing Arthur likes more than having the powerful in his debt. That is how he came to be an MP. Lord Northampton, as Warden of the Cinque Ports and one of the great landowners, controls e elections in many of his boroughs; Romney is one, so he put Arthur into that seat. Arthur will vote the way the Howards tell him.

Why do the aristocracy look down on him? Because his father was in the cloth trade in Leeds, and went to London to pursue that line of business. Arthur followed him into it, becoming rather rich doing so. He then started buying up lands from the Crown (one of the ways the King finances his government), then selling them back to the King, usually at a profit, a few years later. He uses the money he makes to buy more properties, from which he gets rent and other income, and lends that to people like Northampton and Suffolk. The interest rate for this sort of loan is usually about ten per cent, so Arthur does very nicely, thank you.

I am learning a lot by watching how Arthur goes about things, but I hope not to adopt all his methods. One of his favourite tricks is to buy a property for a substantial deposit, the balance to be paid later. Then, having got the property and the rents from it, he delays paying the balance of the price, waiting for the vendor to sue him. He then uses his wealth to run the victim of his tricks ragged through the law courts. He also gets his wealthy 'friends' to put pressure on such people.

What makes this strategy so successful is that he seeks out men who are virtually bankrupt, and who are anxious to sell their estate to pay off their debts. This means that Arthur can offer them a good price, but as he only pays part of it, and never pays the rest, he actually gets the land for far less than it is really worth.

But back to Sir John Savile, and what he came to see me about. He had sent a servant over from Howley Park one morning, with a note asking if he could call on me the next day. I scrawled on it that I should be delighted, and suggested lunch at noon.

Savile arrived on horse-back with a servant, who took the mounts to our stables and was fed in the kitchen. I asked Mother and Margaret to keep the children occupied, to take lunch in the dining room. I ordered mine and Sir John's served in my study. Sir John greeted Mother and Margaret with a slight bow and a few pleasantries, then the ladies made for the dining room with the children, and we went into the study and our .... What did I expect? Just social banter? From Sir John? Hardly. Whatever he said he'd come to talk about, there would be business or politics, or both, in it somewhere.

We ate, we talked of hunting, and the price of wool, Sir John drank two jugs of beer with his food, and I had one small goblet of wine. I was beginning to wonder whether he had turned up just to be sociable after all, and then it happened.

Margaret. 14th December, 1615. Yorkshire

I met a reptile a few days ago. Not a real one. Just a man who seemed like one. Sir John Savile. We exchanged only a few words when he arrived to see Thomas. They didn't have lunch with me and Mother-in-Law. They ate in Thomas's study.

I didn't see Sir John go, but immediately afterwards Thomas came running, yes, running, into the drawing room and took me back to the study. He was so excited.

"Margaret, I think I'm about to step onto the ladder!!"

"Which ladder? And what makes you think so?"

"The power ladder! Savile will put me on it."

And then he related the conversation he had had with Savile.

Savile. I suppose you must have turned your mind to holding public office some day, Thomas. (He waved his left hand in a dismissive gesture). No point in my keeping on calling you

Sir Thomas and you calling me Sir John. We know who we are, don't we, young fellow?

Thomas. We do indeed, John. (A pause).

Savile. Well, what about it?

Thomas. What about what?

Savile. Public office! I just asked you....

Thomas. I know you did. But surely everybody thinks about it?

Savile. (With a laugh). I hope my ploughman doesn't.

Thomas. You know the old chant kids do with the plum stones? Tinker, tailor, soldier, sailor, rich man .... Don't you think they say that even in the shepherd's hut? Even the shepherd's children know it's only men with public office get to be rich and powerful. If they're not rich already.

Savile. But if they think about it it's just a dream. But for the likes of you, it can be true. I mean, take me. I've been Custos Rotulorum here in the West Riding for .... Oh, I don't know; must be years now.

Thomas. Is it worth it?

Savile. Worth what? The effort? Definitely. The pay is paltry, I grant you that, but then I pay a clerk to do most of the grind for me, and he's happy with a quarter of the fees I get. But that's not what makes it worthwhile.

Thomas. Custos Rotulorum. Keeper of the Court Rolls. Not exactly the pinnacle of excitement there.

Savile. But that's where you're wrong. Verily I say unto thee – I just love these phrases out of the new Bible, don't you? Verily, verily, I say unto thee, the record keeping is a bore, but what about the things you find out? I know the details of every serious quarrel between any two people of importance which has gone to Court for miles around. No crime of any seriousness for which men of standing have been tried – doesn't matter whether they were convicted or acquitted – escapes my notice. That knowledge is power, Thomas.

Thomas. Don't tell me you read all the records yourself!

Savile. You're damned right I don't. But I give the clerk an extra pound for every useful case he draws to my attention. It makes him very assiduous - nearly doubles his pay some years. He does all the reading and just gives me a summary.

Thomas. Very interesting.

Savile. Yes, isn't it? I wanted you to know about it because I'm thinking I may give it up soon.

Thomas. Doesn't sound like you, John. But anyway, why tell me?

Savile. I thought it might suit you, with your barrister's training and the cases you've tried.

Thomas. But don't the holders of jobs like this one sell the place to the next fellow to take it?

Savile. True, and you can give me half a year's fee if you wish, though I'm not in a position to sell you this place. You have to be appointed. (He smiles). And you can 'sell' it back to me if I ask for it. (He chuckles).

Thomas. (Roars with laughter). Well now.

Savile. I'll put your name forward.

Thomas paused. I shook my head. "And?"

"So we stood and shook hands. I didn't know whether to take him at face value or not. I thought he was joking about letting him have the job back. At least I hoped he was.

Soon he called for his servant and departed. Straightaway I sought you out, Margaret."

I was stony. "He's up to something".

"Why do you say that? You've never met him before today, and that was only for a few moments."

"Thomas, I've never met a snake, but I'll know one when I see one, and he, believe me, is a snake. You'd better find out more. Go and see Peter Man. I bet he knows something."

Thomas. 21st December, 1615. Yorkshire

Today is the shortest day. I'm acting on Margaret's advice of a few days ago, and I'm sitting once again in Peter's chambers. I'm telling him what I told Margaret about Sir John Savile.

"I can't tell you anything now, Thomas. I'll have to look into it. Savile's reputation is unsavoury, to say the least. I can't understand why he should want to give up being Custos Rotulorum, but perhaps he is just fed up with it, as he suggests. At the moment I cannot see how it can harm you to accept his recommendation for the office, and it doesn't sound to me as though you promised to give it back to him later, even if he thinks you did."

"Very well. I'll accept."

Peter nods. "And as soon as I have news, I'll let you know. In the meantime, be very careful what you say to him and everyone else about this. Whatever you do, don't make him any promises about anything."

"My dear Father used to say 'My lips are as tightly closed as a bull's arse in fly time'. He used to say it about some men's wallets."

Back at home, I go up to see Charles Greenwood in his study. He stays here a lot of the time helping to educate my brothers, and teaching the younger girls to read and write. We became good friends whilst we were on my Grand Tour four years ago.

"Charles, I want you to do something for me."

"Anything which is not illegal, Thomas."

"Can you find some excuse to call on Sir John Savile at Howley Park? See if you can find out why he's giving up the post of Keeper of the Records, and why he's offering it to me?"

"Delighted, Thomas. In fact I wanted to go to see him and his library. There's a new book by Francis Bacon I'd like to read. Sir John may have a copy."

"Why didn't you tell me you wanted it, Charles? I'd have bought it for you."

"I know you would, and I don't know why I didn't think to ask you, but it's as well I didn't or I wouldn't have an excuse to go and see him for you, would I?"

"Very true. What's it about?"

"It's called "The Advancement of Learning," and as a teacher I ought to read it."

"Will you enjoy it?"

"I'm not sure. Bacon is a genius. Some of his work is wonderful but the King said one of Bacon's books is like the peace of God, since 'it passeth all understanding'".

Thomas. 23rd December, 1615. Yorkshire

Charles comes into my study. It is a very cold day, and he stands before the fire warming himself. He is so excited. "Thomas, I have it."

"He told you what this Keeper of the Records business is about?"

"What?"

"Yesterday you told me you'd arranged to see Sir John Savile as I asked, to find out why he wants to give up the job and give it to me. You went to see him this morning. Why are you so excited if he didn't tell you anything?"

Charles gathers his wits. Then the light dawns. "Oh, that! No, the point is he had the new Bacon book .... And he's lent it to me!!"

"Well, that's very nice for you, I'm sure. But what about me? What about Custos Rotulorum?"

Charles is downcast, looking at the floor, which is constructed of the finest, wide, dark oak planks. "Sorry, Thomas. I'm a sinner. I was putting myself first. I didn't do very well there, I'm afraid."

"Come on Charles, I don't think you'd know how to sin if you had Satan for a teacher. What happened?" I go to the side table, take the decanter, pour him a glass, and top up my own. "Here, have a brandy, and we'll try to drive out your melancholy humour. So, what did he say?"

"Nothing much. He's a wily old bird, and no mistake. I tried to be subtle, and made out that it was the book I'd come about, but he saw through that straight away. 'I tell Wentworth about the Custos Rotulorum post two or three weeks ago, and you're round here today asking to borrow a book? And you're a tutor in his house? Do I look as though I was born yesterday?' he says.

"I say: 'But Sir John, I haven't asked to borrow the book. I just wanted to know if you had it.' Then he takes me by the arm and leads me into his library. 'I don't read 'em', he says. 'I just buy 'em and put them in here for show. Bastow', he shouts, and a dusty little man appears at the other end of the library. 'Get this gentleman that new book by Bacon. I'm going to lend it to him, whether he likes it or not.' So he takes me by the arm and walks me back to the other room. 'So is Sir Thomas interested in the job or not?'

"I could see no use in trying to fool him – I just don't have any acting talent - so I say: 'I don't know for sure, but I think he must be or he wouldn't... er .well ... er ...he wouldn't....'

"Sir John laughed. '... or he wouldn't have asked you to find an excuse to come here. I can guess what he wants to know. First, why I'm going to retire from the post, and secondly, why I'm offering to get the job for him. Well, I'll tell you something young feller. If Wentworth thinks there's a catch, he's wrong. There's nothing else to tell.'

"So that's it, Thomas. We're no further forward than a week ago. Sorry."

I pace the room. After a bit I say: "Not entirely true, my friend. We are further forward because we now know just how subtle and clever Savile can be. I shall accept the job, and thank him for it, but I shan't trust him; no, not at all."

I see that Charles is carrying this famous book, and I feign interest when he shows it to me. I never did like heavy reading, and as I have no interest in teaching, I have to draw on my poor theatrical skills for this pretence. Fortunately

Charles soon departs for his room to make a start on the turgid prose of famous Francis, and I sit down at my desk to compose a letter to Sir John accepting his offer and thanking him for it. I shall send it over to him tomorrow.

Thomas. 7th January, 1616. Yorkshire

A letter from the Secretary of State arrives today. I have the position of Custos Rotulorum for Yorkshire, and a salary of 300 pounds a year. Not a bad sum, but nothing to get excited about. What excites me is having my foot on the ladder of official appointments. This post also brings me into a bit more contact with Sir Arthur Ingram, who is Secretary of the Council of the North, a pretty important position. He bought that post from the previous incumbent, I am told, for five thousand one hundred pounds. That is how these offices change hands, but the King's approval has to be obtained. In Arthur's case approval was, in truth, a foregone conclusion. The Exchequer was so empty that he was supplying it with money on loan, or getting other wealthy men to do so. He either gets interest on his own loans, or a commission or backhander from the people who lend the money for giving them the opportunity, and from the Treasury for finding the cash.

Sir Arthur obtained an even more important office. He was appointed Cofferer to the Royal Household. However, he didn't last all that long in that exalted position. He was so unpopular with the courtiers because of his trade background, and his rather shady reputation, that he was drummed out of office.

He told me that this was a rather severe blow for him. "I've never had such a setback, Thomas. I was doing so well with the backing of the Howards, but I fear they are on the way down. As you know, Carr is, or was …"

"Carr? You mean Somerset?"

"Yes, the Earl of Somerset. He was the King's favourite, and now there's a new one. George Villiers. I've been lending money to his backers, so now I have a foot in both camps. If the end is nigh for the Howards, I'll be on the right side with Villiers' sponsors. If he proves to be a power behind the throne, I should be safe."

I could not help smiling. "You'll be safe anyway, won't you, Arthur? You're one of the biggest landowners in Yorkshire now, and you have property in many other counties too. And what about the alum industry? You seem to be in it in a very big way."

"So I should. There's a lot of wool in Yorkshire, and lots of textile making. That's where my father started. You cannot have a successful woollen trade without the alum. When you soak the raw wool …."

"… in a mixture of alum and water it softens the fibres so that they can be dyed more easily. I know that." Sometimes Arthur annoys me by stating the obvious. It's a rather patronising habit he has. "That's why I'm interested in investing in alum, too. There's a quarry of it on the coast between Whitby and Robin Hood's Bay."

Thomas. 10th January, 1616. Yorkshire

I open a letter from Peter Man. He writes:
Dear Thomas,

My enquiries about Sir John Savile have borne fruit. I am not sure that they show why he has offered you the post of Custos, but probably it has something to do with a scandal which is apparently brewing and the Court case which I am told is likely to follow. It will be no ordinary Court case; it will go to the Star Chamber.

It seems that Sir John insulted a fellow member of the Justices' Bench at the Assizes last Hilary term, and then threatened him with violence. It follows that if he is convicted he would be forced out of office anyway. It looks so much better for him to have resigned before there is any trouble.

Unfortunately I have not discovered why he helped arrange for you to step into his shoes, nor why he asked you, even in jest, to hand him the job back if he should want it. We shall just have to wait and see.
Yours,
Peter Man.

I realise that I haven't told Peter that I already have the job. I write to tell him immediately, and hand it to his messenger who is waiting in the hall to see if I have any response for him to take back to his Master. I can't help noticing, not for the first time, that Savile and Reresby, who beat my Father, are very similar men. Violence between magistrates is, thankfully, rather rare. Reresby was fined by the Star Chamber. Perhaps Savile is hoping that, having given the post away, it cannot be taken from him later if he gets it back from me.

Thomas. Palm Sunday, 1616. London

The first Law Term of the year has ended. I have been down here for some weeks representing clients and also dealing with litigation involving my Savile nephews' inheritance; that is, my sister Anne's boys. I shall go home in a day or two. It is not often that I have been away from Margaret, consequently remaining celibate, for so long. That reads badly; I have never been anything but celibate when Margaret is not with me.

Margaret. October, 1617. Yorkshire

Thomas has been away in London. He writes to me two or three times a week. I'd rather have Thomas. His letters are no good in bed. Thank God he's home now for a while. His letters give me news about life in the city and his cases, but it is the society news which is so fascinating. Thomas has been writing to me about a new star in the King's firmament. Every letter for the past few weeks has related more of this saga, and today, after Church, we sit talking about it whilst waiting for lunch to be served. Thomas is excited as he tells me. "This story is so corrupt even the clergy are involved, and you may find that hard to believe, but it's true. It starts with Robert Carr, the Earl of Somerset."

"You always said he was stupid, not wicked."

"He's not been so wicked, but his wife and the people who back him have been. What brought the corruption out into the open was the revelation that Sir Thomas Overbury, Carr's former friend, hadn't just died in the Tower; he'd been poisoned and Robert's beloved, Countess Frances, was behind it. The four assassins she hired were caught and tried for murder, and then all the sordid facts about Frances and Carr became common knowledge."

"So these men informed on the Earl and Countess, then?"

"Yes, Margaret, they did. Eventually Frances and Robert went on trial before the House of Lords, and were sentenced to death, but the King reprieved them, and banished them to live on their country estates."

I shake my head. "That hardly sets an example, does it? I remember something about this."

Thomas smiles. "Of course you do. It was the dominant topic of conversation two years ago. The damage all this did to King James and the Crown was huge. The Earl of Essex, Frances's first husband, is a puritan, and very popular with much of the population. He's a war hero from Holland's fight for freedom from Catholic Spain."

"Indeed, and he was made to 'admit' he was impotent."

"Exactly, and now the King's being seen as ignoring murder by his favourites. He seems to be blind to all of this. He can't see that he's alienating his subjects. Their sense of justice and fair play – looking after the underdog is an English passion – means that all their sympathies were with the Earl of Essex, and now they think the Earl and Countess should have their heads removed."

I'm mystified. "What's all this got to do with - what did you call it? 'A new star in the King's firmament'?"

Thomas holds up his hands, shaking his head, in a gesture acknowledging that he has rather lost his thread. "What made it easier to get rid of Carr is the fact that a new pretty lad has hove into King James's view. His name's George Villiers. He's the King's new favourite."

"Where did this George spring from, Thomas? Have you met him?"

Now Thomas shakes his head. "No, I haven't met him yet - only caught sight of him. Where did he spring from? A lot of powerful people, including Archbishop Abbott of Canterbury and the Earl of Pembroke, were opposed to the hold Carr and the Howards had over King James. How to get rid of Robert Carr? Well, what about finding a new pretty boy for the King to be besotted with? So that is what they did."

I laugh. "Seems to me to be a strange and immoral occupation for an Archbishop."

Thomas laughs too. "Villiers comes from a gentile but poor Leicestershire family. He had so little money that these powerful backers bought him some fine clothes. Then they took him to Cambridge where the King was peregrinating around the country with his Court, living off the local gentry." He starts to peregrinate himself, round and round the dining table. "In Cambridge George landed a part in a play the King went to see. It wouldn't have been difficult for George to get the part, because his backers were funding it, but to be fair to him he could probably have got the role anyway. Why? Because he has what nearly all successful male actors have: tremendous charm when he needs it; reasonable intelligence; a slim athletic figure, and fantastic good looks."

"You'd think that would make him a ladies' man."

"Well, I understand he's not averse to them, but none of them can give him what a flirtation with the King can offer."

I shudder at that. "That's disgusting!"

Thomas laughs at me a little. "Don't be naïve, dearest. It is disgusting to us, perhaps but some men will do whatever it takes to get rich and powerful. The poorer they are to start with, the more they are prepared to do. And don't forget it's the King who's truly disgusting. Rumour has it that poor old James was smitten at first sight. Unlike Carr, George didn't even have to break his leg to attract the attention of the Royal personage. His handsome person was all it took. He was summoned into the King's presence, and the love of James's life was born."

"The Archbishop and Lord Pembroke got what they wanted, then."

"Not straight away. They had to gild the lily a little more, so they bought George even more clothes, and an office which would keep him near the King. Not much of a job; just a Cup-Bearer. But it did the trick. The positive side was that the clothes and the job brought George even more of the King's favour; the negative side was that it attracted the ire of Carr and his coterie."

I think about that for a moment. "I suppose even if Carr is unintelligent, he'd have enough brains to see Villiers as a threat to his power over the King, and therefore over everyone else." I wish it weren't so difficult to keep Thomas in view as he marches about the room.

"That's it precisely, Margaret. He did everything he could to belittle his rival in the eyes of the King, picking quarrels and daily struggles for supremacy of a surprisingly petty nature. Of course that may have been because, lacking any subtlety or real cunning, he couldn't come up with any cleverly devious way of keeping Villiers out of the picture."

"Couldn't the Howards have done that for him?"

"Yes, that hadn't occurred to me." Thomas ponders that for a space. "Be that as it may, whoever thought up one of Carr's tricks made a big mistake. I was there so I saw this for myself." My darling ceases his wanderings and leans on the back of the chair opposite mine. "It was a big banquet at St James's Palace. Somerset had placed all his cronies on the Royal Table with the King. He'd also filled up all the seats on the other tables above the salt. When George Villiers came in, there was no important place for him, so he sat quietly in an empty seat at the far end from the King's dais. He didn't have to sit there long. The King saw him, sent a steward to fetch him to the top table, brusquely told one of Somerset's friends to give George his place, and go and sit in the humble seat from which George had just come."

I cannot help laughing at that. "That just shows Somerset hadn't spent enough time reading the Gospels. Wasn't that Jesus' parable? Wait for the King to exalt you; don't seek the best place for yourself; sit below the salt instead. King James probably didn't realise what an insult he'd given Somerset and his friends, but the signal his action sent to the whole dining hall was; 'Watch out; George Villiers is about!'"

Thomas starts pacing again in the way he has, waving his arms about as he talks. "That's the bull's-eye, my love. From then on the decline of Somerset was guaranteed, and the rise of Villiers set in stone. Once the involvement of Somerset and his Frances in the poisoning of Overbury in the Tower was broadcast, Somerset was doomed. He was swept aside in favour of Villiers."

"So what has happened now, Thomas?"

Strafford

"Once a man becomes a power at Court, he becomes a power in most other fields. Villiers was knighted about this time last year. I doubt anything can stop him taking not just Somerset's mantle, but most of his other garments too. Already a few men at Court are seeking favours from George. That's where the power comes from. If George scratches their backs, he can be sure that they will do the same for him in the future."

Thomas runs his hand through his hair in a meditative fashion. "These events have made a great impression on me. I realise if you really want to do something for King and Country, and be able to go on doing it, you have to keep out of trouble, try as hard as you can to be honest, and maintain a reputation for integrity. Don't foster friendships which may bounce back on you. Don't play 'let's pretend' that your policies are something they are not. Stick to what you believe in; make it hard for anyone to call you a hypocrite justifiably. And try to do what you think is good for England, not just for yourself. What's good for a King is usually good for the people, and vice versa, and what is bad for either usually leads to revolution and civil war."

I smile at my husband. "I hope you manage to abide by all those rules yourself, Thomas, if - when - you get to be a power in the land."

Thomas smiles too. "Well, I'm not perfect, but I hope I can keep most of them most of the time. It's odd though. King James never seems to perceive just how seriously he breaks all these rules, even though he preaches them himself. I do hope he doesn't pass these awful practices on to his son, Charles. If the Prince of Wales inherits them he'll reap the whirlwind, and if I support him, so will I."

I know Thomas would like to be a power at Court, but he is so blunt and honest - I couldn't say he wasn't, could I? - that I can't see him scratching anyone's back. Not in a pleasant fashion, anyway. He might lacerate them if they get in his way or do what he thinks is the wrong thing, though.

Thomas. 23rd December, 1618. Wentworth Woodhouse

A couple of months ago I asked Charles Greenwood if he could come to stay with us for a few months to give me some extra help with legal matters and the running of my estates. That would give Richard Marris more time to go round the farms, check the boundaries and fences, confer with the tenants, and find out why a few rents are seriously in arrears.

I do not care to turn farmers and tenants out when they have been good workers. If they are ill or have been injured somehow, and cannot work, they can't find the rent. I prefer to see if we can come to some arrangement enabling them to pay what they owe over a period. That way I keep a good tenant, which is better than taking on someone new who may turn out to be no use and not able to pay at all. It has worked well, and Smeaton, who is acting as Bailiff, has had far fewer arrears cases to report.

It is always pleasant to have Charles's company. He must feel at home here, because at the beginning of the month he asked me if he could have a friend to stay.

Margaret and I were very happy to agree.

"His name is George Radcliffe. He comes from Overthorpe …"

"Another Yorkshireman then."

"Yes, and another lawyer, too. He was called to the bar at Gray's Inn earlier this year. He's very bright; he was my pupil for a year or so. I think he will do well as a barrister, as he has a devious mind!!"

"Truly, Charles? Then I shall have to try to find him some work."

Radcliffe arrived three days ago. He has a manservant with him.

At dinner we have found him witty, charming, and rather religious. He makes many allusions to Jesus and the Gospels when he talks. His conversation is entertaining, serious and formal by turns. He comes out riding and walking. He is of medium height, looks fit, and is clean shaven. As we both had Charles as our tutor at different times, we have quite a bit in common.

He is a widower, despite his being only twenty-seven. I should hate to lose Margaret that early in life; in fact I should hate to lose her at all. What a morbid thought!

It's going to be quite a large gathering for Christmas Day, as my Aunt, my Mother's sister Mary, is coming for a few days with her husband, Sir Francis Trappes, and two of their children. I understand one of them, Anne, is rather lovely now.

Margaret. 5th January, 1619. Wentworth Woodhouse

It is Twelfth Night tonight, and I have organised a party. Well, there are so many people staying here, or coming this evening, that it will be more like a ball. I don't want it to be as grand as that. I just hope everyone will be happy and relaxed. They will all go home tomorrow, apart from Charles

Greenwood. He'll still be working here. It has certainly been a happy time so far. Our cooks have done a splendid job with the food, and despite the wine flowing freely, no-one has been drunk or objectionable in any way.

I've been particularly taken by George Radcliffe, though I find his formality rather aggravating sometimes. It may be he feels he has to be formal with me, but he has been so kind to my sister-in-law, Anne Savile, that I suggested to Thomas he should talk to her about letting George try his hand at some of the legal problems arising from her late husband's estate. Thomas kissed me and said: "How often we think along the same lines. I've been wondering whether to do that. I've enough to do with Court cases, Parliament, and all our own affairs. In fact, I've been so impressed by his grasp of the law when we've talked about our estate, I've a good mind to ask him to do some work for us, too."

"Then you'll have to ask Peter Man to brief him and see what happens. You're so busy with your thumbs pulling plums from so many pies, Peter won't be sending you to London much longer."

"How right you are, Margaret."

"There's another thing. You know how prettily your cousin Anne has turned out."

Thomas smiles. "Any relative of mine is bound to be attractive. Anyway, what has that to do with George Radcliffe?"

"You can be so blind about some things, Thomas. Haven't you noticed how he always seems to be looking at cousin Anne, or talking to her, or making sure he sits next to her at dinner?"

"Actually, no I haven't. Are you scheming, you old matchmaker?"

"Oh! Get away Thomas. And not so much of the 'old'! I'll wager he sits next to her tonight, and doesn't give her much chance to dance with anyone else, either."

Thomas laughs. "Well on the first point, I heard you talking to the housekeeper about the table plan, so I know you've put them together. As old Higgins used to say, 'Do you think I'm deaf, dumb, blind, and silly?' And what about the second point. What do I get if you lose the dancing bet?"

"I have to make love to you once tonight."

He laughs again. "Fair enough. And what do you get if I lose?"

"You must make love to me twice. I win either way."

I Am Moving Up

Thomas. 30th September, 1619. London

Yesterday I arrived back in the capital ready for legal and other business when the new term starts. Today I go to the Palace in the hope of being noticed and picking up the latest gossip. I am lucky. I pick up a great piece of gossip, and am then noticed by the subject of it.

When I say gossip, I don't mean rumour or scandal. This item is true. Villiers is now Earl of Buckingham!! He is still charming, very friendly, and anxious to help people who are willing to help him, but he seems to have no political motives. He is not yet a power behind the throne, or even in front of it, as Somerset was, but it is coming, I am sure. His influence comes from the fact that the King is charmed by him, and will give him anything he wants, either for himself or for anyone who seeks his help.

As I'm wandering about in one of the ante-chambers, he comes in and notices me. I have no idea how he knows who I am, but someone may have pointed me out to him. Come to think of it, I saw Sir John Savile in another room earlier; he probably manoeuvred the Earl in my direction, judging by what happens. Rumour (and I mean rumour) has it that Savile is a sycophant of Buckingham's, though he probably thinks he is the Earl's friend! Margaret was right. I don't trust Savile. He is a snake, as she said.

Buckingham comes up to me with a slight polite nod of the head; I make him a rather deeper bow. He must be over six feet tall, slightly taller than me, very fair, and very handsome indeed. He is beautifully dressed in a regal blue velvet doublet over a startlingly white linen shirt with ornate lace cuffs and collar. No wonder the King loves him. Women must gasp with anticipation!! Heavens, it sounds as though I love him myself. Not a bit of it, but I fail to see why a man should not appreciate a person of beauty, no matter what their sex.

Villiers. Sir Thomas, is it not?
Me. It is, My Lord. I trust you are well.
Villiers. I am, I am. And you?
Me. I should be better if I had a position at Court, My Lord.
Villiers. Then you must let me know if any particular place might suit you, and I'll raise the matter with His Majesty.
Me. You are too kind, My Lord.
Villiers. Too kind? Too kind, Sir Thomas? Can one be too kind? Perhaps not. But I should be grateful if you could see your way clear to doing me a kindness.
Me. If I can, it would be an honour.
Villiers. Your neighbour, Sir John Savile, has asked me to remind you to honour a promise he says you made him some time ago.
Me. A promise to do what, My Lord?
Villiers. A promise to do with the post of Custos Rotulorum for Yorkshire, I believe. You are the Custos, are you not?

Me. I am, My Lord. When Sir John resigned from the position, he offered to put my name forward which I was soon offered and pleased to accept. I recall no promise.

Villiers. No promise. No promise, you say? Sir John tells me that when he arranged for you to get the office, he asked you to resign in due course if he wanted the position back. He says you agreed.

Me. My Lord, I am embarrassed. If I tell you the truth so that we can both act with honour in this matter, I shall probably risk offending you and Sir John.

Villiers. You need have no fear of telling me the truth. I know from Sir John that his enemies caused him such trouble in Star Chamber he felt it prudent to hand over his office as Custos until the air had cleared and he could resume it.

Me. Then I must disabuse you, My Lord. Sir John is an ambitious and arrogant man who ….

Villiers. *(He smiles disarmingly so that I cannot possibly take offence).* And you are not Sir Thomas?

Me. *(I cannot help laughing).* I am indeed, but I hope that I am not also unscrupulous and hot tempered. Savile's hot temper is the cause of the trouble. He apparently assaulted a fellow magistrate, Sir Edmund Sheffield, who was President of the Council of the North at the time, and in other ways brought disrepute on the office of *Custos,* which is why Sir Edmund referred the man to the Star Chamber.

Villiers. Interesting. Interesting. It never occurred to me to ask Sir John specifically who these enemies were, nor why they were his enemies.

Me. And you will be aware My Lord, that in his judgment on the case, Lord Ellesmere …

Villiers. The late Lord Chancellor.

Me. Indeed, the Lord Chancellor. In his judgment he said that Savile was disorderly and passionate in his behaviour, which ill became a man in his position.

Villiers. I wasn't aware of that. Savile did not mention it. Didn't mention it. Are you suggesting that he misled me?

Me. You must draw your own conclusions, My Lord, but it seems to me that the conduct which took him to the Star Chamber, caused him to resign and led to my getting the office, makes him singularly ill-suited to that post.

Villiers. And the promise? The promise to let him have the office back?

Me. There was no such promise, My Lord. I recall that he made a joke about my doing so, but he laughed, I treated it as a jest, laughing too, and I promised him nothing.

Villiers. Thank you, Sir Thomas. One might be forgiven for thinking that it would be inappropriate to restore a hot-tempered, unscrupulous and disorderly man to so important a position.

Me. Indeed, My Lord.

Villiers. Hmmm. I must apologise if I have given any offence by raising this matter with you when I was not in possession of all the facts ... not in possession of all the facts.

Me. No offence taken, My Lord, and I know none was intended. You would have had no reason to doubt or question Savile's word.

Villiers. You are gracious, Sir Thomas, and I shall be more circumspect another time.

Villiers is very pleasant. Unlike Margaret, perhaps he doesn't always know a snake when he sees one. He walks away, greeting and chatting with place-seekers and fortune hunters as he goes, charming all. I dare say I shall have to watch out for the reptilian Savile henceforth. So should the Earl.

It will also pay me to keep my eye on this Earl of Buckingham. He is, as I say, on the verge of being a real power with the eye and ear of the King. He has not only supplanted Carr, Earl of Somerset. He has also seen off the Howards in the shape of the Duke of Suffolk and the Earl of Nottingham. They were Carr's backers, and used him to gain control of the government after Robert Cecil died in 1612. After Carr's disgrace, Suffolk's wife tried to foist onto James an effeminate fool called Monson. This act of procurement was not a success, but it made Villiers see the red mist.

It also made him take his first political step, although whether he saw it like that is another matter. He sought out Sir Arthur Ingram. Ingram is another reptile. He may have started out as a barrow boy in London, but he's a very rich power-broker now, and a member of the Guild of Drapers and Haberdashers. His particular talent is as a go-between in financial matters, and he was well-known to serve the Howards in that capacity. His loyalty is not as developed as his monetary acumen.

Approached by Buckingham for information, he therefore had no difficulty in revealing that there were certain irregularities in the way Suffolk, as Lord Treasurer, discharged his duties. Buckingham then went to Lionel Cranfield, a senior figure at the Treasury, and between them he and Lionel persuaded the King to set up an inquiry. This inquiry was held in Star Chamber. It found that Suffolk had declined a pension from Spain but acquired one for his wife for a thousand a year; he had his builder paid from the Treasury for work at his homes; large sums of Treasury money had gone missing for which he had no explanation, and similarly with money which was supposed to go towards the Irish debt. The Earl of Nottingham was by that time senile, but the corruption in the Admiralty, which had enriched him, was laid at his door as Lord High Admiral. He and Suffolk were dismissed from their posts, and Suffolk was smacked with a huge fine.

The fate of Nottingham was especially humiliating, since he had been the commander of the English fleet which (with the assistance of the weather) had defeated the Spanish Armada thirty years before.

As I see it, nothing now stands in George Villiers' path to control of the King and government policy if he wants it. It seems like blasphemy to me (though Kings don't get prosecuted and in any case James is Head of the Church) that the King is supposed to have said that "Christ had his John, and I have my George." Arthur Ingram told me the King came to the christening of one of his sons and said this to the guests!!

I suppose Arthur Ingram's about fifty or so now. He has a reputation as a fixer, a crook, and this extends even to his matrimonial adventures. Everything is money to him, it seems. After his first wife died, by whom he had had children, he married a young widow, Mistress Holyday. Of course, I did not know him then, but this is what I have been told. Arthur had been knighted by the King in July 1613, 'for services to the Crown', mainly consisting of lending money, or finding men who could lend it and getting them to do so.

Knighthood raised his status above tradesman, even if it couldn't make him a gentleman, but this enhanced status meant he could look around for a new and profitable wife.

Apparently Mistress Holyday was a pretty and rather delicate creature, with one very attractive feature so far as Arthur was concerned. Her deceased husband had been a rich merchant in London. On his death he had provided her with an inheritance of sufficient capital to produce an income of three thousand pounds a year. How did Arthur get her to marry him? He could be sly and wily in business and politics; perhaps he could turn these talents into charm if he needed to.

He would definitely have needed to. He must have been over forty then, and he was never what you could call handsome, or even attractive, but short, corpulent, and coarse. She, on the other hand, had apparently been besieged by a host of admirers, and it was said that in picking Arthur she had chosen the worst of them. They were married in September 1613.

The new Lady Ingram did not have much luck. Within nine months she gave Arthur a son, and then died four months later. But Arthur was three thousand a year better off. He had all the luck; but then he made a lot of it, even if the making was far from admirable.

Over the years he had lent a lot of money to Sir Edward Grevile. Now Edward was a real gentleman from an old family with estates in Warwickshire. He owed money to others as well as Arthur. And Edward had daughters, including one called Mary. Arthur told Edward he would buy his estate for 21,000 pounds, and marry Mary. He should have paid more for Edward's land, but Arthur had knocked off the dowry in fixing the price, so he did very well.

He let Sir Edward go on living in the house and grounds, but Arthur enjoyed the rents from most of the farms and other properties on the estate. Fortunately for Mary she and Arthur were happy, and she bore more children for him.

I do not criticise Arthur for getting married and remarried in rapid succession. That is how things are, especially in the upper classes. Rich men do not look after their own children on a day to day basis. That is what a wife is for, and if you lose one, you look around for another. What varies from case to case is how much cash is involved, and whether it is more important than any other factor.

Thomas. 1st November, 1619. Yorkshire

I have been home a month.

"Your father is dead, Sir Thomas."

I do not move. I might not have heard. I stand leaning, palms down, on the stone balustrade, looking out from the rear terrace of the house over the Yorkshire landscape. One foot is thrust forward, knee bent, the other leg straight. The servant might think I look much as a sea captain must look on the poop deck of a galleon, scanning the horizon for ships, or squalls. Not that Smeaton would really know what a sea captain looks like. He's only ever seen a galleon in some of the pictures in the house. He's never seen the sea, but he has been to Sheffield twice. Some of the people in the village have never been out of it.

He tries again; "Sir William is dead, Sir Thomas."

I straighten and turn to the old steward with a distinctly unemotional expression. "He's been dead for five years, Smeaton."

Smeaton gives a little bow. "Sir," he says.

I move to him and put a hand on his shoulder, and smile sadly. I pause. "Why did you feel you had to remind me he is dead?"

"The way you were standing, Sir. You looked like you expected the Master to come walking up here through those fields, and the park, just like the old days."

"You must have been reading my mind." I look away from Smeaton, and back across the park and the fields beyond. That was exactly what I had been thinking. How I wanted my father to come striding, or riding across that park, as he was wont to do before he became ill. He was only about forty-four when he died. That wasn't so very old. How could he have been taken from me so soon?

Tears roll down Smeaton's cheeks. "Sir William was a fair Master, Sir Thomas."

"He was a good Father, too. Too good in many ways. Even if he left me nine brothers and sisters to feed, and a Mother to care for."

Smeaton dries his eyes on his sleeve. "And you've had the Lady Anne to look out for, and her two children; and her a widow not long before your Father died."

This makes me laugh, short and sharp. "Why, what a Job's comforter you are Smeaton. As if I could forget my big sister and her brood!" I run my fingers through my short, dark hair. I begin to stride back towards the house.

Smeaton, somewhat shorter than my five foot eleven, does his best to keep up, but his rather rotund figure and fifty-nine years make this a struggle. "Sir," he pants, "shall I call the staff into the Hall so that you can tell them the er, the er...."

"...the news?" I slow down as Smeaton comes up and I say, "Yes, do that. I'll speak to them as soon as I've seen my Mother." I stop, and catching Smeaton by the arm, look him straight in the face. "Smeaton, I'm not still grieving for my father. But I do still miss him. And now I could do with his wise counsel."

Smeaton starts crying again. "I know, Mast... Sir Thomas. I haven't been steward here, and a servant before that, for nigh on forty year without knowing you're a close family."

I turn aside to wipe my own eyes with my sleeve. I can't bring myself to use a handkerchief in front of even so loyal a servant. "Thank you, Smeaton. My Father and grandfather counted on you. I count on you, too, even with Mr Marris here."

Before Smeaton goes off in search of the staff I ask him to show me tomorrow how the fishpond has developed. I stand still a moment, staring at the Tudor house as though never before had I seen the oblong stone blocks rising to the red bricks of the first floor, with large rectangular windows. With a sense of wonder I find myself thinking the same thoughts I had when Dad died: *"This is all mine now. All this Manor of Wentworth; those at Gawthorpe and Thornton Risborough too."* I recall that I blushed with shame. "By God, Thomas," I recall muttering to myself, "how can you say that? Your Father only dead a few days and all you can think about is the money?" As I do so another little voice whispers to me: *"But you have to be realistic, don't you, Thomas?"*

Entering through the double doors from the terrace I make straight for my Mother's bedroom. I have never had the heartlessness to ask her to go to live in the dower house next to the Church in Hooton Roberts, which Father had had built twenty-one years ago. As I run up the oak staircase I stumble as another old thought struck me: I was only twenty-one when Dad died! I recall thinking then: *"How am I to do it all? A Mother, nine brothers and sisters, and two nephews to provide for, and four manors to run from which to secure enough of a living for all of us! With Dad dead I really need to retrieve my digit from the fundamental orifice."*

Mother is sitting by her window, reading. She looks up.

"Mother, I am on my way. I've been appointed a member of the Council of the North!!"

"Why Thomas, your Father would have been so proud of you! So very proud. And so am I. But why has this come about? Or should I ask how it has?"

I am slightly shocked. Mother's question is one I had not yet considered. I scratch my head, then my chin, and begin to stride about the room. "I'm not sure. I've worked quite hard at being Keeper of the County Records, and I've kept my eye on the clerks who help me. I think I have a fair reputation for honesty locally, and I'm known to work hard."

"Nobody gets these places without patronage or influence from on high, my son. Who watches out for you?"

"I really don't know. Perhaps…. Mother, you've surprised me. You're more political than I thought."

"Thomas, your Father may not have gone far politically – well, to be honest he never tried. But he was very wise and knew all the nuances of the system. I could hardly be married to him all those years without learning something, now could I?"

I smile. "No Mother, you couldn't. And yes, Dad was wise. I've always missed him, but being on the Council without him behind me will be so hard. I shall be sorely in need of his guidance."

"You will, Thomas, but you have Charles Greenwood and Christopher Wandesford to talk to, and they are sensible young men."

"You're right, Mother; between the three of us we must have almost as much in the way of brains as Dad did." She smiles now. I pause. "I wonder. If I have a patron, it might be Buckingham. He might have put my name forward as a quid pro quo for letting him see that Savile is an untrustworthy reptile."

"Perhaps. I fear you may have acquired an enemy there, Thomas."

"That's what Margaret thinks."

****

Then I go down to tell the staff, all gathered in the hall as Smeaton promised, that since I am now on the Council of the North, we may have a larger number of important visitors to deal with in future. I shall rely on them to care for the strangers within our gates.

The Council is a body appointed by the King to rule the Northern half of England for him. Because he is two hundred miles or so away in London the King needs men he believes he can trust to carry out his policies, keep the peace, and be able to deal effectively with emergencies. If it takes a messenger, or a team of them, two or three days to get to

London with a message, and another two or three to get back with the King's orders, without such men a real disaster could occur in the meanwhile.

Mother says she's proud of me. Father might well have been proud of me if he had still been amongst the living. Although I am pleased to be on the ladder, I'm far from satisfied. I want – or rather, lust after – a place at Court. I go there often enough – in fact, as often as I can. I'm getting known, but not sufficiently. Perhaps, in many ways, I do myself few favours.

I'm not fashionable. I have my hair cut the way I want it to look. Everyone else has theirs done to ape Prince Charles or Buckingham. I'm a bit too puritanical for that. I favour black clothes with a little white linen showing, and very little gold and jewellery. Most courtiers go about looking like a dummy out of a goldsmith's shop – and that's just the men!

I don't mean I am a Puritan. Although I belong to the Church of England, I'm not really enamoured of High Church ritual. It seems a bit too much like Popery to me, but that appears to be the emerging trend. In any case, it is the King's choice, and Laud's so, hypocrisy aside, I swallow it. No, I don't dress in style, I don't worship in style. And I can see that I annoy people, especially a lot of important people.

I lack that easy-going way of talking to people I don't know well. Upper-class people have ways of speaking, phrases they use, expressions, which are instantly recognisable to those in the know. They use them, and if you don't respond in the right way, with the same sort of speech mannerisms, they know you're not one of them, and then they treat you differently. They use subtle ways to humiliate you, and to let you know that you're not quite good enough. Well, that's how I feel.

The graduations of society are numerous, and largely to do with property and wealth, or the lack of it, as well as sheer 'class', which is what most of the real aristocracy possess - Dukes and Earls from families whose ancestors have been Dukes and Earls for generations.

The mistake I'm making is to think that I'm as good as they are, and to try to demonstrate that that is so. I tell people about my family, and the claim (or myth or legend, it may be) that I am descended from John of Gaunt. It is boring. And vain. And looks like inferiority making a cloak for itself. I can see that. For the most part people take little notice, but occasionally someone lets me know they've heard enough; that they are fed up with it. One Lord told me: "If you were King you'd be so insufferably high and mighty, I'd become a rebel!"

Being on the Council of the North is not exactly getting high and mighty, but Arthur Ingram has been its secretary since 1612. What he doesn't know about money and business and property up North isn't worth knowing. He's been Controller of Customs for the Port of London since 1601. Men don't get big salaries for these jobs. Their task is to make sure the customs dues and taxes are paid for the King, and they are expected to reward themselves by taking a percentage of the revenue they collect. It is a system open to all sorts of corruption, and men like Ingram can make a fortune out of it. And he does.

As Arthur was so embroiled in the financial chicanery surrounding Parliament and the King, he was able to prevent the suppliers of goods and services from swindling the King.

He knew how to do that, and how to profit from it, too. Anyone who wanted to do business with the Court, from selling meat to the cook or bedding to the housekeepers, had to go through or be paid by Ingram or his minions. To keep him sweet they supplied him for free with most of what he wanted, or just added to their bill the amount of any bribe they paid him.

Of course, the Court soon got fed up with having this lower class *nouveau riche* merchant sucking up to everyone. Being so lacking in subtlety with his manners and his sharp practices, he was sent packing. Did he vanish from sight? Not at all; he used the money he had made to buy property and develop it, and become richer still. Over the years I expect I shall learn a lot from him.

Henry Clifford. March, 1620. London

Thomas has been here quite a lot lately. He is a hive of activity all on his own.

He is desperate to get some sort of office under the Crown. He may be a Member of the Council of the North, but he says he wants a really important post down here in the capital. Mind you, I don't think he goes about it in quite the right way. He's not sufficiently suave, or even diplomatic.

What he tells people is whatever he thinks. The fact that it might upset them never seems to occur to him. Let's take an example.

There's a rather low life money broker at Court. His name is Sir Arthur Ingram.

It seems his father was some sort of tradesman in York, and Arthur came down here to make his fortune. His methods of doing so are, to put it mildly, rather suspect. I came upon him and Thomas recently. They were talking about Thomas's desire to buy into the peerage, apparently something Arthur Ingram knows how to arrange – provided some of the silver sticks to his own palm. Being an Earl's son, I find this kind of talk rather odious, and it annoys me that Thomas indulges in it. On the other hand I recognise that if he wants to get on, he has little choice.

Anyway, I wanted to change the subject, so I asked Ingram how his litigation with Sir Edward Waterhouse was going. How anyone can boast about conduct which is little better than criminal, I do not know, but that is what Ingram did. He explained that he had been buying a lot of property in Yorkshire, and had agreed to buy two manors from Sir Edward. There were some problems over the title deeds, and Ingram, who had taken possession of these manors, and was enjoying the rents and other income from them, used these problems as an excuse to delay paying most of the six thousand pounds purchase price.

Sir Edward was already hard up, which is why he wanted to sell in the first place; his finances just went from bad to worse whilst Arthur held on to the property, the income from it, and the purchase money. Arthur was very proud of his conduct. He clearly thought this was the right way to conduct business. Thomas was clearly appalled. He told Ingram, in front of me, that haggling over the price after the deal had been struck, and trying to beat the seller down, was dishonest and dishonourable, and conflicted with his own sense of justice and fair play. It was a repeat of what Ingram had done to Sir Edward Grevile.

Ingram has boot-leather for skin, so he laughed, and told Thomas that if he wanted to get rich, he'd have to learn, and Arthur would be the one to teach him. Unfortunately not everyone is as tolerant of Thomas's forthright utterances, and he will make enemies, and lose friends.

Mind you (I wish I could stop saying that), Thomas has made some very good friends at Court, and I don't just mean me. Archbishop Abbott thinks highly of him, largely because their religious views are similar. Sir George Calvert, another MP for Yorkshire, like Thomas, and now one of the Secretaries of State, is close to him. Lord Doncaster is a friend, and so is his wife, Lucy; she was a Percy, a sister of the Earl of Northumberland. Lucy was and is the most beautiful woman at Court, and I cannot help noticing that Thomas seems rather interested in her, even if he is married to my sister, Margaret. Not that he does anything about it. I hope he never does. But I digress.

Back to Sir Arthur Ingram. Thomas might learn a lot about making money from him, but he would have to abandon his principled approach to business, and his desire to deal honestly with his neighbour, as the parable calls our fellow man. That would be a pity.

Thomas may be stiff and lacking in warmth to those he does not know well, but his frankness and candour are what make him what he is, such a refreshing change from the oily front presented by those who tell you what they think you want to hear, and not what they believe, or what you ought to know. Thomas is a formidable character, and you know exactly where you stand with him.

Margaret. 9th September, 1620. Yorkshire

Thomas arrived home from London yesterday. He was exhausted, but that did not stop him talking about Parliament and Government, and his anxiety to get back into Parliament. We sat at dinner, just the two of us. I could not bear to share him with anyone else when I had not seen him for weeks. I had had the servants lay our places close together, with a pentangle candelabra near us, shedding what I hoped would be a romantic glow.

Romance was not what occupied Thomas, however. He was full of encounters with Buckingham, whose gradual engrossment of the power of the state on behalf of the King proceeds fairly fast, it seems. He was full of praise for Prince Charles. He told me the Prince was becoming more confident with each passing day, but remained a contemplative, reserved, and somewhat hesitant character.

"Undoubtedly his friendship with Buckingham is working these changes. Before Charles's brother Henry died, he was so shy, whilst Henry shone like a handsome beacon. The favourite is so easy-going, and charming, he is not awed by anyone, and the Prince looks up to him and goes about with him, so to some extent he is put at his ease too. This makes him easier to talk to, and the readier to enter into conversation."

I was intrigued. "Why should the heir to the throne be shy? Who is likely to worry him, or be condescending to him?"

"Difficult to say. His brother was such a young god, with so much energy, spirit, and sheer joy about him, Charles must always have been in his shadow. Henry was so popular, too. Charles is too diffident to attract that kind of adulation. There's something else, too."

"What's that?"

"I'm not sure, really, but I just get the feeling that he doesn't trust people."

I smiled. "But you just said he looks up to Villiers. You don't look up to people you don't trust."

"True, but that's different. To Charles, Villiers must shine like a sun which has replaced his brother."

This time I laughed. "Then Charles can only be a planet. Not very encouraging for the man who is born to be King,"

Thomas paused, and looked at me thoughtfully, before saying: "You're right. Perhaps, when he is King, he's going to need someone bigger and more decisive than Villiers to help him."

"And I wager you know just the man, and he's sitting right opposite me at this table!"

Thomas laughed in his turn. "Don't be silly, Margaret."

"Don't tell me I'm silly, Thomas. I know you. Who wants the best place he can get at Court? Who thinks constantly of the best way to run Yorkshire and the country? Who has ideas about getting the most out of the King, Lords, and Commons, for the benefit of the country? And who honestly thinks that no-one could do it all better than he can?"

Thomas looked very serious: then he slowly smiled. "Sometimes, my love, you know me better than I know myself."

"I haven't known you for weeks, Thomas. Take me to bed."

And he did, but he fell asleep as soon as he lay down.

Thomas. 9th September, 1620. Yorkshire

I'm having the most marvellous erotic dream. I'm lying on my back. I can feel long, soft, warm hair floating across my thighs, my groin. Moist lips are wrapped around my member, while a tongue glides over the helmet so exquisitely that I shudder with the sheer pleasure of it. I am in one of those odd states when I know I am asleep, know I'm dreaming, and do not – emphatically do not – want the dream to end. This tongue is imparting so elemental a hedonism that it has a likeness to some sort of torture, I shudder, and shudder again. Then again. And it wakes me.

It is Margaret's hair on my thighs. It is Margaret's mouth inflicting this incredibly enjoyable torture. As I open my eyes I can see that her beautiful buttocks are near my face, and her knees are either side of my waist, and I can feel her aroused nipples pressing into my chest. I want to seize her and make love to her. Yet I don't. I want her to go on doing this until I can take it no longer, and come gloriously. My cock feels like a skittle held upside down, with the thick end at the top, she has aroused me so.

I feign sleep for a minute, and another, and a fourth and fifth. I cannot keep it up. Her entrance is so near my face, I just raise my head slightly and lick it. She is wet; excited. She emits a sigh somehow, but doesn't take her lips from me. Maybe I only feel the sigh. I lick slowly with long strokes, and stick my tongue in deeply. I lift my hands off the sheets, and slide them, palms up, between her body and mine, and hold her breasts, and run my thumbs round her nipples, which harden further.

I begin to moan. My body stiffens as I feel the beginnings of orgasm, thinking she will recognise the signs and stop. It is more than I can do to stop her; she continues manipulating me in her warm sanctuary, and I burst forth. She turns around, and smiles at me. She is so beautiful. I think: *"I'll make her pregnant this morning; I could make love to her all day."* But I go straight back to sleep.

An hour or so later I wake, Margaret is gently playing with me, stroking herself – stroking what she calls her Parliament. She's been calling it that for some time now; in fact, since I got into the House of Commons again. When I asked her why she called it that she said: "Thomas, you're a Member now, and I want my Member in my Parliament."

I need no prompting. I kiss her nipples; I assist her with the stroking; I introduce my member to the House as soon as she's ready, which is almost at once. Please God, help me make her pregnant this time! A child borne of such passion, such love, must surely be happy, have the brightest of futures.

Thomas. 12th December 1620. Yorkshire

A few days ago the most abominable news spread through England. It was about the King's beautiful daughter Elizabeth. At the start of 1614 she had married Frederick, Elector Palatine of Germany. In 1619 the Hungarians had risen up against the Austrian Empire and its Emperor. They didn't want to be ruled from Vienna any more. They wanted to be free, to have their own king in Prague. They asked Frederick to be their monarch, and Frederick accepted. His principality, the Palatinate, was on the Rhine, a long way from Hungary, so he had to go there.

The English people were delighted. Frederick was a Protestant standing up to the most powerful Catholic ruler in Europe, if not the world: the Emperor of the Austro-Hungarian Empire, allied to Spain, with huge colonies in North and South America. The national wish was, still is, for an English Army to go to Europe to fight alongside Frederick and his Hungarians. However, King James does not want a war. For one thing he knows wars are very costly. Secondly, he knows that even if the people want war, they would not want higher taxes to pay for it; Parliament, if called, would not vote for more tax. Thirdly, he wants to marry Prince Charles into the Spanish Royal Family, believing that he would then, with the help of the Spanish King, have enough clout to secure a peace between Frederick and the Emperor.

In the end all this daydreaming on both sides came to nought, because on 20th November 1620, at the Battle of the White Hill outside Prague the Emperor's army defeated Frederick's forces utterly. That was the news which made us all so sad. But it didn't mean that the King will send an army, or that Parliament and people would pay for it, even if that is what they say they want.

****

All that is not as remote from my story as it may seem; it is in fact quite significant. It shows me that politics, and politicians, can behave quite stupidly, defying their own intelligence. One side wants to do something they do not want to have to pay for, cannot afford, whilst the other side wants to try to get the same result by a different means that costs little; neither side will listen, no-one will give way. It is a dialogue of the deaf. No-one can admit that the other man's idea might be better; working together is hardly ever tried. This discovery will make a difference to the way I try to do things if I ever have any real power.

****

However, I am cheered up by the fact that the King has called for a new Parliament to be elected, and I am to stand as a candidate again. I've asked Sir Arthur Ingram to help me. I know that wily old bird Sir John Savile will do all he can to defeat me, so I need an equally wily old bird of my own to make sure I win. I have another good card in my hand: Sir George Calvert will be the other MP for Yorkshire if we get in, and he is a Secretary of State, one of the most important people in the land. On the other hand, whilst he comes from Yorkshire, he hasn't been here much for a long time as his office requires him to live in London and travel about with the King. That may mean local voters do not pay much attention to him.

None of that bothers Sir Arthur. He says he can drum up a large mob to shout for me and Calvert on the hustings. He tells me to ask the Sheriff – who has to summon the freeholders to vote – to be firmer than usual in telling - ordering would be more like it - the people to vote. He also wants the Sheriff to tell us which men don't turn out for us. I think that may be going a step too far, but there's little point in owning a dog and barking myself; I'll do what he says, even if this dog might come back to bite me.

The hustings from which the candidates make their speeches, seeking the votes of the electorate, are noisy, and can be violent, places. Violence is common.

In Yorkshire, for example, if I were speaking in Ripon, say, or Rotherham, my supporters would be there, shouting for me and Calvert, and cursing Savile and any other candidate. And then a bunch of thugs from Savile's side might tear in, start clubbing my supporters, an affray would get going until the constables and the Sheriff show up. The next day, Savile or one of his colleagues might be speaking in Hallam, my men might go and attack his people whether I wish it or not. When I say clubbing, that is exactly what I mean; all these bruisers carry big sticks, clubs, even worse weapons, and the bloodshed can be frightful.

And it isn't just violence. Some big landowners like me - well, not exactly like me - pay people to vote for them; some - as I've said before - threaten their local people with losing their farm or cottage if they do not vote the 'right' way. None of the ordinary farmers can afford to fight a big landowner, like an Earl or someone with a huge estate (I am getting that way) through the Law Courts, so these threats can be very real.

I don't go in for threats myself as I am always interested in small people getting justice. I have no desire to be so ostentatiously a complete hypocrite.

Thomas. 31st January, 1621. Westminster

The State Opening of Parliament was today. King James rode down on his horse with Prince Charles, the Prince of Wales. It was a splendid sight, though nothing like as grand as a French King would have; after all, the French monarch barely needs to seek the approval of his *Parlement* for anything, and is not answerable to or likely to be criticised by it, as our King is. The royal pair was accompanied by a score or so of armed retainers in royal livery.

It is splendid, too, that he brought the Prince with him. He'll have to run the Kingdom eventually. It's a good idea to give him something more than a mere inkling of how to go about it.

On the way to St. Stephen's Hall the King did something he doesn't usually do; he waved to his subjects and blessed them. It was a common touch he rarely displays. I may not be a top-of-the-tree aristocrat, but I don't see myself as one of the people either. Even so, I can see the political advantage of making the people think you love them (better still if it's genuine), especially when you are the ultimate power in the country. I hope that is a lesson not lost on Charles.

However, what followed in Parliament is no guarantee that he will learn anything, unless it is how not to rule a country. The King talked in a relatively kind but patronising way to the Peers and the Members, almost like a gentle Father lecturing a wayward son on his behaviour. He is pedantic. He'd probably like to give them a book like the one he wrote for the instruction of his deceased son, Henry, the *Eikon Basilike*. He just told us what he expected of us, and nothing about what he will do for the people. He spoke of the tragedies being enacted in Europe, seeking our support (more like a demand, in truth) for his foreign policy. As it happens I agree with his policy (peace, not war), but he did nothing to try to persuade the rest that he is right. Having offended many he asked us for unstinting aid, by which he meant plenty of money.

I am a loyal subject, and believe in the over-ruling power of the Monarchy, but I was not at all impressed by this performance, even though I shall do what I can to smooth his path with Parliament. Still, I was quite nauseated when that highly intelligent, eloquent, sycophant courtier and lawyer, Francis Bacon, stood to praise the King, told us all to remember our duty to this wonderful ruler of ours, to revere him in a fitting manner. If my own feelings were anything to go by, if I am any judge of how both Houses received this tripe, the King did himself no favours at all. Fulsome Francis will have fuelled the flames.

How many of these men, Lords or Commons, have any real idea what is going on in Europe, or what to do about it? Clearly they are upset about the fate of Frederick and Princess Elizabeth, hate to think of the consequences for the Protestant states if the Emperor and the Spanish King win more battles such as the White Hill, but they have no solutions except a war they do not wish to pay for. Many are also very worried by the way England's trading position is, they say, going from bad to worse. The country's finances are diabolically poor, and that makes it hard for the King to get taxes, and difficult for the MPs to vote for them even if they wanted to (which they do not), and virtually impossible for the people (other than the rich) to pay them.

There are more discharged soldiers in the streets and byways, some begging, some turning to more violent and desperate measures to feed themselves. Poor people are everywhere. I am rich, but I cannot help them all. I do what I can on my estates, but I am resolved that when and if I get any real power, I shall see what I can do to make the Poor Laws work as they should.

All these problems just drive the King and Parliament further and further apart. The King says his policies don't work because he is given no loans or subsidies, and hasn't had any for nine years. The Parliament says his policies are stupid so they won't give him any cash. Obstinacy on both sides rules the roost. Sitting down to negotiate a way forward never seems to occur to anyone.

The King wants a marriage between Prince Charles and the Spanish Princess. He thinks if Spain is his ally, he will be able to get them to halt the war against the Protestants in Germany, Hungary and Holland. That would be an inexpensive policy, if it worked. The last thing Parliament, come to that most of the country, wants is anything to do with Spain at all except to send an army to fight the Catholic powers. Even if the King agreed, no-one would give him the money for a well-equipped army.

After the Opening Ceremony, and the King's address, when the King and Prince had departed, I decided to talk to my friend George Calvert about these things, and what might be done. "Were you impressed with the King's Speech, George?"

George pondered; he is not ponderous; he's small and neat, with brown hair worn fairly long, a pointed brown beard, but he always ponders. I suppose you don't normally get to be a Secretary of State if you don't. At last he said: "The King's right, of course. We have no power to make him do anything. Starving him of money to carry out his policies simply makes him resent having to have any sort of democracy at all."

"We just don't seem to have any control over what the Commons do."

Unusually quickly George came back with: "We need a leader of the House. It was different under Good Queen Bess. She attracted a group of MPs who followed her lead and her policies and …. er …."

"Manipulated?" I suggested.

George laughed. "That's somewhat Machiavellian, but let it serve. We have a number of clever men who could do the same sort of manip – let's say organising – it sounds better – the conduct of the King's business in the House."

"But even so, Elizabeth was always short of money. Well, that's what my Father always used to say."

George acknowledged that with a nod or two. "Yes, but she avoided calling Parliament as far as she could; when she did so, she was so seductive with them. She'd harangue old Salisbury and other ministers in private or in Council, but she never talked down to Parliament or the people. She always struck exactly the right note."

"You'd expect that from a skilled harpsichordist."

"Indeed you would. Maybe that's why she enjoyed more harmony than King James manages. But back to business. As I said just now, we need a leader to knit together those who support the King."

Was that my cue to enter stage right and dominate the drama of Parliament? That is what I shall try to do. It will be hard. Somehow I must seem to be on the side of the House at the same time as I persuade it to do what the King desires. I can see myself getting crushed between these two massive rocks if I fail.

Thomas. 5th February, 1621. Westminster

A few days ago, being worried about Roman Catholics and some Puritans, the House resolved that everyone has to attend a communion service in St Margaret's Westminster, and must take the sacraments. Anyone who fails to do this will be excluded from the House. We are supposed to think this will help ensure the safety of the Kingdom.

A couple of days later we passed a law that no Catholic should be in or near London, but must retire to his home in the country-side, nor may he move more than five miles away from it. On top of that we decided that no Catholics should come within ten miles of Parliament, or the Courts of the King and the Prince of Wales, even when they peregrinate the country. This is bound to cause trouble; the King raises money by selling indulgences to the wealthy Catholics excusing them from attending the Church of England. If they obey Parliament's new law, the King's cash will dry up. It remains to be seen whether he will give it the Royal Assent.

Parliament's purpose with these new laws is to guarantee that we do not see men of all faiths and none sitting in Parliament, but only those who follow Jesus in the way we think He besought us to do. Any advanced degree of toleration would shock Jacobean England to the core.

Thomas. 15th February, 1621. Westminster

The first sessions of this 1621 Parliament hardly do the Members any credit. The first ten sitting days are mostly taken up with debating our Parliamentary privileges, as well as what we see as the King's attacks on them. He had assured us at the opening ceremony that all our privileges, including Freedom of Speech in the House, were safe with him. We nurse our grievances as if they were sick children. We spend days deciding how to put our worries to the King, instead of just doing it.

Sir Edward Coke, a famous lawyer, red haired, large enough to remind me of portraits of the last King Henry, tells the House that "The Prerogatives of Princes grow daily, but the liberties of subjects stagnate, and if once they are lost, they are in danger of never being regained".

At the same time the House should consider properly the King's request for money; it fails to do so. Yet on the question of Spain, he had the Lord Chancellor explain to us that he had spent one hundred thousand pounds of his own money on help for the Elector Palatine, and thirty thousand on ambassadors to try to negotiate. He also told us he had calculated that sending a military force to help Frederick and Elizabeth would cost three hundred thousand pounds the first year alone; if Parliament would not vote the money, he could not afford it.

We have a debate about the gradual rise and fall in the value of money. Trade is bad, the country seems to be poor. The landed gentry in the House (including me) complain that there is not enough money in circulation, that the price of land is falling, and our rents with it. I can vouch for that. I don't think I have ever been so hard up in my life. A ridiculous and trivial reason for the disappearance of the currency in England is the fashion for jewellery, and gold ornamentation and gold thread on clothes, because gold bullion and coins are melted down to adorn the apparel of the rich!

The serious cause of this lack of cash is what we call the "Balance of Trade." In 1620 we sold only one million, one hundred thousand pounds worth of goods abroad, but imported two hundred thousand more than that.

At last we have a serious debate about money for the King and the government of the country! It is mixed up with our grievances. It is said by some (and I agree) that the greatest grievance is the King's need for money, and Parliament must find some for him. Without that, the loss of the Palatinate would be certain, and someone says that "foxes have holes, but the King's daughter, Elizabeth has no place where to lay her head." However, it is pointed out that an army of at least twenty-five thousand foot and five thousand cavalry would be needed. No wonder the King could not afford it.

Parliament would have to be generous. A small subsidy would be like a plaster which, covering only a tiny area of a huge wound, would do no good.

In spite of a lot of talk to that effect, the House steers clear of being generous. Instead of giving an adequate subsidy or two for war to help the Elector and Elizabeth, and another to relieve the King's needs, the House gives two smaller subsidies "as a free gift and present of the Love and Duty of his subjects."

Calls for three grants, enough to enable the King to take realistic action, are rejected.

Thomas. 17th February, 1621. Westminster

Yet another attack on Catholics!! Both Houses, Lords and Commons, have the Lord Chancellor deliver a Petition to the King. He is asked to take it seriously because it comes from both Houses, based on Law and Religion. Parliament is worried about the Papists bearing arms; practising their religion openly; spreading their corrupt faith, chiefly through their priests and the Jesuits; and flocking together, especially in London. Their avoidance of the Law and its Penalties allows their numbers to increase.

The King replies that any existing licences for Catholics to be excused Church of England worship will be looked into by the Privy Council; that disarming the Papists is already happening; that only foreign ambassadors can hear Mass; that if English Catholics attend these ceremonies they should be arrested; and, finally, that whilst the laws against the priests and Jesuits should be enforced, he does not believe, any more than the late Queen Elizabeth did, that men should be made to die for their religion.

We have more fun in the afternoon. The conflict between the different Law Courts is the subject of debate. The Common Law Courts have different rules, different remedies from the Courts of Equity, and apply the law in different ways. The results would be comic, if they were not so expensive and disastrous for the litigants. Mr Fuller and Mr Hall had a dispute and Hall sued Fuller in the Court of Wards. The Court found in his favour, and sent Fuller to prison for disobeying the Court order.

At the same time Fuller sued in the Courts of Chancery, which gave judgment for him, and sent Hall to prison. So both men are in the Fleet Prison!! This is a system of Justice?

Margaret. 21st February, 1621. London

I really shouldn't tell Thomas "I told you so" quite so often. Thomas says I've been insufferable the last few days. He's joking, of course, but in a way he's right.

I haven't been able to resist poking fun at him about George Radcliffe. I told him right at the start that something would go on between his cousin Anne and George, and it did. Soon after that Christmas party of ours three years ago George was invited to stay at the Trappes' home in Harrogate. A few months later he was at a house party at their other home in Nidd.

He's got a busy legal practice in London now, when he isn't in Yorkshire doing work for Thomas's sister Anne (not to be confused with the cousin!) and her boys, and he's doing more and more for Thomas. Christopher Wandesford has effectively replaced Charles Greenwood, who has moved on to other things. Between them George, Christopher, Richard Marris, and Peter Man more or less run our estates and business affairs for Thomas, whilst he deals with politics and the North, and looks out for more opportunities for business and acquiring more land. I do admire his ability to get other people to do things for him and let them get on with it. I have a horrid feeling as time goes by he will find it harder to do that. He does like things done his way, and to have his hand on the details. These four men do what he wants. Others may not be so willing and loyal.

George Radcliffe has been lucky to make a good living in the law in London, and also in York, where he was able to see cousin Anne regularly

But I digress. The point is that today was George and Anne's wedding in Harrogate. We should have been there, but Thomas is just too busy to get away from London and make the long journey up to Yorkshire, and North Yorkshire at that. I dare say it would have been lovely, but Harrogate will be so cold now. It's bad enough down here; just thinking about going back to the snow and ice makes me shiver.

Thomas. 26th February, 1621. Westminster

I was a very busy boy last week. The Commons has been considering the uses and abuses of the licensed trade in liquor. Many MPs have been worried that there are too many unlicensed and disorderly Inns and Ale-houses around the country. Behind some of this is resentment at the granting of Patents by the King for cash. Once upon a time the responsibility for controlling the licensed trade was in the hands of the local magistrates, but the King granted a Patent to Sir Giles Mompesson to regulate the Inns. This led to much corruption of which, it was suggested, Sir Giles was the beneficiary.

It was alleged he had been charging inn-keepers fees for permission to build a new room on their inn, or a new staircase, or any other improvement. He was supposed to enforce the licensing laws against disorderly houses, and take action in respect of Inns and Ale-houses which had been opened without permission. Mompesson was said to take bribes from the owners of such inns, taking no action against them, even when other inn-keepers complained. He was also said to be charging exorbitant amounts for granting licences to build new inns.

He defended himself as best he could against these allegations, including saying that he was entitled to do some of it under an old law of Edward VI's from the 1550s. He came unstuck, though. When it was put to him that he had threatened a magistrate named Drake who had closed down an Ale-house where the owner-brewer had plotted the murder of a guest staying in the tavern, he denied it. He denied he had granted the murderous publican a new licence, and that when Drake objected to that and took the brewer to Court, Mompesson threatened to make his life a misery. This was a course he was said to have taken with anyone who objected to his unscrupulous, criminal behaviour, with which usually he succeeded.

How did he come unstuck? What he did not know was that I had been given the letter in which he had threatened Drake. Making his life a misery was his euphemism for having him beaten up, or even assassinated, a practice he was alleged to use frequently. I insisted the letter be read to the House.

The House has to decide what to do with this villain, but today we learn that he had issued no fewer than 3500 writs against inn-keepers, and had had about a hundred of them outlawed. Bearing in mind that an outlaw was, as the name suggests, outside the law, he could be killed by anyone! Pretty drastic for merely having refused to pay bribes to Sir Giles, you might think.

Margaret. April, 1621. London

Thomas has been so worried, although hardly anyone but me would know it. It's that snake, that ghastly Sir John Savile. He's been trying to get the House of Commons to declare that the election of Thomas and our friend George Calvert was fraudulent. What a hypocrite! He started this nonsense in February, about a week after the King opened Parliament.

So Parliament set up the Committee of Privileges to look into it.

From what I can make out, during the election, Savile was bribing anyone he could think of to vote for him or his candidate. He complains because, he says, Thomas asked the Sheriff to word the summonses to vote very powerfully so that men knew they must vote. What is wrong with that? I'm only a woman and don't even have the vote, but surely, if you can take part in an election which may express your views and wishes, isn't it only right that you should do so?

If you don't, how can you complain when the King's policies are not what you want, if you have no MP to speak for you? If the King's proposals are what you want, shouldn't you vote for someone who can support them?

Still, I have to admit that perhaps – and I only say perhaps – Thomas should not have told the Sheriff to let him know who did not give their support. Of course, this is the problem with the way the voting is organised. On polling day, the men go to the village green or a square in town, and they have to hold up their hand for the candidate they fancy, so anyone can see who voted for whom, and the would-be MP who didn't get that vote may send some toughs round to give them a pasting.

Maybe one day women – well, upper class women - will get the vote, and we'll have voting on pieces of paper so nobody knows who voted for this man or that.

Anyway, Thomas tells me that it is all over now. The Committee decided he and Calvert had done nothing wrong, but that Savile had done the right thing in reporting what might have been an abuse. Clever really, to leave honour satisfied on both sides.

We had Calvert to dinner the other night. Considering he is so small, he contrives to look extremely elegant, a description usually reserved for taller men. He was not happy about the way things are going in the House. "I just don't seem to be able to hit the right note about the King's need for money, do I, Thomas?"

Thomas, as usual, was blunt. "That's not the problem. The Members abhor the King's foreign policies. Until he agrees to send soldiers to fight on the Protestant side in Europe they will not help. Even so, they did vote him some subsidies."

Calvert laughed. "Just about enough to put on two of those masques the Queen loves, but hardly enough to secure an alliance with Spain, which he wants, or a war against Austria, which they want."

"You're right, George, but I shall go home to Yorkshire to make sure that the money that has been voted is raised promptly there. I don't see how the people can hope for fair and competent government if they do not co-operate with the King and pay the taxes honestly."

I chimed in. "But won't the MPs see that as just bowing down, knuckling the forehead, to the King? The way I see it, they think that if they pay the piper, they ought to call the tune."

George laughed again. "Lady Margaret has ...."

"You can call me Margaret without the 'Lady'. Thomas will not wonder if you have inappropriate designs on me, nor that I have wicked intentions about you if I drop the 'Sir' when talking to you, George."

Thomas agreed, and George smiled his acceptance. "Margaret has more brains than many of our colleagues in the House, Thomas. How will we men fare if women are educated, get the vote, and can enter Parliament?"

I hated Thomas's reply. "There are some things I prefer not to contemplate." But then he improved it a little; not much, but a little. "I have enough trouble dealing with the problems we already face than frightening myself contemplating those beyond the horizon." I punished him for that, by denying him the chance to make love to me that night. Well, I said "no" for ten minutes or so. If I'd held out much longer I'd have been as unhappy as it made him. Sometimes it would be advantageous if I didn't love him and enjoy lovemaking quite so much.

Next week we shall go home and Thomas will make speeches telling the people in Rotherham and other towns to give the subsidies happily to the King if they want good government to last.

Thomas. April, 1621. Yorkshire

Back home for a short while, very busy making speeches, and seeing people who matter; not much time for people who don't. Well, everybody matters, really, especially those who can vote, but there are very few people who truly count if you want to be successful in politics. You can always tell when a politician is conversing with someone who matters, because he looks interested. When he talks to someone who doesn't matter, he looks animated when he is speaking, but when the nobody speaks, a sort of glass screen comes over the politician's eyes, and you know at once that he's not really taking any notice. Unless you're telling him how wonderful he is, of course.

What do I learn as soon as I get back here? Why, that Sir Arthur Ingram is buying an estate called Temple Newsam, just outside Leeds, for twelve thousand pounds. He's buying it from the Duke of Lennox, who was given it by King James. Of course Lennox is the King's cousin, and a Scot, so James favours him, as he seems to favour most of his own countrymen. Come to think of it, the fact that George Villiers is not a Scot but still became the favourite, ousting Somerset and all comers, is yet another tribute to his looks, his skill, and his tenacious grip on the Royal Household.

Temple Newsam is a huge estate, including two coal mines. Rumour has it that Sir Arthur intends to build himself a palace on this new estate of his. The rumour is almost certainly true. I heard it from Peter Man, my solicitor, and he is rarely misinformed.

But twelve thousand pounds? Where does Arthur get the money? I spent fifteen hundred on some land at Kirkby Malhamdale in 1618, but there was more money about then than now. And I bought the manor at Ledstone for about five thousand pounds in 1617, and rebuilt the house in what I hope has been a stately fashion, but twelve thousand? In fact he is to pay half of it now and the other half in 1624. Even that would be incredible if I did not know Arthur's business methods.

Thomas. May, 1621. London

Back in the city again. The weather is warmer and the streets stink. It is a shame that the centre of power has to be here. Life would be so much more pleasant and kinder on the nose if Parliament met in a building in the fields of Yorkshire. I'd accept a field in Sussex or Northampton, or far away Devon! Never mind. I wasn't forced to come here. I volunteered, didn't I?

It's been a very busy few weeks. At home I met with deputations of fishermen from Whitby and other places on the coast, makers of knives and forks from Sheffield, and spinners and weavers from all over the county. They are very worried about trade. We should be worried about it, and them too, in Parliament. The wool and cloth business is one of the country's biggest exporters. If we don't do well there, the King's subsidies and taxes are a lost cause.

Even the cutlery people matter. They have been famous for three hundred years, since Edward III carried a Sheffield knife all the time, and left it to someone in his Will. The steel they make and the quality of their knives seem to be getting a fine reputation everywhere, not just here, but in Europe too. I'm told some of it even goes across to America, to the colonies in Virginia, because no-one there makes any of these things.

The fishermen's labours are an important source of food, especially in winter when there are no crops, all the edible cattle having already been killed. This subject cropped up in the February sittings. It emerged, as a result of my talks with the fishermen, that many of them sail all the way to the fishing grounds off Newfoundland on the other side of the Atlantic. They may be away for weeks on these hazardous enterprises. They pack their catch in ice, and sail home to sell the fish in the London market at Billingsgate, and in Whitby, and Hull (good Yorkshire ports, those), in Grimsby, and Great Yarmouth, and ports and harbours on the west coast.

I speak in the House about all these things. I point out that as the services of the fishermen are extremely important, their trade and their prices should be protected. This is not just because of the food they produce. They are marvellous seamen, able to turn out for the navy in time of war, and their small trawlers are useful as auxiliary vessels, for harassing enemy shipping, and as fire ships to be sent amongst enemy fleets, as was done against the Armada.

Regrettably, too many of my Parliamentary colleagues care for nothing but their own money-making schemes and scratching each other's backs to concern themselves with what is in the best interests of the country, let alone the people on the bottom rungs of the ladder. Consequently such matters are ordinary Commons business, and do not usually arouse much passion. Not so with questions of religion, nor money, which the King needs always.

The King tries to raise cash by selling monopolies, and the House pursues Francis Bacon and a couple of others for being involved. Those others have been obliterated, but Bacon is on trial over the scandal. Poor Francis; the House in hot-bloodied pursuit of a victim is a shocking sight. I hoped it wasn't one I'd come to know myself.

The victims on the religious side are the usual suspects, the Papists and the Puritans. The Catholics are always in trouble because they do not go often enough to the services of the Church of England, but every now and again the same charge is levelled at the chapel and meeting-house worshippers. The member for Tavistock in Devon, John Pym, recently supported the making of a new law to enforce proper observance of the Sabbath Day. Its target was the Catholics; the object was to make more of them attend 'our churches', not 'theirs'. As usual, it also aimed to have fewer games (such as football and wrestling) and other entertainments on Sundays.

A Mr Sheppard, an unpleasant looking man with a predatory nose and a pock-marked face, whose constituency I can't recall, was outraged that we did all we could to fence the Roman worshippers in, but left the Puritans (who go to the 'wrong churches' too) alone. Being a devoted Protestant myself, of a Low rather than High Church order, with few truly denominational preferences, I much resented this attack on fellow Protestants, as Pym did. Albeit they may be Puritans, I cannot see that they represent any kind of threat to England. They have no Pope, no King of Spain, willing, indeed anxious, to reduce me and my compatriots to the status of Popish satraps.

Mr Sheppard's views outraged me, and I vented my feelings in the House. "The Puritans are not an enemy. They have no desire to enslave England as yet another Spanish colony, or bind it with superstitious hocus pocus. For the most part they are honest Protestants, as we are, hard-working and loyal. Another Member may well say that we do not make mousetraps to catch Puritans, and maybe he thinks we should, but his views do nothing but offend our Protestant friends, and give comfort to those who would forfeit the religious freedom we value."

But back to finance. Not only does the Commons fail to get King James to attack Spain: he inflames them even further by continuing to sell weapons to the Spanish from the Royal Armouries and Arsenals. The fact that this gives employment and income to the country and to many people employed in the industry is ignored. Can Parliament accept that with a good, if disgruntled grace? After all, he is the King. No. Happily for the House and the King a whipping boy – almost literally - has appeared.

A bankrupt lawyer recently published a pamphlet making fun of the King and Queen of Bohemia, Fredrick and Elizabeth. Not a very tactful thing for him to do, when you recall that Elizabeth is James's daughter, and the darling of the Protestant cause, here and in Europe, but a really stupid thing for him to have done when you know that he is a Roman Catholic.

In the petty way of many politicians the Commons decides it has to punish this unfortunate, if very misguided, fellow, because it cannot punish the King. He was to be hauled before the House and tried by it in its capacity as a Court. The King then makes the situation even worse by taking the matter over himself. As a result one of the most tumultuous debates I have so far witnessed takes place. I use my legal training to argue in my speech that the King was legally entitled so to act, and that the Commons could not and should not take the matter any further.

This hardly increases my popularity in the House, but I am attracting attention. Perhaps the Monarch may receive reports that I'm not opposed to his policies, and support them whenever I feel it right to do so.

It is now Whitsun, and the King has called for the adjournment of Parliament. A large number of members is totally opposed to this move. They want to be able to go on taking the King to task over money, and Spain. The atmosphere during this debate is only marginally less toxic than during the debate about the punishment of the Catholic lawyer. I try to pour oil on the waters, to calm the rather savage breasts of those endeavouring to keep the House in session. I am not shouted own, but attended to as I say:

"It was undoubtedly wrong of this Catholic gentleman" (there were sudden yells of "Gentleman? Traitor rather!"); "…very well – I agree with the Honourable Member that the man is a traitor to have spoken so of our beloved Princess Elizabeth and her husband, the Elector. But she, the Queen of Bohemia, is our venerated King's daughter; if he feels it proper to overlook such treachery, is it for us to seek revenge on her behalf?

"Let us consider what it is we are really complaining about. Are we so desperately anxious to punish a foolish man for being a Catholic, and for speaking his mind in a partisan, Catholic way? Are we not speaking our minds in a Protestant fashion? Do we only do so because we have the freedom and privilege of the House to protect us? Or are we rather protesting against the King because he has not rectified all our grievances?

"What are those grievances? That he sells the rights to monopolies in goods, such as soap and cloth, to people who will fill his coffers, without which he cannot govern? That he chooses not to victimise the followers of sects, Roman or otherwise, whose religious practices are not ours? Does it lie with us to criticise him for taking money from those who can pay and are willing to do so, when we refuse him loans and taxes and grants? Is he not the Father of the nation, and are not we all, Anglicans, Catholics, Puritans, all his subjects, and does he not care for all?

"If we fail to do as he wishes, is it right for us to moan that he does not do what we desire? He is our benevolent ruler and guide. If we do not do our duty by him, how can he do his by us, if we withhold the means by which he might do so?

"Gentlemen, we are debating the adjournment of the House. Let us not fall out with our Monarch. Let us not depart with a mistaking, a misunderstanding, a rift, between us and the King, and between the King and his people.

"We have before us a dozen or so excellent Bills to consider, some proposed by the King or his officers, and others of our own suggestion. All are worthy to be passed. Instead of consuming the time in rancorous debate achieving nothing, or 'signifying nothing', as the playwright says, let us do some honest business, and please His Majesty with our endeavours, rather than aggravate him with our intransigence."

I feel that this is the best and most important speech I have yet made, and certainly the longest. Quite how successful it might be, is not for me to say, since other older and wiser heads than mine speak to similar effect.

Thomas. July, 1621. Wentworth Woodhouse

I'm delighted to say that the House did calm down, and a lot of good work was done before we went away for the summer. I've been spending a lot of time since that Parliamentary episode learning as much as I can about foreign affairs. I've met men who have extensive experience abroad as ambassadors, emissaries, to various European Courts. The complexity of foreign diplomacy, negotiations, and treaties never ceases to amaze me.

Hardly any event in India, say, or China, or the Americas, affects England at all, save in matters of trade, and that not significantly. The King, it is said, wants to have the Spanish Infanta for a wife for Prince Charles. The Spanish King Philip would be glad indeed to have England for an ally in his war with the Dutch. In England this policy is deeply unpopular because of the hatred of Catholics and Spain. In fact, it isn't the King's policy at all now.

If there were a Spanish match and alliance, if the English sided with Spain against Holland, there would be a serious disadvantage. Holland is a Protestant country. So is England. Holland is the only ally Frederick and Elizabeth have found in their struggle with the Holy Roman Empire. England would be incandescent with fury if the King took us to war with the Dutch. On the other hand, the Dutch are our greatest trade rivals, their ships, their navy competing with ours on every sea and ocean. Many of our merchants outside Parliament want Dutch vessels sunk, but those same merchants are well represented in Parliament, and totally averse to paying taxes for war!

These and similar arguments rage throughout England, with Parliament moaning about monopolies, the lack of war against Spain. The King bewails the lack of money, the failure of Parliament to grant taxes, its pestilential interference, as he sees it, in foreign policy, which he regards as his province alone.

There are many acrimonious debates, in which I normally side with the King whilst trying to mollify his Opposition, but my words usually fall on deaf ears. I try saying what I hope has a Biblical flavour, about trampling on the King's favour like squeezing olives for the oil but letting it all run away. These debates repeat themselves in an endless procession, doing no good to either side. There is little point in my going into detailed descriptions of them; suffice it to say that there is no war, which pleases King James; there are no more taxes which doesn't, but keeps Parliament happy, whilst it bemoans the fact there is no war.

Thomas. August, 1622. Stratford

Parliament resumed last November, adjourned for Christmas, started up again after the holiday, the quarrels between the King and both Houses, especially the Commons, going on unabated. If anything they are getting more and more vitriolic. It is so bad that even an overture for peace from one side makes the other more intransigent and unreasonable. I still try for calm, for reason, but I have had no more success than the year before.

I have been busy in London for my sister's boys, and in Yorkshire on my own behalf. My estates grow and prosper.

When I returned to London last month I had a fever, and this running of the bowels from which I seem to suffer from time to time. The summer was so hot that Margaret and I decided to move into the country nearby where the smell of the kennels (the open drains running along the centre of the city streets), the putrefying fish at Billingsgate and the meat at Smithfield markets could cause no offence. We rented a small, elegant house in Stratford, a rather lovely small village in the flat Essex countryside a few miles to the east of the city.

We took to walking in the lanes and woods, riding in the fields, over the commons, picking and eating blackberries in the hedgerows. Sometimes, dressed in shabby clothes we went out like farmers or workers, walking to an alehouse, having a drink or two, and dining on whatever fare might be on offer. It was romantic, laughing and joking with each other, sometimes with the locals. I don't think the locals were fooled much. Neither of us was as grubby as we should be if we really worked in the fields or on haystacks, hedging and ditching, but they took it in good part. The inn-keepers and their servants seemed not to mind the tips we gave.

We walked home hand in hand like man and maid, or with our arms around each other; we were both slim and fit enough to make that possible. Of course, the touch and feel of my beloved so close, so happy, so pretty, alluring, led to the inevitable when we got to bed – which was as soon as we got indoors. Nipples, and breasts, and legs, and skin, and softness, at least one hard thing, blessed release, relief, kissing, stroking, then more of ….

And it was there, in that bed, a few days ago, that the greatest tragedy that had ever befallen me until then overtook me. Margaret died. Yes, God in His Wisdom (if that is what it was, I think heretically every now and again) took her from me.

Strafford

We had not been in the Stratford house longer than a few weeks when she began to feel unwell. She became very hot, sweaty, sometimes seemed not to know me or make any sense. I sent for a physician, who, saying it was a fever, bled her. It did no good. I sent for another, and he bled her. Since all illnesses seem to be different, I do not understand why these medical men think – and apparently believe – that taking someone's blood away is going to do them good. I resolved not to let her lose any more blood this way.

I sat with her, and slept by her side constantly. We relied on fervent prayer together. At times I could not hide my despair; I strode up and down the room, round the house, back into the room, perhaps on my return found Margaret praying alone, if she were not sleeping fretfully, or mumbling incoherently in the grip of the fever. The servants brought our food; I fed her myself when she was too weak to hold a cup or a spoon. God knows I tried to be cheerful for her sake, but I was cold, dead inside, try as I might to keep hope alive. In our eleven years together neither of us had ever been seriously ill; I felt I could not bear it, but somehow I did. Perhaps our prayers gave me strength even if they didn't help her. I remembered that when I met George Radcliffe, learned that he was a widow at twenty-seven, I marvelled that he could lose his wife so young. Now it might happen to me at twenty-nine! What was worse was that Margaret was the same age: so young to die!

Eventually the day came when I had to send a manservant for the village Rector, who came to give my beloved her last Communion, in which I joined her, kneeling by the bed. I knelt, not just out of piety, but because I was exhausted with the vigil, weak from fear of losing her. It may seem wrong, inappropriate, to dwell on it now, but we had continued to enjoy the fullest conjugal bliss right up to the onset of her illness. Despite being an MP, a landowner, on the council of the North, and having many interests, none of that seemed to matter; there had never been anyone whose company I enjoyed more, whose companionship was more dear to me. I felt as though my soul had departed with hers.

Henry, Lord Clifford. October 1622. Yorkshire

I was very much saddened by the death of my sister Margaret. Our marriages, estates, and affairs of state kept us apart in fact but not in spirit and affection. I know from her letters that she and Thomas were very happy, and so it always seemed whenever we saw each other.

But Thomas has not just been saddened; he has been devastated. His letters to me are such outpourings of grief as I had never imagined he had the sensibility to compose. I feel for him deeply. It would be different, perhaps, if he had more intimate friends to whom he could turn for comfort and company, but he doesn't. He is possessed of few friends. He has me, of course, and Christopher Wandesford (we three were boys at school together). He has George Radcliffe too, but they are not close friends, as far as I am aware. Apart from being friends of Thomas's, Christopher and George have only one thing in common: each is married to a cousin of his.

Why do I not think of Thomas in terms of sensibility? God knows he was sensitive enough to Margaret, caring for her endlessly, conscientiously in her sickness. I think it is because until one knows him, he seems distant, even arrogant. He cannot tolerate fools or foolish talk. He can't make light, or what is known as 'polite', conversation, but is usually serious in the subjects he picks, even though he can be witty about them. I was thrust into his company at school, learned his virtues, his loyal qualities first hand.

Thomas almost never speaks diplomatically. He says exactly what he thinks, even if it causes offence. I do not think he causes offence intentionally. If he wishes to be insulting, of course his directness makes his intent perfectly clear. It is just that he expresses himself precisely so that his meaning is as clear as daylight, and if the cap he describes fits the people he is talking to, wear it they must. This is not the way to charm your path to others' hearts.

Of course, he has not the comfort of children from my sister. As her fate shows, and the Bible tells us, we none of us know when God will summon us home, and God forbid that Thomas should die a widower. He still helps his sister Anne, all his other brothers and sisters, and Anne's two boys. He has amassed a fortune, seeking to make it grow larger and larger. What would happen to them, and to that fortune?

I have to reconcile myself to the idea that, miserable as he is at present, he must look for another wife. Is that disloyal? I think not. If my darling were taken from me, could I care for my daughter as a woman devoted to me would do, should I choose wisely? Could I live the celibate life of a monk, but surrounded in society by women? Not a hope. If I were to die now, would I want my wife to live on as a widow? How could I be so selfish? She is still young and beauteous, and I should be glad, up in Heaven, if, luckily, that is where I go, to think that life with me was enjoyable enough that she would be happy to risk another marriage. She would not make a good nun, and I should not wish it upon her.

And Thomas is a mere twenty-nine years old. He is vigorous, fit, strong, and from the hints Margaret used to drop, and the alacrity with which they used to retire to bed together, exceeding lusty. But then if my sister Margaret was as keen on conjugal relations as I am, this lustiness was a shared interest. She loved him too well to want him to be miserable because she is no longer there.

No. I fancy Thomas will not remain single long.

Christopher Wandesford. November, 1622. Yorkshire

My wife Alice and I, having spent some weeks in London for Margaret Wentworth's funeral, and in keeping Tom company, have returned home at last. We have been very sad. Tom always spoke of Margaret as a most obedient, loving wife, but that almost makes light of her virtues. She was in fact a tower of strength to him. She was intelligent. She easily held her own in a discussion of the issues of the day with me and Tom, George and Anne Radcliffe, and Henry and Frances Clifford when we all dined together.

Tom has changed since her death. He was always serious and proud, although he could be very entertaining. Margaret's passing has humbled him somewhat. He is quite different from the bold, confident orator who proposed the toast at my wedding to Alice Osborne. Like me and Tom, Alice is off-spring of a Yorkshire gentleman, and as it happens, one of his cousins. He is altered from the joking, generous man who accepted the role of godfather a year or two since to our eldest son. Then he never seemed to need anyone but Margaret, and me, Henry, and George, but above all Margaret.

It must have made both of them sad that when he could be godfather to a child of mine, they could not beget one of their own. The pride I take in these sons of mine is almost a passion. I know Tom would dearly love to have a son, or any children, but particularly a son. He is so adamant about building up his family's status, his family's fortune, his family's reputation, that it only makes sense if he has "an heir of his own body," as the old saying goes. By contrast, I have hardly anything to leave anyone, except the debts with which my Father burdened his estate, which constitute the reason I am poor by comparison.

Now he seems to be so lonely, depressed. He rouses himself in company to make jokes and appear to be jolly, but there is none of the spirit that used to move him and delight the rest of us.

Thinking about 'the rest of us', it occurs to me that we are quite a disparate bunch: Tom, mainly so serious, consumed by ambition, rich, getting richer; Henry, son of an Earl, rich, a Lord, fairly idle, good humoured, given to music and poetry; George, poor, like me, but, unlike me, very religious, extraordinarily intelligent, very lawyer-like, methodical and organized. And me; bookish, studious, rather quiet, almost shy, reluctant to think a bad thought or utter a bad word about anyone.

I suppose the biggest contrast is between me and George. He can be very interfering (a trait I find it odd that Tom should tolerate, when he himself likes to get his own way), pedantic, and, believe it or not, quite likely to let all sorts of cats out of the bag; almost a gossip really, one might say. Except when he's doing a case, or negotiating one. If his opponents can guess what he's thinking then, they must be very clever indeed. However, that side of him is more than off-set by his frank talk; he is always brave enough to say what he thinks. That may be one reason why he and Tom get on so well; you always know exactly where you stand with both of them.

Thomas. 19th March, 1624. Westminster

I'm back in Parliament again as MP for Pontefract in Yorkshire. That devil Savile and his son are MPs for the county. No-one ran against them. I have a large number of business interests as well. I need to keep busy, since I continue to miss Margaret so much, and, to be forthright, I still want to "get on." One of the businesses is the alum trade, which I have mentioned before. Sir Arthur Ingram is, as I have said, also in this game. It is a curiously complex business. It is known as the alum farm, and we are the farmers. The King farms out to us the right to dig up this special earth, for which we pay him rent for the right to produce the alum for the wool and cloth trades. We have people dig up the ground in which the alum is found, and get others to process it for us to sell to the cloth manufacturers.

Unfortunately, the King tells us how much alum he wants us to produce, and sometimes it is more than we can manage. And the rent we pay can be high. Ingram is in this Parliament too. He tells me he has been paying 9,000 pounds a year to the King for his share of the farm. I'm not that far into the trade, but we usually make money out of it.

A couple of years ago, Arthur was not doing so well, though. He has friends in all the high places because he does so many people favours. One of his patrons is Lionel Cranfield, the Lord Treasurer, one of the most powerful men in the kingdom. He was elevated to the Earldom of Middlesex in 1622, just about the time Arthur was having trouble with the alum farm. These two have been doing business together for decades, mainly lending money to hard up members of the aristocracy and gentry.

Ingram, swapping favour for favour with Cranfield, got him to persuade the King to lower the amount of alum he expected Arthur to produce. In return, Arthur now represents Lionel in the House of Commons. It has been a very interesting Parliament.

Arthur presented Lionel, the Earl of Middlesex's report on trade to the House. Arthur got a shock. Middlesex turned out to be rather unpopular. MPs exposed the report as sleight of hand to obscure a new book of customs dues Lionel has imposed, and the House said these rates will decimate the economy (a trifle hyperbolic, perhaps).

Arthur then asked the House to raise a lot of tax for war with Spain. As usual, the Commons wants war with this Popish neighbour. The Duke of Buckingham and the Prince of Wales are clamouring for it, but the members do not want to pay. I'm not keen on war myself, and I have no desire to ask my constituents to pay heavier taxes for it.

What emerged in this debate was that Middlesex had fallen out with Buckingham. At first sight that seemed odd, because Lionel achieved high office by sponsoring Buckingham to replace Robert Carr as the King's favourite, and then becoming one of his acolytes. Buckingham is no fool, as Robert Carr was. He plays his cards (and the King) very skilfully. He sees people like Lionel Cranfield rise, and that is good so long as they do not oppose him, but if they cross him, they are doomed. Lionel has made two mistakes.

First, he spoke out against the Spanish war, which meant he had set himself against the policy Buckingham and the Prince of Wales espouse. The fact that his view was also the King's did not help him, since the King is putty in George Villiers' hands. His second offence looked even more serious to Villiers. Cranfield, sensing that he had been losing influence with him, tried to get another pretty boy into the King's embrace. This young man, Arthur Brett, was a relative of Lionel's. Other people have tried this tactic, as I have mentioned before. Indeed that is how Buckingham got there.

But no-one can repeat that trick with Villiers in control and the King entering his dotage. Brett was sent packing, and Cranfield was doomed. Buckingham saw the virtue of sacrificing him in an attempt to assuage the hatred Parliament feels towards Villiers himself. This is an amazing side of Buckingham's mind and talents. Whilst his idea of any kind of policy is farcical, he is extraordinarily astute at making use of people, playing one off against another, taking personal advantage of any opportunity that comes his way. If he could do that for the benefit of the country, England would be in better shape and much the richer.

George Villiers is, of course, a Duke, and Lionel only an Earl. That difference matters. On top of that, George is the King's favourite, and the Prince's hero. Lionel did not stand a chance. George persuaded the King to let the Earl of Middlesex be impeached by Parliament.

He was accused of fraud and abuse of his position as Lord Treasurer over the customs farm. I've already written about the alum farm. The customs farm was similar. The King has no effective civil service which could collect and administer taxes and duties for him. What he does is lease to rich men like Cranfield, and Sir Arthur (and me), the right to collect the tax and customs duties, in return for ready money in pretty large amounts. The farmers are expected to collect more tax than they pay over in rent to the King. They are also supposed to pay over to the Treasury a large percentage of what they collect. The system is rife with corruption.

The farmers, in many cases, keep more than they should, and falsify their accounts to cover themselves. The case against Cranfield was that he knew what was going on, and took advantage of it. A man called Dalison short-changed the King by over 13,000 pounds, but still managed to get into debt to Cranfield for a lot of money on loan. Lionel then 'bought' Dalison's land and property from him, allegedly to pay off the man's debts. That may even have been true. The fact Cranfield was also selling baronetcies didn't help him.

The trouble for him was that Arthur Ingram was also involved in all this, and when he was called to give evidence, he shifted any blame which should have attached to him onto Cranfield's shoulders. The odd thing was that Dalison's land had ended up in Arthur's hands. More Ingram luck? Or was it simply that as Buckingham had been gradually falling out with Cranfield ever since he had been made Earl of

Middlesex, Arthur's betrayal of Lionel made little difference?

Even so, although Arthur helped Buckingham by giving evidence against Cranfield, it did him no good, because Buckingham saw him as part of Cranfield's gang of crooks. Having helped Cranfield destroy Suffolk and Nottingham a few years ago, Arthur Ingram has turned the tables on Cranfield.

In a curious, shameful, way, I admire Arthur Ingram for an ability I lack, and do not think I could ever acquire. He trims his sails to any wind, telling any tale that suits. Had he supported Cranfield at the trial, he might have shared his fate: fined and banished from all power and influence. As it is, he now has no patron to protect him from his own rivals. But nothing is likely to stop Arthur from making more money, getting richer, acquiring more and more land. He is just extraordinarily cunning.

Thomas. July, 1624. Yorkshire

Two very interesting things have happened. One has a big effect on me, and the other slightly less so. The lesser one is, however, extremely unfortunate for Arthur Ingram. The first thing is related to Buckingham. Earlier I wrote that Cranfield was doomed because he had spoken out against the Spanish War. He was also advocating peace with Spain. That, of course is the King's policy; he doesn't want war at any price. Why is this bad for me? Because I have been taking the same line, in other words, supporting the King, and it follows one could say I am critical of the Duke and the Prince by implication.

This means I am now *persona non grata* with the Duke, and to some extent with the Prince. Life is going to get a lot tougher. I have to review my position. Do I continue to support the King, promoting peace, or change sides, advocate war, and hope to win Buckingham's approval again? If I were sensible, I'd go with the Duke and the Prince. That is definitely what Arthur would do. After all, the Duke is the King's favourite, and James is hardly likely to protect me against his beloved. Contemplating the death of the monarch is treason, but James is old, unwell, and likely to pass away leaving the Prince as King in the not too distant future; anyone who thinks that Charles would abandon his own policies and Villiers for me should be caged as a lunatic.

The second thing that has happened is that Arthur has lost his share of the Alum farm. In spite of having Middlesex, the Treasurer, as his erstwhile patron, it has been discovered that Arthur embezzled a huge amount of money from the Crown in respect of the alum farm rents and profits. His lease of the farm has been forfeited, but fortunately for him he has been able to negotiate a "composition" with the King. In other words he has agreed to pay 20,000 pounds compensation; in return the King will not pursue him any further, or have him prosecuted.

No wonder he was able to find twelve thousand for Temple Newsam two years ago! And more cash to start building his palace.

The effect Ingram's self-inflicted misfortune has had on me is to show me just how profitable these financial farming practices are, and that defrauding the King is deepest folly. I have decided that somehow I have to get into the farms in a big way, whether it is an alum farm, an English customs farm, or even an Irish one. Imagine getting into all three!! Arthur would still be essential to such a venture because he has all the right contacts, knows so much about how it all works. For some legal reason I don't yet understand, the farmers (or their contractors) have to make the alum at 8 pounds a ton, but are allowed to sell it for 24 pounds. That is a huge profit. The wages of the workers make little difference to the profits. Most of them are paid about 8 pounds a year. How does anyone live on that for digging all day? Only with the greatest difficulty. I may care about that, but Arthur would not lose a moment's sleep over it.

The process and the materials are cheap. The alum is not hard to dig, and it just gets mixed with urine. Imagine earning your living by going from house to house collecting piss! But then in London, the night soil men come round in the morning collecting the shit and taking it out to the market gardens for manure. I suppose they do that in other towns, like Leeds, and Bristol; rather better than emptying the chamber pot out of the bedroom window into the street, as some offensive persons do.

I must bide my time and ask Arthur to help me buy the farm when an opportunity arises. There's no point in worrying about it now; a new lease is already being granted to someone else.

Thomas. March, 1625. Yorkshire

Dad died eleven years ago. I was twenty-one, William was nineteen, John was sixteen, both of them were at St John's College Cambridge. They went on to study, as I did, at the Inner Temple. Fortunately, Father had given William his own estate, but I still had to support the others for quite a while. Five of my brothers being then under eleven, I had to pay the better part of the cost of educating them; it was not cheap, since I wanted all of them to be cultured, as befits a gentleman. The overriding consideration was that it was Dad's wish too. He had made some provision for all of the boys, but it was not enough.

I sent George, Mathew, and Philip to University College, and I paid for John to go to Italy on the tour six years ago. Two years after that I supported Michael and Robert to live and finish their education in France. And now John is dead. It is hard to believe, as he is - was - so young. On the other hand he was such a quiet fellow, preferring books and study to lively company, sport or politics, that his absence is not as noticeable as the loss of William or George (my dearest brother) would be.

How can you be dead at twenty-seven? I still can't get over how often it seems to happen: Radcliffe's first wife, then Margaret at 29. John had not married; in fact I think he had never had a girl, and would not have known what to do with one. But if John should not be dead at twenty-seven, how could Michael have died two years ago, even younger? I wish I had known Michael better, but he was much younger than I. I was away on business, politics, and with Margaret, so I had little time for him, or the other younger ones. Success certainly comes at a price. Should any of us bother?

Despite success, my finances seem in such a mess. Yet if I sit down and think about it rationally, things are not so bad. I owe about seven thousand pounds, but as I could clear that with two years of my income if I had nothing else to spend it on, I can hardly say that I'm on the verge of bankruptcy. I'm still trying to get a decent Crown appointment, with a good salary plus the chances of private profit that go with it, but I've had little luck.

If I didn't buy other land and property I should not owe as much as I do, but the property I buy produces more income. There are many who would like to be in my shoes, with my coffers. Kit Wandesford and George Radcliffe would be delighted.

I live well. I have fifty servants who run my country houses at Wentworth Woodhouse, Gawthorpe, Harewood, and Ledstone. Feeding fifty costs a good deal; when any of my brothers and sisters come to visit, there may be forty people in the house. According to the housekeeper's account book, food alone costs about 900 pounds a year for the family, the servants, and my guests. On top of that there are clothes for the household, tools for the farms, fodder for the horses and cattle in the winter, and wine for the table. I spend a fortune travelling to and staying in London to attend the Courts and Parliament. And, joy of joys, I am married again.

I was very low and miserable for a long time – or so it seemed to me – after Margaret's death, but after a year or so I decided I must find another wife, try once again to have some happiness and children. I had little luck at first.

I flirted with a daughter of a rich City merchant for a time, hoping to get her twenty-five thousand pounds of dowry. It was not an inappropriate match as her father is a knight, and very respectable, but it came to nothing. In any case there was no love in it. Then I made an approach to young Lady Exeter, the daughter of the Earl, but that fizzled out too. I did not know why.

Thinking the third time might be luckier, I made suit for a cousin of Margaret and Henry's. She was the widow of the late Earl of Dorset. Her maiden name was Lady Anne Clifford. She was about thirty-four, so it was not the ideal prospect for begetting an heir and other children, but she had plenty of money. She was quite attractive, too, and if she had Margaret's appetite for love-making, it might have been a good match. But it did not get that far. Then in September last year I found out what my problem was – or should I say wasn't?

I was telling Henry Clifford about my approach to Lady Dorset, when he said: "Well, old friend, you don't stand much chance there. Not with what people are saying about you."

"What are they saying?"

"That you are impotent."

"What absolute rubbish. Henry, you know it's rubbish. Margaret and I could barely keep our hands off each other …"

"And certainly not when you were bare." He paused. "That was in incredibly bad taste. Forgive me." Another pause. "I know, Thomas, I know; sometimes Frances and I could hear the two of you through the bedroom walls, and it would set us off. Not that that was a hardship. But you and Margaret never had any children did you?"

"No." I felt embarrassed.

"You've not even got any bastards, either, have you?"

"Certainly not! Not that I know of, anyway." I didn't feel as confident as I tried to make that sound, not because I do have bastards, but because I could see where this was going. That's where it went.

Henry stated it clearly. "Well, maybe you can get it up, but maybe your powder and shot are no use. To be blunt perhaps your emissions are …."

"Alright Henry, I get the picture. The women or their fathers don't want me because they think I can't get anyone pregnant. But that's not fair, because Margaret didn't get pregnant either. It could have been either of us with the wonky apparatus, or neither. Just very unfortunate."

"That's chivalrous of you, Thomas. Few men are prepared to admit the fault may be theirs. Most blame the woman as a matter of course."

"But how does that apply to your cousin Anne of Dorset. She's a bit old to have a baby anyway isn't she?"

"Is that one of your seduction lines, Thomas? I don't recommend you use that as an argument for her marrying you! In any case, I dare say she would love to have a child of her own."

"It's alright for you to take the piss out of my situation, Henry, but I'm serious. What am I to do?"

Henry was contemplative for a while. "I'll give you a tip. You know the Earl of Clare? He's not old aristocracy like Dorset, or my family. He paid Villiers ten thousand pounds to have the King confer the title Baron Haughton on him in 1616, and another five thousand to become Earl of Clare last year. It's an Irish title, but he is rich. To come to the point, he has rather a sweet daughter called Arabella. She's …"

"Ugly and fat? And older than your cousin Anne?"

"From chivalry to crude and ungallant in a few seconds, Thomas? Actually, I understand she is only 16, and when I saw her with her father a few months ago, I thought her extremely pretty. I'll go a stage further than giving you a tip. Frances and I are having a house party at Skipton Castle next month, and I'll ask Frances to invite you. Clare and his family are coming anyway."

"I'm sorry if I was being crude and ungallant, my friend. I was just slightly taken aback that you should be shying me away from your cousin and acting as a matchmaker."

"Nothing altruistic about it, Thomas. First, we are old friends, and I should love to see you happily married again. But Anne has some sort of a claim to the Earldom or one of the family titles and much of what goes with it. Frankly, I should not relish having someone with your energy and ambition becoming enamoured of Anne and increasing her chances of taking it all away from us, especially if you get her with child!"

"Ambitious I may be, Henry, but even I do not stoop to the level of disinheriting my best friend." We both laughed.

October saw me at the house party at Skipton. It was a grand place, and Henry's artistic temperament, the artists, actors, musicians he gathered about him ensured the twenty or so of us who were invited had a very entertaining time. Clare, with his wife and daughter came: she proved to be most beautiful indeed.

She had the thickest, most abundant, shimmering auburn hair I had ever seen. It curled entrancingly almost to her waist. Her blue, almost violet, eyes, had a luminescence about them that was, to me, irresistible, encircled as they were by long dark lashes. She was not exactly shy, but had a ladylike reserve which much became her youthfulness. I cannot say it was love at first sight, but at the end of our stay, it had been more than enough for me to ask her father if I might call upon them. He agreed, but I felt that he was somewhat reluctant, partly because of the rumour about my abilities as a stud, and partly because of the differences in our ages, as I was thirty-one. On the other hand I could sense that he was tempted, because I was not a bad catch, whether in terms of class, status, income or estate.

I was invited to visit them at Haughton Hall, which is the main family seat at Bottamsall in Nottinghamshire. In November I went there. There were few guests, so I could enjoy Arabella's company alone, walking in the grounds, or sitting in the library. It was a chaste courtship. There was none of that sudden outburst of passion which had distinguished my pre-marital flirtation and mutual seduction with Margaret, the memory of whose loss can still upset me greatly.

Arabella curtseyed as I bowed when we met in the morning; I kissed her hand, as I should have done with any other lady. When we walked in the grounds she occasionally took my arm, once or twice she even let me hold her hand. When the family and I parted for the night, Arabella and I repeated the bow, curtsey, the kiss with which we had graced the morning, before retiring to our rooms.

I was charmed to discover that she was well-educated; when she learned that I had spent much time in France, she spoke to me in French. When I told her I could speak some Italian, she surprised me by conversing in Italian, too. She exuded gaiety, with a light, delightful laugh; and her voice, as Lear remarks, 'was ever soft, gentle, and low'. Certainly it is 'an excellent thing in woman'. Even nagging is not nagging in a quiet and melodious voice; Arabella never nags. She makes her points gently, intelligently, hardly surprising with her pedigree.

The Earl of Clare is a Holles, a very well-respected political family. Thus Arabella is even well-informed about political matters, and had heard much good conversation.

As I left I was invited to visit their other family seat at Clare Place in Nottingham in December. I accepted. At the end of that sojourn, I chanced to be alone in the library with her. Her parents were saying goodbye to a couple of other guests. I was nervous. This was not bold Margaret; this was a shy young girl from whom no clues as to her affections or sexuality had emerged, or at any rate been discerned by me.

We were sitting before the fire, on the same sofa. I was already holding her hand. We had been talking about hunting, the paintings in the house, her wish to visit Italy. We were perfectly pleasant, but my mind was not on those things, as I suspect she knew. If her intelligence did not tell her so, her intuition would have done. Suddenly, I could restrain myself no longer.

I raised her hand to my lips, holding it there for some little while, longer than ever before. I kissed it several times; hearing no protest I then lowered it and spoke: "Lady Arabella, you cannot, I think, be indifferent to the fact that I have fallen in love with you. I should be … I cannot … I wish you to be my wife. If you could, in due course, find it in your heart to say yes, I should like to speak to the Earl about it very soon."

"Yes".

"Yes what?"

"Yes, I shall marry you."

"Yes? But you haven't had any time to think, have never given me any sign, except perhaps that you do not find my company uninteresting."

"Sir Thomas, I need no more time. If my father did not find the idea of you as a son-in-law tolerable he would not, I assure you, have invited you to our homes twice. Please speak to him as soon as you can. I should very much like to be married, and I should very much like to be married to you. I cannot say that I love you, but I am sure love will come. I am also sensible of the fate of girls in our class who do not marry someone they like when they get the chance. Their fathers or mothers choose someone, marry them off to that someone, and a life of misery and boredom, or both, may be all they can look forward to."

"You are not very …"

"Flattering, Sir Thomas? No, but like you I can be blunt and honest. I find you very handsome, forthright, and ambitious, and I know I can support you in your endeavours. I am in no doubt that love will come, and if you truly love me it will come quickly."

I was amazed by this speech. That this sweet little thing could express herself so clearly, so well - far better than many of my colleagues in Parliament - quite took my breath away for a moment, but that gave me the opportunity to consider the essential truth of what she had said. "Then we shall make a good team, Madam, and I shall speak to your father in the morning."

As I rose from the sofa, still holding her hand, she rose too, and standing on tip-toe, to my even greater surprise, kissed me gently on the lips, then turning away, said goodnight. I could not move as she left the room in her graceful way. Graceful she was. We had danced together much at Skipton, to Henry's musicians; when not dancing with her or another, I had barely been able to tear my eyes from her.

In the morning, when the servants were packing my things, loading the carriage, I asked to speak to the Earl, and he took me into the library. He is of medium height, with thick iron-grey hair, rather stout, and stern, but not altogether unkind. He poured wine for us both, came straight to the point. "You wish to marry Arabella, I suppose."

"Yes, my Lord, I do. She is beautiful, cultivated, charming and …"

"Yes, yes, I know all that. I've lived with her for sixteen years. Let's get down to business. You want a dowry for her?"

"Well, it is customary in …"

"Yes, of course it is. I wasn't born yesterday. Well, I propose to make six thousand pounds available with her. Take it or leave it; I do not indulge in haggling, and it is my best offer."

I cannot hide the fact that I had hoped for more, but I was not in a mood to haggle. I was inflamed at the thought of Arabella in my bed, I loved her, and (mercenary and shameful thought) the dowry would almost clear my debts, though I should have married her without that. "I should not insult you by seeking to haggle, sir; nor would I wish you to think that I expected you to pay me to take your daughter away. I have told her that I love her, and I tell you the same. Your consent is vital to her happiness and mine."

The Earl was, if anything, even more blunt than I am. "I should hope so too. Anyway, I hope you will both be very happy, but don't come complaining to me if you are not. Marriage is a chancy business at the best of times, let alone when you are old enough to be her father. And let's face it, I just hope that you are in working order, and that you will be a father. I hear rumours."

"Groundless, I assure you," I replied with rather less confidence than I felt.

And so Arabella and I were married on 25th February this year of Our Lord 1625. Are we happy? I am ecstatic; I think Arabella is too.

George Radcliffe. 29th March, 1625. Yorkshire

James VI and I is dead. The news reached here yesterday, and the bells have been tolling in all the Churches. Long live King Charles. I feel sorry for James. He was, by all accounts, highly intelligent and learned, but he just had no real political intuition. When he could see what should be done, he had insufficient self-control and authority to make others do it, especially his favourites. He must have been quite worn out by what Charles and George had been doing over the Spanish business. He'd failed to unite England and Scotland and establish a single religious atmosphere based on tolerance, which was his desire.

He was no tyrant, and had had no inclination to be one. He had done no harm, but he had achieved little or nothing good, either, apart from the King James Bible. How will King Charles fare? Buckingham has not benefitted James, nor the country. God forbid that matters should go on in like manner under Charles with Villiers in charge!

Thomas. April 1625. Yorkshire

Three weeks after our wedding, King James died. He was carried off by an ague, Charles became King, and our ruler, whilst being largely ruled himself by Buckingham.

The Prince and Villiers had, eighteen months or so before James's expiry, been to Spain in a vain attempt to seduce the Infanta and the Spanish court into a dynastic marriage. It was a ridiculous policy, not to say a disaster. They had lurched from wanting war with Spain one month to trying out James's desire for a Spanish matrimonial alliance the next. The Spanish are far from stupid, and Buckingham was said to have behaved appallingly, insulting everyone, even persuading Charles to invade the Royal Gardens to speak to the Infanta, as a result of which she was terrified. The prospects of marriage, flimsy to start with, vanished completely. The loose and frivolous ways of James 1st's Court were not to be tolerated in Madrid.

The Prince and his favourite returned to England from Spain in shame, but to acclamation from the King's subjects, who had not wanted a Spanish marriage or Queen in the first place. There was feasting in the London streets, which was understandable. Less so was the way the London mob greeted a terrible tragedy which occurred not long after Charles got back to London. At a hall in Blackfriars, where a huge Catholic congregation had assembled to hear a firebrand Jesuit preach, the floor collapsed, many people fell from the upper floor to ground level, at least a hundred died, many more suffering terrible mutilation, losing limbs. The mob stood around, doing nothing to help them, jeering, abusing them.

The King and Buckingham then tried for a French Princess for Charles. This proposition was almost as unpopular with the masses as the idea of a Spanish Queen being thrust upon them had been. Both were Catholic. To make matters worse, Buckingham carried on a scandalous flirtation with the French Queen. We have been fighting the French on and off for ever, and in one case for about a hundred years almost continuously. I spoke out against this match in the House and locally, although I tempered my remarks to some extent. After all, the French and Spanish hate each other more than the French hate us and we them. The French have not sent an Armada to invade us as the Spanish did almost forty years ago. That being so, there was some logic behind the Royal thinking. But why can't the King have an English wife, or even a Scottish one?

The last King Henry had six wives, four of them were English. It was the English girls who gave him children, a son and a daughter, unless you count the daughter born of Katherine, the Aragonese Princess. The memory of Queen Mary is not that fond in the bosom of my countrymen after all the Protestant hangings and burnings she instituted. Charles ought to find himself a girl like my Arabella.

Whilst the negotiations for Charles to wed the French Princess were afoot Buckingham organised (for want of a better word) an expeditionary force to fight the Spanish, but it was another inspired disaster, only worse than invading the Royal Garden, since this time many men died. How Charles can remain devoted to this totally incompetent nemesis of his is quite beyond my comprehension. Whenever Parliament met I spoke out against these so-called 'Royal' policies, which were, in truth, just adventures of

Buckingham's vanity, supported by our new King. Of course, this was just about the worst thing I could possible do if I want advancement at Court. With Buckingham in charge of King and country, I could get nowhere of any significance.

Christopher. May, 1625. Yorkshire

King Charles seems to be making a very conscientious start to his reign; long may it continue. A week ago he issued writs for the summoning of Parliament, so elections have been held. Thomas stood, hoping to represent this shire. Our neighbour, Sir Thomas Fairfax, who was a candidate too, has been a great help to him, and with Sir John Savile as his opponent again, he needed a lot of help. Yesterday was election day, and what a day it was! Sir John was up to his tricks, as usual.

In the days before the election he had bribed, with drink or coin, or both, many of the workers in the cloth trade around Leeds and Halifax to support him by rioting, as they do not have the vote. Quite what he hoped to gain from a riot I'm not sure, unless he anticipated that if his support was violent, our voters – I say 'our' because I have been campaigning for Thomas – might stay away from the meetings and the ballots.

Then yesterday, when all the 40 shilling freeholders who intended to vote gathered in York to do so, Savile struck again. Somehow he started up a rumour, aimed at Thomas's likely voters, that the election might last half the week, so some of them left. When they had gone, a crowd of Savile supporters, with a mob from the taverns, charged into the voting area shouting for him to be elected. Fighting broke out, and the Sheriff cleared the area to prevent further violence.

How Thomas happened to corner the Sheriff in the Guildhall I do not know, but the Sheriff, when he emerged, declared that Thomas and Fairfax were the winners. Savile was furious, and the city and countryside are buzzing like a hive with gossip that Thomas persuaded the Sheriff to decide in his favour, or worse – blackmailed, bribed, or even threatened him. Thomas will not talk about it. Parliament is due to be opened in about three weeks.

I marvel that Thomas feels he can afford to go. His income is at full stretch, or so he says, and he has spent freely on being elected for the county, though I am told Savile has spent more. He will cause Thomas more grief shortly, I doubt not. I do not imagine the new Lady Wentworth will be anxious to see Thomas leave for London.

Thomas. May, 1625. London

I am back again in London for the opening of the new Parliament. When I arrived in Westminster I learned that Savile had presented a petition to the House to have my election set aside on the grounds that I had forced the Sheriff to declare in my favour. Of course I deny that. Granted, I sought the Sheriff out after the disgraceful riotous, drunken conduct of the mob Savile is proud to call his electorate, but I merely told the Sheriff he had to do something. Having cleared everybody away from the hustings and the courtyard where the voting was taking place, he had prevented anybody being chosen as MP for the county.

Did I bribe him? Did I blackmail him? Did I bully him – something I am said to excel at? I decline to defend myself against these scurrilous suggestions; I was there and Savile wasn't, so the Sheriff did the only sensible thing, declaring that Fairfax and I had won the seats.

That did me no good at all when I walked into the House. I was unaware of the rule that when an inquiry is afoot as to the validity of an election, the Member whose seat is disputed is suspended until the result of the inquiry is known. As soon as I walked onto the floor of the House to take my seat, Sir John Eliot, one of the greatest orators we have, caught the eye of the Speaker. Dressed entirely in black, without a shred of colour, he was scathing of my presence.

His voice is marvellous. There are no better voices on stage anywhere in the country. "Mr Speaker, if we ignore our own rights and privileges, it hardly behoves us to criticise others outside the House who would take away the benefits of free Parliaments. What greater disgrace or contempt can be shown the House than that of the Member for Yorkshire who has just entered here. There has been no greater affront since Cicero declaimed against the invasion of the Senate by a non-member.

"But stay; did I say 'Member for Yorkshire'. I crave the pardon of the House, Mr Speaker, for this man is no member but an interloper. I call upon you to have him expelled!"

And expelled I was. Immediately. I have never been so humiliated. I have tried to familiarise myself with the rules and procedures of Parliament, but clearly I have more homework to do. I shall not make a mistake like that again.

****

I almost forgot. King Charles married Princess Henrietta Maria of France ten days ago in Canterbury. Instead of a Spanish Catholic Queen, we have a French Catholic Queen. There have been no riots about that so far, but it will not take the people long to be in some turmoil about it, not now the French King and his grey eminence, Cardinal Richelieu, have resumed persecution of French Protestants. War with Spain will not be enough for Buckingham. He'll want to attack the French as well. And to think that this French marriage and the treaty that goes with it were rushed through in the teeth of the feelings of the people and Parliament!

Royal policy goes from bad to worse. At least James was wise enough to be able to exercise some influence over his favourite's whims, but Charles sees no fault in his George at all. Already I hear rumours that the royal marriage does not go well. It seems the Queen is jealous of Villiers, who is rude to her French friends, her servants, and even her relations, part of the French Royal family. His arrogance knows no limits. The King takes his side, not hers, and dismissed her servants when, as Catholics, they spurned the English Protestant servants. He replaced the French ones with English.

Christopher. July, 1625. Yorkshire

I am exhausted. Another election, and this one a whirlwind of a campaign, but thankfully very short. Tom came back from London in what must have been one of the fastest journeys ever, saying he had been turned out of the Commons; an MP for the county had to be chosen all over again. This time there were no riots, and no violence of which I am aware. The Sheriff didn't need to be told what to do, and at the hustings Tom was chosen as one of the two MPs almost unanimously. If I am tired he must be nearly dead, or will be by the time he arrives back at the Commons.

Sir John Savile must have had apoplexy at being defeated like that.

There is an outbreak of the plague in London, Tom tells me, and Parliament is meeting in Oxford, so that is where he will go. The King and Buckingham have gone there too, with the Court, which has undergone a number of sudden changes since James's death.

First, Charles is elegant, polite, distant, and always conscious of his dignity. He has a studied, practised air and posture. He never forgets he is a King for an instant, unlike his father, who was scruffy, dirty, smelly, and crude. James was undignified, and familiar. He never put on an act. With him what you saw was exactly what you got. He told you exactly what he thought, so you did not need to "read" him. With Charles it is almost impossible to guess, let alone know, what he may be thinking, or what his feelings are. This, of course, is what I am told. I have never met this King.

He also splashes less money about than James was wont to do, so the Court has become less corrupt, there is less vice and wantonness (at least, in public), whilst austerity and correctness of behaviour is now the order of the day. This is not surprising, since Charles is rarely at ease, standing on his dignity and trying very hard to be and look every inch 'The King'. This naturally imposes a straitened atmosphere, and many courtiers are unhappy at this change. They delighted in the bawdiness, the luxury, the money, the intrigue, and they haven't enjoyed losing it.

I've heard all this from Tom, and Henry Clifford, and others who've been to Court. Even Sir Arthur Ingram has remarked on it. Of course, it makes no difference to Tom. He's disgusted by blatant corruption, and the appointment to high office of totally incompetent men, just because they are friends of Buckingham's. He has no time for extravagant masques, public flirtations, and private liaisons.

Thomas. 15th August, 1625. Wentworth Woodhouse

I arrived in Oxford a week ago, and went straight to the Hall where the Commons sat. It was like a bear pit every day. The Speaker could barely control the business of the House. MPs from all over the country, but especially from the South and West and the harbour towns of Dover, Portsmouth, Plymouth, and Falmouth, were furious at the press gangs roaming the streets and dragging away the menfolk, without regard to anyone's family obligations. With no man in the house, there is no money, and if the women cannot find some work, it matters not how lowly, they cannot pay the rent. With no home, they are thrust onto the streets, often with small children. They are forced, as a result, into whoring and other crimes. Last week, the House was told, a woman was hanged in Bristol for stealing a loaf for her children, and was feeding the smallest at the breast as she was taken to the gallows.

But she was from the lower classes, so the House did not get as surly about that as it does about the billeting of soldiers and officers on some of the Members and their rich friends. There was uproar about that. Quartermasters rove the countryside requisitioning food, horses, uniforms, and arms for the soldiery, which adds to the chaos, and the fact that these things are done for Buckingham's vanity makes it all much worse. If anyone in the House thought Villiers could be trusted to fetch a victory at Cadiz they kept very quiet about it.

Of course, that uproar was despite the desire of Parliament for the war with Spain! I still tried to persuade the house to give the King the money supply he needs, and in return get the King to remedy grievances. It is amazing that he has been given anything, but I reckon that from his point of view, what he has been granted just looks insulting.

Almost from time immemorial Parliament has granted the monarch the right to tunnage and poundage on all foreign trade for the rest of his life as a matter of course, and has not fettered that right with restrictions. This Parliament has granted King Charles these Customs dues for one year only, and stipulated that he cannot increase the rates by his decree. That is for the running of the Kingdom. And money for the war? One hundred and forty thousand pounds! How can anyone, let alone Buckingham, fight a war with a treasure chest as tiny as that? Yet, as I say, hate Buckingham as they may, the MPs want war.

Lack of Parliamentary logic didn't stop there. The country wants war with Spain because the Elector Palatine and his wife, Charles's sister Elizabeth, have been driven out of their home by the Emperor of Austria. Granted, the King of Spain and the Emperor are related, and they both owe fealty to the Pope. Granted, Spain fights on the side of the Emperor, but this fight is on land in Northern and Central Europe. None of the MPs seems to grasp that fighting sea battles with Spain (as they wish our navy to do) will never force the Austrians to restore the Palatinate to Frederick and Elizabeth, or help the Bohemians, where the war started.

I might not have tumbled to this idea myself if I had not chanced to meet Sir Thomas Roe, one of our most experienced diplomats, who explained it to me, saying that he had had discussions with some well-placed generals who hold the same views. As a result, I find myself in something of a paradoxical situation. On the one hand, I hate the idea of war, with Buckingham in charge of it. On the other, my natural inclination is to support the King. In the debate I said: "If we deal with our grievances, and the business of the country, then we can do what is necessary for the King, and I shall do as much as any man".

In any case, Parliament can now do nothing. The King dissolved it on the 12th. It only met for a few weeks. I am back home.

The last straw for the King was when it became widely known that the Marriage Treaty with France broke a promise Charles had made to the people. He had given us his assurance that, whilst the Queen and her family could follow Catholic rites, there would be no softening of the laws against the practice of those rites by English Catholics. The Treaty contained a secret provision that was intended to make life easier for the recusants, and when this was revealed Parliament went wild.

Will Buckingham's expedition to Cadiz achieve anything? I doubt it very much.

Thomas. October, 1625. Wentworth Woodhouse

News has reached me here that the King may soon call another Parliament. It will be his second. If it is more successful than the last it will be a miracle despite what Buckingham has now persuaded the King to do. The law is that the Sheriff of a County cannot be one of its MPs, because it's the Sheriff's duty to announce the winner at the election, and he can hardly declare that he himself is the winner.

Christopher Wandesford called on me with the revelation that I have been appointed Sheriff of Yorkshire, by the King, at the request of Buckingham.

"But why me, Kit? I know I have spoken out against the Spanish War, and Buckingham's policies – if that's what they can be called – but I am far from being one of the real troublemakers in the House."

"Villiers cannot brook any sort of criticism, Tom, and the King won't hear his friend denigrated to the slightest extent. Certainly you're not the worst of the opposition, but you are getting a name for yourself. You speak your mind openly and honestly. Indeed, when shown Villiers' list of proposed Sheriffs, the King apparently said: 'Ah, Wentworth. He's an honest gentleman'. Whether he meant it or was being sarcastic, I cannot say, but I suspect it was the former. He's not known as a humourist."

I was downcast. Kit sympathised. "Look, it gives you more time at home with Arabella. You haven't tired of her charms already, have you?"

That made me laugh. "Far from it, old chap. And I must look on the bright side, mustn't I? It'll do me no harm to stay at home for a while, consolidating my position in the county, doing my duty, and keeping, as far as I can, tranquil and appeasing."

"You appeasing? Hardly!"

"Perhaps, but I can at least try. After all, it's my aim not to oppose the King's prerogatives and powers, and never to do so outside Parliament. No man is strong enough to stand against the King outside Parliament."

Christopher was very serious. "Certainly not. That's why we have to fight to protect our privilege of free speech in the House. Without that we dare not utter a word of reproach to the King about Buckingham or anything else."

I asked him who else was on the list of new Sheriffs, he told me as many as he could recall, and one was Sir Edward Coke. The penny dropped. "The King has taken me and Coke and the others out of the running for a Parliament by making us Sheriffs, and he thinks that will shut us up, and silence the opposition. Doesn't Buckingham realise real hotheads are just waiting to take the lead in the Commons? Coke and I and a few sensible types may have spoken firmly against Royal policy, but we were keeping the cork in the bottle."

Now Kit was biblical. "Jesus warned against putting new wine in old bottles. The likes of Sir John Eliot will burst this Parliamentary bottle asunder. There's one major subject for debate in this Parliament, and that is the removal of Buckingham. No money for the King will be forthcoming unless he yields to that."

"Charles will never, ever, do that, Kit. He would rather go without the money, and keep his George."

Thomas. December, 1625. Wentworth Woodhouse

Buckingham's venture to Cadiz was a complete and utter failure. The fleet left England in October. It turned out that the canvas and rigging on many of the navy ships had not been renewed or overhauled for thirty years. The food supplies were inadequate, and much of what there was had rotted, largely due to the corruption which always seems to accompany the provisioning of armies and navies, and partly to the unsavoury conditions in which the food was kept. Water was in quantities too small for the number of men

I received a letter from an officer with whom I was well acquainted. He was adjutant to Sir Edward Cecil, the Commander of the army expedition. He wrote:

My Dear Wentworth,

I am barely able to find the words to describe the futility of the venture from which I have just returned. Before we set off Cecil was elevated to Viscount Wimbledon. He was, of course, chosen by Villiers. He was not a completely inappropriate choice, as he is a very experienced soldier, but he has never commanded a naval expedition, nor anything as large as the force then at his disposal. I felt throughout that his diffident personality gave him little sway over his subordinates.

When we reached Cadiz many of the ships' captains were too frightened to make any serious effort to capture Spanish ships, and some simply turned tail and ran before the wind. In their favour I think a number of them could not be blamed, since their vessels were merchantmen and colliers from Newcastle and the North, the crews had never been in a battle before, and had been press-ganged to serve.

Nevertheless, some of the Navy ships made it into Cadiz harbour which, having weathered a heavy bombardment from the fort guarding the entrance, managed to land some marines who succeeded in storming and taking the castle. This triumph enabled the main army to land, but thirst and a shortage of water – the poorest of planning to land an army with nothing to drink and little to eat – induced the soldiers to raid the local wine-cellars. They became hopelessly drunk, and had to be sent back to the ships, achieving precisely nothing!!

We then took to sea again, Wimbledon intent on intercepting a flotilla of treasure ships bringing gold and silver bullion from Spanish Mexico, but the old rigging was beginning to fall apart. It could not possibly stand the strain of fast sailing to catch fleeing vessels, and certainly not the major stresses of a battle. To make matters worse, we ran out of food, and were throwing men who had starved to death into the sea! On my ship the water for the men was so foul by then that even the ship's cat would not drink it.

Before we reached English ports we were caught in a storm, and lost more men and a couple of small ships. Who do we have to thank for this? Why, our Lord High Admiral, of course, our George, Duke of Buckingham.

Sir John Eliot, one of the wisest, but now one of the most inflammatory of our MPs, changed from being a supporter of Buckingham's to feeling much about him as I do. He was Vice-Admiral for Devon at the time of this travesty. He told the House that starving men died in the streets of Plymouth and the villages of Devon and Cornwall when the remnant of the Cadiz fleet came home. The West Country – Eliot's country - was the heart of the English navy, and proud traditions and seafaring heritage were in their sailor's blood. He said; 'Our honour is lost, our ships are sunk, and our men have perished, but not by the sword or the cannon, but by those we trust. The Lord High Admiral is a cancer in the King's estate, the moth in his goodness, the rust that enters in."

Thomas. March, 1626. Yorkshire

Kit called on me again last week. He had been in London, taking some of my Sheriff's reports to the King and Buckingham. I have been sending copies to Buckingham as well as His Majesty because it is essential that, if I am ever to be rehabilitated at Court, I restore my reputation with both of them.

"Your reports are well received, Tom. They both remark that, as far as a Sheriff can, you are following government policy, supporting the raising of revenue for the Treasury, dealing efficiently with prosecution of those who avoid paying, and pursuing the Catholics for fines for non-attendance at Protestant services. They seem to be well pleased, from what I hear."

"Splendid news, Kit. Let's hope it does some good. There's not so much call for me to stand up against Buckingham in this role as there is for an MP. Mind you, I could have been Sheriff and an MP if I were prepared to be more devious than I am."

"Devious, my friend?" Kit smiled at that. "No-one can be as straightforward in what he says as you are, and be devious at the same time."

"You cannot judge from what I say what goes on in my head, Kit. You have no idea what devious schemes are afoot there. In any case, I'm talking about others' deviousness, not mine. One of my fellow Sheriffs of equally recent appointment, also with me in the last Parliament, suggested that, if I should secure his election here in York, he would do the same for me in, well, let's say Gloucester, or Bury St. Edmonds. It's only in our own counties that we cannot be Sheriff and MP."

"It is certainly devious, but clever, even so. And you turned him down?"

I nodded. "As you know, my every inclination is to try to do good for myself – yes, I make no bones about that – and the Kingdom, by working with the King, not against him. There is a much better chance of doing that from a position of power and influence than by being his ranting enemy."

Kit, always very alert and attentive, was suddenly more so. "An opportunity to do just that may arise soon. You know about Lord Scrope?"

"Of course I know Scrope. You can't be on the Council of the North for a few years and not know its President. And I am the Vice-President."

"That's not what I asked, Tom. I know you are the VP. Of course you know Scrope. What I said was 'do you know about him?'"

"I've heard he's under pressure from the Commons because he goes easy on the Catholics. I am trying to pursue them and he is letting them get away with it."

"That's it, Tom. He is supposed to be considering resigning. You're Vice-President. You're the obvious choice to replace him. Why don't you write a letter to the King now, asking for the job?"

"Do you think I'm back in his good books sufficiently to do that yet?"

"Nothing ventured, nothing gained. The worst that can happen is that he says 'No'. How can you lose by it?"

That stopped me. How indeed?

So we sat down and I dictated to Kit, he made some useful points, and I then wrote out a version for dispatch. It hardly seemed appropriate to send the King a letter in someone else's hand asking for the most important job north of the Wash.

That is not the only star above the horizon. Arabella is pregnant! I am overjoyed, but than a sad thought hits me: *Why couldn't Margaret and I have shared this excitement?*

****

A few days later I have a letter from my brother-in-law, Denzil Holles, who is a Member of Parliament.

Dear Thomas,

I regret to say that at the opening of Parliament King Charles did it again. He has offended all but the most devoted Peers and MPs. Here, as best as I could note it down, is what he said:

"You may remember that in the time of my Blessed Father you persuaded him, and me, to break off the Treaties with Spain. We did as you wished. Now that you have everything you wanted, and seem to think that I have gone so far with you in war against the Spanish that there is no retreat left open to me, you start rolling your own dice and making the rules of the game as you go along.

Strafford

"I pray you, make no mistake and do not deceive yourselves: this is not a Parliamentary way, nor is it a fitting way to deal with a King. Sir Edward Coke has told you that it is better to be killed by a foreign enemy than to be destroyed in battle at home. For my part, it is better for a King to be invaded and almost destroyed by a foreign army, than to be despised by his own subjects.

"Remember that the power to call, permit the sitting, and the dissolution of a Parliament is entirely in my power. If I find the fruit of a Parliament good, I shall let it sit; if I find it evil, it will not continue a moment longer.

"Remember also, that if this Parliament persists in the errors of the last one, and you delay doing as I ask, you deepen those errors and make your position and mine irreconcilable. By contrast, if you mend your ways cheerfully, and consider the distressed state of Christendom, and the desire you and I have to aid our beloved sister Elizabeth and our brother Frederick, and the parlous state of the affairs of this Kingdom because of the war, you will do yourselves honour, and I shall be encouraged to go on with Parliaments."

Isn't that arrogant? Verily, I understand that kings may be entitled to be arrogant, but it is not an auspicious beginning to a plea to us to open the nation's coffers to him, is it? Does he think this was diplomatic? It was so offensive to most of us – Lords and Commons – that even those who might have spoken up for the King were too cowed to say a thing.

How could he say to us: "Now you have everything you wanted"? Has he not heard that the thing we want above all *else is the end of rule by favourites in general, and Buckingham in particular?*

What good does he think Parliaments are to us if we cannot ask for what we want with some expectation of getting it, but have to dig deep in our purses for Buckingham to waste as he wishes? And all that manure about being despised by his subjects; respect has to be earned, or doesn't he know that? Probably not; he just thinks we should show respect no matter what he and Buckingham do.

With the affection of your brother-in-law, and my love to Arabella,
Denzil.

Thomas. 7th June, 1626

The early Parliament of 1626 went very badly for Charles, the Lords and Commons, and, of course, the people. Nothing of note was done. Perhaps the only positive thing to come out of it was that as no money was voted, the people were spared the necessity of paying further taxes. However, if the nation doesn't pay any tax, it can hardly complain if it gets nothing it wants. And if you wish to balance the books, why would you go to war at every available opportunity? There is no more expensive pastime in the universe.

That is Charles's trouble. He has to have war because Villiers wants it. The people want it too, but not with Villiers in command, so they would not pay, even if they wanted to. It might be different if Charles were better at explaining why he needs the money, and had another commander. If he coaxed the funds out of Parliament, as Queen Elizabeth used to do, rather than demanding it as of right, he might get it.

Of course, she had favourites too, like Essex and Leicester, but she did not let them dominate her or the country. They were her servants, not her masters. They were not her advisers; for that she had brilliant men like Lord Burghley.

Even so, I can see that because she called elections, and managed Lords and Commons to do her will, she encouraged an expectation that that is how things would be. Her father, King Henry, well, he would never have let anyone, let alone Parliament, forget that he was in charge. Persuasion was not his way either, any more than it is for Charles, unfortunately, but Henry was magnificent, huge, majestic, clever, very cunning, and overawed everyone, so it worked for him. It doesn't work for Charles. He is small. He is very dignified, and gracious, but no-one could pretend he's majestic. He looks more like an ambassador from Spain.

Arabella. Yorkshire. 9th June, 1626

Could anyone burst with joy and happiness? I believe so, and it will be Thomas if he goes on as he has yesterday and today. He is charging about the house, and into the village, he tells me, grabbing hold of anyone he sees, and telling them that I have given him a son!! He even ran into the inns and taverns, threw gold coins on the counters, and told the landlords to serve all the customers at his expense. Then, of course, when this got out, there was a stampede for the ale-houses.

He has been sending messengers, grooms, and servants out by horse to all the neighbouring seats of the gentry announcing this event. Anyone would think I have done the greatest thing since the Virgin Mary!!

But a virgin I am not. In February last year, after our wedding and the celebratory dinner and dancing, Thomas and I were put to bed by our families. Thomas's brother George was there. I have never been so embarrassed or nervous in my life. Here I was about to embark on a voyage I knew nothing about, having been told very little by my mother or anyone else. In fact I have no idea whether my mother enjoyed intercourse or not. Perhaps if she had, she would have been more informative. However, at least she did not tell me I should hate it.

I was going to bed a man whose appearance before me had always been fully clothed. I had seen dogs and cattle and sheep doing this 'thing' that I was, I knew, now expected to indulge in, but they seemed to get little pleasure from it. Would it be the same for me? Would I have to stand silently bent over as a mare does when serviced by the stallion, motionless except for the impetus his thrusting induces? With my family looking on?

I need not have feared. Thomas came to my rescue. He spoke to my father as our families stood around the bed; "I'm not a callow youth, my Lord," he said. "I have run this course before, and would spare Arabella any indignity she might feel at being watched as she runs it for the first time. Please be so kind as to leave us to ….er …" My new husband very delicately left the last words unspoken, but my father seemed to acquiesce gladly, and gestured for everyone to leave the room. Someone called "Good luck!!" and someone else giggled, but the door shut and my blushes were now a private matter.

Strafford

****

No. I am not a virgin. The sight of blood on the sheet next morning did not deter me. We had made love three times that night.

I started on his body as soon as I awoke next morning. We have continued like that ever since, until my swelling belly, full of the baby, made ordinary lovemaking rather difficult and uncomfortable for me. Thomas was so considerate, and we pleasured each other with our hands and mouths - how astounded I was when he taught me that - and the night before William was born he came into me from behind, so softly and stroked my pleasure button with one hand round my tummy and the other on my breast, that we both came and then fell asleep, until I was woken by the baby's kicks and then the start of the birth.

I shan't go into that. I dare say what happens is familiar to most people. When I told Thomas last December that I was with child, he was so happy he cried, and was afraid to make love to me, so I had to take him to bed and show him that it was just what I needed and wanted. I have never seen him as happy as he was at the thought that we really were going to have a child, and that, despite the rumours, he had fathered it!! At least, I had not seen him so happy until yesterday and today.

We shall have him christened William after Thomas's father, and every few minutes Thomas starts pacing about saying, and even shouting: "I'm a Father. My lovely wife has given me William. I have an heir at last!!" or words to that effect, and in as many combinations as you might imagine. I'm still in bed of course, but the servants tell me that The Master cannot even sit to his dinner for more than a few minutes before having to get up and shout the news to someone he has probably told ten times already.

Thomas is said to have a cold and hard image in public and in business, but that is not what I see at home.

There is only one small blot on my landscape at this time; Thomas will be leaving home next week for London and Parliament. For my sake and the baby's he doesn't want me to go with him, though I know he would like me there for his own happiness. He says that London is an unhealthy place for little ones, and as Margaret died there, he does not want it to be the scene of more grief. I should be distraught if we lost this gorgeous little boy, and I think Thomas might lose his reason.

Thomas. 10th June, 1626. Yorkshire

I am a father. I made a baby, after all these years! I have the most wonderful, beautiful, soul-mate for a wife. I'm sure I'm a new man. I have never known such joy, such sublime content.

At the same time I'm still me. Ambition still drives me on, but I am getting nowhere. I ought to be like Sir Arthur and other time-servers, and speak up for the Royal policies, but I am still me. I have to say what I think, what I believe. My period of keeping my opinions to myself is at an end. I was not appointed President of the North. The snake, as Margaret used to call Sir John Savile, has found the ear of Buckingham again. Clearly I have not.

Savile is cunning, no doubt about it. It turned out to be true that the King wanted Scrope out of the job, and hoped to appoint a replacement who would please the Commons, but Savile got to Buckingham, advised him to persuade the King to leave Scrope where he was, and – and this is the bit that really hurts – appoint him, Savile, as another Vice-President!

My situation is worse than ever. Scrope knows I applied for his position, so there's no love at all lost between us now. Of course, having kept Scrope in the job, Savile has become his right-hand man. He's not only added to his power in the county by this move; he has also secured the grant of a charter for his town, Leeds. This is important, since it gives the town its own measure of self-government, with all the opportunities that affords its leading lights – not least Savile himself – to make more money by fair means or foul.

Where does that leave me? Shall I take Savile on at his own game? Shall I sit quietly for another few months or years hoping the sky will clear? I don't think I can do that. I was doing pretty well as a Member of Parliament last year, had a lot of support from the patrician landowners, not just here in Yorkshire, but in many parts of the country. I shall just have to reassert myself in that role. I may be wrong, but I felt that Coke and I were leaders of the House. If I can win that reputation back, perhaps the King will see that I'm not so much an enemy as an ally he ought to embrace.

I have to go into opposition, and see where that leads me.

George Radcliffe. July, 1626. York.

Today I have seen Thomas as angry as I have ever known him. It is hardly surprising. He was sitting in office as *Custos Rotulorum*, presiding over the Court in this city, when a messenger, dressed in Savile's gruesome brown and yellow livery, approached the bench, and sought permission to hand him a letter. Thomas invited him to come forward and took the missive, breaking the seal. He asked the Court's indulgence whilst he read it, and his face turned red with passion, but he kept a grip on himself as he rose to his feet.

His restrained stateliness and powerful voice dominated the gathering. "My Lords and Gentlemen, I have just received, even as I sit here, His Majesty's command depriving me of this office of *Custos* in the Commission of the Peace. I shall, of course, dutifully and cheerfully obey. Still, I could wish that my successor had chosen some other time and place for the delivery of this dismissal. This Court is not the arena for the attempted humiliation of its President, nor a theatre for the showing of poorly contrived insults which do nothing to enhance the dignity of this Court and its proceedings.

"Nevertheless, as they chose this feeble method of trying to disgrace me in the opinion of the people of Yorkshire, I shall endeavour to erase it, and maintain the reputation I hope I enjoy amongst you of an honest gentleman, which I might lose if I behave otherwise. There are too many amongst us who value honesty not at all. I do not wish to be one of them.

"Many may think that I could have stayed in this seat if I had kept my opinions to myself, but to buy my place with my silence is a price I am not prepared to pay. I am not told of any wrong that I have done, but of this I am certain: I am not guilty of those 'virtues' which have given my successor this post."

He then left the Court with all the magnificent dignity of which he is possessed. As I hurried after him I heard whispers from all sides: "Wentworth blames Savile!" "Savile and Wentworth are at it again!" "Sir John has had his revenge!"

Thomas is not a swearing and cursing man, but as I came up to him on the steps of the Court as he awaited his carriage he was uncharacteristically crude. I have no need to reiterate the language he used, but to say that he made it clear he is not terribly fond of Sir John or Buckingham puts it as mildly as I can. My sympathy fell on deaf ears, but he did not take his temper out on me. I just let his anger subside as we got into the coach and started for Wentworth Woodhouse.

At last he was calm. "How was London, George? How was Parliament?"

Thomas did not need to know about London. "Parliament does not improve, Thomas, unless more chaos is what is needed."

"Eliot is leading the impeachment of Buckingham, isn't he? How is that faring? I remember Arabella's father telling me in February that we would see some real hobgoblins emerging from the witches' brew in the Commons without Coke and me to keep a lid on the cauldron."

"He was right, Thomas, but don't misunderstand. Eliot is a fine speaker; orator even. But that isn't enough. As you said, attacking the favourite will get nowhere with the King."

"But with impeachment the King has no role to play," Thomas said. "He doesn't have to sign it or assent to it in any way. If Parliament upholds the charges, and a majority votes for it, Buckingham is doomed." He chuckled a little.

"This is so ironic. Old King James told Charles and Buckingham that they would have a bellyful of impeachment when they used it to get rid of Cranfield, you remember?"

"I remember Villiers sacrificing his friend Cranfield. He'd had him made Earl of Middlesex not long before. If you have friends like Buckingham you have no need of enemies. What is that old saying? 'Greater love hath no man than this, that he lay down his friends for his life'? Mind you, some of our lawyer friends in London told me they think the impeachment is badly drafted, and can't succeed."

"Then Eliot is a fool and has done his cause no favours." Thomas was judgmental. "The King will never let his friend Villiers be impeached. In consequence, he'll get no money from this Parliament; he'll dissolve it."

Thomas, August, 1626. Wentworth Woodhouse

The King has dissolved Parliament again! He gets nothing out of Parliament, and Parliament gets nothing from him. It is a waste of time. Yet he cannot govern without it since he cannot run the country without money. He must have money. What will he do to get it?

It follows that the impeachment of Buckingham is as dead as a shot duck floating in the lake. The news from Westminster is that the atmosphere between the King and Parliament is calamitous. The country will go to the dogs at this rate.

Henry Clifford. April, 1627. London

Thomas has surprised us all. Amazed us is more accurate. A little while ago he was telling his friends that he would not tangle with the King unless driven to it, and not even then except in Parliament. Well, there is no Parliament, and he has tangled with the King so decisively outside the Commons that he is in prison for it.

He is in the Marshallsea. If you have to be in prison, it's not a bad place to be, and George Radcliffe is there with him, so he has congenial company. Indeed it is a prison for gentlemen, in truth, and there are plenty of gentlemen there at present. Would you believe most of them are imprisoned for debt?

Mind you, it is a special kind of debt. Last year the King could not get the Commons to give him any money, so he decided to take it. He issued Royal Proclamations ordering the aristocracy, the gentry, and wealthy merchants to lend him what he wants. People are up in arms about it all over the country. Well, I say up in arms, but no-one is actually carrying his musket about with evil intent. The proclamations are the subject of meetings and speeches, some pretty wild. Everyone is clamouring for another Parliament, but what good that will do, judging by the last two, is difficult to imagine.

I was up at Wentworth Woodhouse a week ago with Frances, visiting Arabella, who, as you might guess, is not too happy with Thomas two hundred miles away in prison. She told us she is expecting again. I have come to see Thomas, to tell him Arabella is well, and I want to find out why he has chosen incarceration.

We are out for a walk with George Radcliffe. Yes, we are allowed out of prison for a walk. The country hereabouts is fairly flat, and the prison is just west of Southwark, and within an easy stroll of the Thames. The prisoners at Newgate Jail would hardly recognise this as a prison at all. Because it mainly houses men from the upper classes, and because most of them are wealthy, they can eat as they wish, they can have proper beds, and fires, and books, and lamps or candles by which to read them. And they are allowed out for walks, like this one. Because they are gentlemen their word that they will make no attempt to escape is accepted, and they don't.

Thomas is adamant. "Why should I try to run away, Henry? I'm here because I shall not pay this 'loan' to the King. Loan? I have to say I think that's a joke. He is forcing men to make a loan because he cannot raise any revenue, since there is no Parliament to grant him taxes, and every time he calls one, the mood of resentment over grievances is so strong that MPs will give him nothing. How can he pay back a loan? What can he pay it back with?"

"Have you heard that people are calling it the Forced Loan?"

"Yes. A couple of new prisoners arrived yesterday. They said that's its popular title."

"But why choose this course, Thomas? Only a few months ago you were saying ..."

"No need to remind me, Henry: that I would only stand up to the King in Parliament, and even then only if forced to. Well, I think this Forced Loan has forced my hand. I'm not just *talking* about a principle. I am standing firm on it, come what may. My conscience will not let me do otherwise."

I find it incredible, not that Thomas will abide by a principle, since that has ever been his way, but that he will run the risks. "You stand no chance of getting back into favour at Court like this, Thomas. The King's heart is so inflamed by this business, he vows he will never forget it, will bear the memory against all the defaulters, and punish them severely. Your health may not stand imprisonment for long. You know you are of a nervous disposition. Freedom to move as you will has always been essential to you."

"You think I do not care about that? Or that I have not seen Arabella and little William for weeks? Of course I care. Yes, I may never recover my standing with the Court, though goodness knows it has ebbed low these many years, but I am taking a calculated gamble. Tell me, though, how is Arabella? Is our new child flourishing *en ventre sa mere*?"

"She is the picture of very rude health for a lady of her quality, Thomas old fellow, and sends you her love, and this package of letters which I would ask you to read later. You spoke of a gamble? What gamble is that?"

"Let me ask you a question first, Henry. How do men speak of me now?"

"Very well, for the most part. There are, of course, a few who think you are just a trouble-maker, but the majority say you're the leader of the landed men and the aristocracy in Yorkshire, and elsewhere. Your quarrel with Savile has boosted your standing vastly, because people see you as representing them against the trade interests of men like Savile, who's no better than a merchant, and not truly nobly born into the bargain."

"Precisely. It's not as though I can't afford to pay the loan; none of the gentlemen in here with me is that hard up. Part of my gain from my gamble is that these same men, and many outside, will see me as a sort of martyr for their cause. They live on the rents and produce from their lands and their tenants. Most of them are not at Court, and have no hope of gain from the King. They do not get charters for their towns or villages, as Savile did for Leeds, increasing his wealth. My lands and my money are mine, not to be taken by the King when and if he chooses, unless an act of Parliament says so. These men feel the same about theirs."

I see now where Thomas's argument is heading. "And Parliament doesn't say so. They feel, as you do, as I do, that if the King can help himself to what he wants, the rights and privileges, not only of the gentry, but of all England, will be gone forever. If enough men resist the loan the King must call an election."

"And I shall be back in the House, and shall lead it again, but not like a trouble-maker, as you put it, Henry. I hope that with men like Coke I shall be able to secure redress of our grievances, and persuade the Commons that we really do have to give the King some money, but in the proper, lawful way. My other likely gain is that the King will realise I can help him if he will employ me properly, and that forcing me into opposition is not in his interests."

I point out that the huge risk is that the King will never employ Thomas in any truly important office. He might also be kicked off the Council of the North.

"Again, precisely. That is why it is all a gamble."

I ponder this a while. "But you cannot stand for Parliament in prison, nor when you are still Sheriff."

"My office as Sheriff ended with imprisonment, so that obstacle is out of the way. I don't think the King will keep us in prison for long, as this time he'll appreciate that if he does, the House will be full of more hot-heads, the election will be seen as rigged, and his chances of getting any money will be gone."

That makes me smile. "Do you think he will get his taxes and grants even then?"

Thomas becomes very serious. "He may not. After all, I am here on the King's command. There has been no trial. I have not been found guilty of any crime. Many men have paid up in the face of being put in prison without a hearing. Some of my wealthier tenants or their sons have been conscripted into Buckingham's army as punishment for refusing to pay. There is enormous resentment of this new style of government which has hardly been seen in England since Magna Carta."

I nod. "And remember the five knights, imprisoned for refusing to pay the loan, as you are, with no trial, but solely on the King's warrant. Their application for *habeas corpus* was rejected by the Judges who ruled that it did not run in the case of 'His Majesty's special command'. Have you heard that the King dismissed the Lord Chief Justice for advising him that he was acting illegally? And that old Archbishop Abbott has been stripped of his powers, if not of his actual office, for his comments?"

Thomas looks shocked. "No, I have not. What is he supposed to have said?"

"He told the congregation in Canterbury Cathedral that when he heard about men being called to arms because they would not pay, he was reminded of King David sending

Uriah to his death in the front line of the battle so that David could take his wife, Bathsheba, and bed her. Abbott got into more trouble for refusing to licence a priest called Sibthorpe to publish a sermon saying that it was the Christian duty of the citizen to pay what the King demanded, even if he did so illegally.

"Buckingham and the King liked this sermon as it made the case for what the King was doing. When Buckingham tackled Abbott about this, the old man said: 'I cannot agree to this, nor with Sibthorpe. If I do, and the next day the King commands me to send him all my money and my goods, I must obey him. Sibthorpe bases himself on weird interpretations of Apostolic Succession. He's wrong. The apostles never demanded money with menaces, and neither does the Church'."

Thomas contemplates this for a moment. "Then Abbott is an even braver man than I thought."

Arabella. October, 1627. Dartford, Kent

We now have two children. Anne was born a week ago, and I am with Thomas here in the country, and very happy. July was hot, and August hotter. London was a cauldron, and Thomas and the other prisoners were being boiled alive. A few of them wrote to the King to ask permission to move into the country, still on terms of imprisonment, and still on their honour not to abscond. Their petition was granted, and they were housed in some pleasant dwellings here in this village.

Thomas immediately sent a messenger to ask me to join him, so William and I, with a few servants, travelled here by easy stages. I was seven months gone, and rather large. The journey was not pleasant for me, though William thought it a great adventure. Anne is well, and I love feeding her. I do not favour giving my little ones to wet-nurses, as my milk is for my children. God made it so.

I know why a lot of ladies of my station in life employ these nurses. It is because they stop having their monthly courses while they have a baby at the breast, and this stops them conceiving as soon as they might. They treat themselves – or their husbands treat them – just like breeding cattle to produce a reliable number of heirs. Neither I nor Thomas thinks like that.

In any case, we rediscovered after William was born that bedroom passion when I am not pregnant is a lot better than when I am. I just wish that I were ready for some lovemaking now, but I am not quite recovered from the birth. I do long for it so, and I can tell that Thomas is getting quite desperate. He loves it that my nipples have grown larger and darker as a result of feeding William, and that they are doing so now with Anne. He gets so randy; I bring him off with caresses and licking, which gives him relief, but he hates my being left out of it, and I am almost as desperate as he is, but I remain too sore to let him do anything about it.

Still, there are plenty of things to occupy us. He gets letters from his solicitor, Peter Man, and his steward, Peter Marris, and he tells me what is happening on our lands. He is very angry about some tenants who've been forced to go in the army, and sympathises with others from this part of the country and the South of England. They have had Buckingham's troops billeted on them. They even have to feed these soldiers, since the King does not.

Thomas tells me the Forced Loan has raised about two hundred and ninety thousand pounds, which is a lot, but less than half of what the King expected. Thomas thinks Parliament will have to be summoned again. He is looking forward to that, but I am not. It just means, as far as I'm concerned, that he will be away from home and me and the children for another long period. It was bad enough when he was in the Marshallsea. I just hope he doesn't end up in prison again, as he is bound to speak out against Buckingham. My feelings get so mixed up.

Part of me really resents it that he puts me and the children at risk of losing him, and of being persecuted by the King's servants. Yet at the same time I love him for his courage and standing up so firmly for what he knows, or believes, to be right, and he makes me sinfully proud.

How do I know he will speak out about Buckingham? Well, last week, my brother Denzil came to dinner. He's good-looking with the same auburn hair and blue eyes as mine, but he looks like a man, not a girl. In an emerald green doublet and a large white collar he appeared very dashing compared with Thomas's usually more sober attire. He and Thomas get on very well, and both are opposed to what the King lets his favourite do. Denzil was talking to Thomas at the table. "Can you believe it? Villiers is still fighting the French on an island near La Rochelle. He thinks he could help the Protestant Huguenots defend themselves against Louis's army. Thirteen is an unlucky number. Well, having Louis XIII on the throne is certainly unlucky for you if you're a French Protestant."

Thomas shrugged. "Maybe, but Protestant though I am, through and through, I can't see how we can help them much. Villiers still has us at war with Spain, and he can't get enough cash from Parliament for that, let alone a simultaneous war against France."

Denzil leapt in again. "And what a crazy policy! What was the idea behind getting Charles to marry Henrietta Maria if not to get us a powerful ally who hates the Spanish as much as we do? How does Villiers think he can – we can – afford to fight the two most powerful countries in Europe at the same time?"

"God alone knows, Denzil. It's not as though the people are really behind him over these wars. They may want to assist the Huguenots, but the quarrel is really about two things. Villiers lent King Louis some ships which are now being used to fight the Huguenots, and not Spain and the Emperor. That has angered King Charles. The second thing has angered Louis: Charles has broken the marriage treaty and is not allowing more tolerance for Catholics. Besides, I don't suppose Villiers' outrageous flirtation with Anne, Louis' Queen, when he was in Paris as an Ambassador a year or so ago, has been forgiven either. On top of that the fuss people make about the conduct of Buckingham's troops and sailors around our southern ports is growing."

"I don't think 'fuss' is a good word for it, Thomas. It suggests that they are having an unjustifiable moan. It is really serious, let me tell you. You don't feel it so much up in Yorkshire, but from Kent to Cornwall – the South coast - there is uproar."

Thomas laughed. "But this is Dartford, Denzil, and Dartford is Kent. We do hear the news here."

Denzil seemed not to hear, and is, in any case, unstoppable when in this mood.

"Trade is virtually non-existent. At home wagons get waylaid by bands of hungry soldiers looking for food, and clothes, and bedding. And because the Spanish navy is out looking for our merchant ships, fewer are sailing abroad. Although we're supposed to be on good terms with the Dutch because they're helping Frederick and Elizabeth try to get their Palatinate back, that doesn't stop their ships attacking ours over exports, and ours doing the same to them. Nobody can sell anything."

I decided to make a comment. "But that only affects the merchants, doesn't it? Are there enough of them to cause uproar?"

Both men looked at each other and then at me. They smiled, but I can tell they are serious. Thomas says: "That's not the worst, or even the whole of it, Arabella."

Denzil interposed. "Not by any means, dearest sister. Farmers can't get a decent price for their sheep and cattle, if they have any left after the army and navy have taken what they want."

"But the King pays them for it, doesn't he?"

"Unfortunately not. He just doesn't have the money, and Villiers can't control the troops."

It is odd that most of the time, when talking of the Duke, Denzil and Thomas call him Villiers instead of Buckingham, as though his title means nothing to them. It is their contempt for him I suppose. Denzil continues: "So we have many farmers and their labourers on the side of the merchants. And then Villiers, with the King's warrants and orders, billets soldiers and officers on the gentry, and expects them to feed these troops; they don't get paid either. So now we have the gentry on the side of the farmers and merchants. But it doesn't stop there. Some of the officers force their attentions on the ladies of the house, or the servant girls, and the soldiers do the same in the fields with girls from the farms and villages, and some of these women get raped. Parliament is unlikely to vote much war tax in these circumstances."

Thomas took a turn. "I've heard it said that in some villages the number of unmarried mothers is rising fast, and that a chicken that hasn't been stolen by the army is a very rare bird."

"So it is Thomas, so it is. As one of my farmers was on his way home from market with a pair of new boots, he was set upon for the boots by two sailors, whilst a third stole the eggs his wife was carrying home. People are furious with the war and Villiers. If you are elected when Parliament is called, you'll have a busy time of it, and no mistake."

"Have no fear, brother Denzil, I shall talk." Thomas replied. "But I have nothing against the King. He's just a fool to let himself be controlled, perhaps even bullied, by an idiot like Villiers."

Now I know. My husband will put himself in the forefront of the struggle to preserve the liberties of England. God help us!

Thomas. 27th December, 1627. Dartford

Today is a good day, and it started last night, when Arabella felt really well, and we were able to make love in whole, not in part, for the first time since Anne was born.

Then today I was released from imprisonment, and Arabella and the children and I must return to Yorkshire as soon as possible. It is obvious the King will shortly call for a Parliament, and I must be at home to organise my re-election.

It is impossible to believe the King thinks a new Parliament will do his bidding when he clings to Buckingham. Buckingham took the army to relieve the Huguenots in La Rochelle; it was a complete disaster for us, for him, and for the Huguenots. I had a letter from a friend the other day saying that "Buckingham has returned with no little dishonour to England, excessive charge to our treasury, and great slaughter of our men."

On the 29th of last month Denzil wrote to me about this saying; "Since England was England it received not so dishonourable a blow." At the beginning of November the ships brought home the tattered remnant of Buckingham's Army (if that is what it could be called). I had a visit at Dartford from one of the commanders, Sir Edward Conway, a charming but very military man, soon afterwards.

As we sat at our dining table drinking mulled wine, he told a harrowing tale. Buckingham set sail with about a hundred ships and almost seven thousand soldiers in June. This fleet arrived off the Ile de Re, an island which guards the entry to La Rochelle Harbour, on 10th July. "It was a good plan to start with. If we could take the two forts on Re it would be very hard for the French to keep us out of the harbour. Buckingham had listened to and taken the advice of his generals."

I could not help myself: "That makes a change. I thought he never listened to anyone".

Sir Edward chuckled, and continued: "One of the Forts is the Fort de la Prée, and the other is St Martin, which is the one he chose to attack first. We landed not far away on the

12th, and the French attacked us ferociously straight away. We were nearly thrust back into the sea. When you think how ill-equipped and trained our men were, it is quite amazing that we didn't all drown, but they fought very hard and we got ashore. Buckingham was hoping that the Huguenots would help, but they did little."

"They may have feared they would fare worse at the hands of King Louis if they did."

"True, Sir Thomas. Anyway, we got to St Martin and started the siege on the 17th. I can only say how much one has to admire, albeit reluctantly, the courage with which the French garrison fought and kept us out. We made little progress. After nearly two months I made a note in my diary. It read: 'The army grows weaker every day; our victuals waste, our purses are empty, ammunition consumed, the approach of winter grows, our enemies increase in number and power; and we hear nothing from England'."

I was appalled. "But didn't you get any supplies or reinforcements?"

"Yes, we had one small flotilla arrive with a few hundred equally inadequate soldiers, some food, clothes, ammunition and gunpowder, but it was not enough. Then, to add insult to injury, a French fleet arrived outside the fort to unload reinforcements and supplies for them. The morale of our men was devastated."

"It seems the whole expedition was a hopelessly planned mistake, Sir Edward."

"That's an understatement, though as I say, Buckingham's original idea was good, and I have to admit that when he decided we had no alternative but to retreat and withdraw from the island, he conducted the evacuation from

Loix, at the other end of the island, very competently. It won't save him though. We boarded ship on 30th October but with only three thousand men – less than half the Army which left England five months earlier."

Sir Edward is right, of course. Villiers may now be doomed. Denzil is likely to be elected for Dorchester, where he lives, and I should get in for Yorkshire again. I cannot believe the King and Villiers will find many friends in the Commons.

Thomas. March, 1628. Westminster

My brother-in-law and I are back in Parliament. Perhaps I should say a bit about Denzil. He takes after his father, the Earl of Clare, in being opposed to Buckingham, which put them at odds with James, and now with Charles, although I understand that when young, Denzil was one of Charles's chosen companions and friends. He's about the same height as me, but his beard is just a small dot under his lower lip, whilst mine is a pointed one much in the style of the King's. All three of us have a full moustache.

The Earl's family have estates in Cornwall, as well as at Haughton in Northampton, and when Denzil married Anne, his father gave him property in Cornwall. Her father, Sir John Stanhope, settled Dorchester Priory on them, and that is where, in the main, they dwell. He first became in MP in 1624, but I did not know him well. Indeed, he did not make much of an impression in the House then. He was MP for the constituency of Mitchell, which was near the Cornish family estate.

Strafford

I began to know him better when I courted Arabella, his sister, and since our marriage we have become firm friends. He is of a keen intellect, well educated at University and in Gray's Inn, and such a treasure of a son to his father as I hope William grows to be for me. Not, I hasten to add, that William is not a treasure to me already, but he is too young yet to make much of a mark on anything but his parents' hearts.

Denzil began to show some heart and spirit in the 1626 Parliament, speaking out against Buckingham and his Spanish war policy. He has an unerring eye and instinct for foreign affairs, seeing clearly that where the Duke leads, shame for England and the monarchy will follow. However, he and I differ over these policies in one major respect. He is more violent in the expression of his opinions, and seems to care little for the monarch, whoever he may be, whereas I endeavour to speak more moderately, with a view to bringing the King and people closer together, to heal rifts rather than dig them deeper. Despite that we gain a great deal from our discussions and the ideas we can bounce off each other.

I hope that we are able to work together in this Parliament. Denzil is MP for Dorchester this time, and I again for Yorkshire, as we expected. He is as opposed to the continuance of the wars with Spain and France as I am, so endeavouring to rid ourselves and England of the Duke is essential. Bearing in mind the King's devotion to him, this task will take all the patience and skill of pushing the proverbial pea up-hill with our noses, but it has to be attempted. It is a bonus that we have Sir Edward Coke here in the House to help us; he is not Sheriff of his County now.

Buckingham deserves, even more thoroughly than previously, to be removed; he has further humiliated us all by sending his brother-in-law, Lord Denbigh, back to La Rochelle recently, in another futile venture to assist the Huguenots. The same sort of ill-chosen rabble passed muster for an army, and, of course, after the retreat of October, their morale was at its nadir. The sailors would not attack Richelieu's moles and booms across the harbour entrance, and the fleet turned back having achieved nothing apart from the depletion of yet more of the King's tiny store of bullion.

Now the troops are ashore, and so are many of the sailors. There is pandemonium all along the South Coast, with more rapes, robberies, murders, foul deeds of every conceivable variety. The men have not been paid for months, yet rumour is rife that Buckingham is planning yet another expedition against France. His constant desire is for a mighty victory to wipe out the memory of all his shameful defeats and failures. He is like an insane gambler who thinks that having lost his fortune at the tables, he will, with one more roll of the dice, cover himself in gold and glory. The trouble is, he is not playing with his own fortune, but ours – the nation's. It is not his life that is at risk. It is those of the poor benighted souls who have to go and fight for him.

It is not as though all the money and lives lost have done the French Protestants any good. Louis pursued his policy of starving out the citizens of La Rochelle, entering the gates of the city in triumph some weeks before Christmas. That, of course, as Denzil is fond of saying, just adds to England's shame.

If we can rid ourselves of Buckingham we may regain our honour.

My Career Begins.

Thomas. 26th March, 1628. Westminster

Six days ago, King Charles opened this, his third Parliament. He set the tone for it at once, telling us that if the House did not grant him the money he needed and wanted, he would take it in any event "by those other means which God has placed in my hands." He'd already done this once with the Forced Loan. Some of my fellows interpreted this as a threat, but I do not see it that way. I'm sure Charles thinks only in terms of what he believes to be the Divine Right of Kings to rule, and the obligation of the rest of us to be obedient, do what he says, and pay up.

This means he wouldn't think of threatening anyone. In fact he more or less said as much at the end of his speech. He told us: "Do not take this as threatening, for I scorn to threaten any but my equals".

That may not be a threat, but insulting it most certainly is! We know well enough that we have only one King in England, so he has no equals here. He thinks his word – "I want this or that, and you will give them to me" – is all that is required, no matter how tactlessly that word is expressed. Having rather stunned, shocked most of the House, he withdrew, and left us to our usual debate on his speech.

No-one was taken off balance by Sir Edward Coke rising to his full magisterial height and immediately putting a Bill before the House calling for the protection of the citizen from imprisonment without trial. Moderate as I wish to appear, even I could not object to that, having so recently been incarcerated with him and George Radcliffe and others arbitrarily, without any sort of trial, in the Marshalsea for non-payment of the Forced Loan. I thought Coke's method ill-chosen; I decided to keep my powder dry until a more opportune moment came.

That moment is today. I know exactly what my strategy is; I have discussed it with Sir Edward and Denzil. What we intend to do is persuade Parliament to present a Bill of Rights to the King. There's another man in the House who merits watching, whom we expect to support us: John Pym from Somerset. He's a gentleman farmer and former collector of the King's rents. He's been in Parliament before as MP for a place called Calne in Wiltshire. He's the Member for Tavistock now. He is no more a friend to the Duke than Denzil and I. He's small, rotund, rather like Ingram. He's very astute, a brilliant political strategist, several years older than me.

I stand in the centre of the benches along the wall of the Commons. I have chosen this position because I can be easily seen from every part of this huge room. I feel all the weight of being an MP for the largest, and by no means the least, of the counties. The murmur of the voices of other members and the Speaker seem to come from off stage in the darkness, as though this were a theatre. Wintry daylight barely lights the space.

Sir Francis Seymour, from a very old aristocratic family, at last opens the debate on the matter of supply. He harkens back provocatively to what the King said a week ago, repeating much of what the Royal Speech contained on this subject, giving his reasons at some length for voting no money, and ending: "If his Majesty shall be persuaded to take what he will, what need have we to give?"

There is uproar, with shouts of "Hear, Hear," "That's telling him," and more besides until the Speaker makes himself heard above the din and members settle down again. Someone with the courage to speak up for the King then asks us to forget all that, come to agreement, make peace – in other words, give in and vote the money!

The Speaker then calls Sir John Eliot. There is absolute silence. His authority hangs over from the last Parliament, and the attempted impeachment of Buckingham. He is very powerful, and his oratory can inflame almost anyone, but that is not what we need just now. I must wrest control of the House from him and his followers, and find a surer path for it to follow. Sir John tears into the Royal – or should I say Buckingham's – policies. He refers to those who have spoken of the oppressive conduct which many of them and their constituents have experienced.

He says, in effect, that we should not concentrate on the trees, but on the wood. "In this dispute it is not just our lands, our goods, our chattels which are at risk, but everything which, as Englishmen, we call ours. These rights, to a fair trial, to a jury of our peers, to *Habeas Corpus*, our freedom of speech in this House to give voice to the concerns of the men of our cities and counties, to decide here, with the King, Lords, and Commons in Parliament assembled what taxes we shall pay, what advances and grants we shall make the King for the government of the country, are the privileges that made our forefathers free. We acquiesce in their removal at our peril, and that of all generations to come."

There is thunderous acclamation for that; fortunately he has not proposed any insurrection or violent course be adopted.

Then another Court acolyte, Sir Benjamin Rudyard, a weak fellow, catches the Speaker's eye, and in a weak voice and weaker speech, asks the House to trust the King, and aim for unity with him. He says there is a crisis of confidence; he asks: "Men and brethren, what shall we do? Is there no balm in Gilead?" Steeped as we all are in the Bible, this offers no solution, and he is greeted with a sullen silence.

I catch the Speaker's eye and he calls upon me. "The Member for South Yorkshire."

Me. Mr Speaker. This is the third Parliament in which I have had the honour to represent the county of York, this time with my colleague Thomas Fairfax. When last this House met, we were asked to grant subsidies to His Majesty for war with France to assist our Protestant brothers, the Huguenots. His Majesty declined to remedy our grievances - we denied him the subsidies. Instead, he forced loans from those who would pay.

A Member. Stole, more like. Mr Speaker, I refused to pay and went to prison.

Me. True Mr Speaker; the Honourable Member and I were imprisoned, with many others, in the Marshalsea and elsewhere for that refusal. Some say the thief went free.

A Member. And was it put to good use, this forced loan? *(General laughter and scornful comments greet that interjection).*

Me. It might as well have been thrown in a pit. Villiers, our glorious Commander in Chief, our …

A Member. He may be *your Villiers*. He's certainly not mine!

Me. I stand corrected. Members need no reminding that the Duke of Buckingham attacked La Rochelle, was defeated, and achieved nothing but the loss of much of his ill-provisioned Army.

A Member. That was no Army. It was a rabble.

Me. Aye, a rabble, but none the better for being led, or perhaps I should say misled - by Buckingham. *(A chorus of "Right, Yes, True, Hear Hear" is my reward for that).*

A Member. And he followed it up by sending Denbigh there with another rabble and no result at all.

Me. It is our privilege in this House to lay our grievances before His Majesty and seek to unburden our country of the yoke Buckingham has laid upon it.

A Member. He should be impeached.

Me. Let us not move too fast, Mr Speaker. We are fortunate to have a good, a noble King, but the advice His Majesty gets and the Counsellors from whom he gets it are not always of the best.

A Member. What course does the Honourable Member suggest, then? They say King James liked to have his arse licked. Is that to be tried again?

Me. Mr Speaker, I leave that to him who suggests it, and resent the suggestion that our rightful King, King Charles, might welcome such advances. No, Gentlemen, we should address the King regarding our grievances in a way which will advise His Majesty on those courses which, to us, seem fit. We must make it plain that forcing loans from the people contrary to the will of this House is bad; that billeting troops on unwilling folk to induce them to pay is unacceptable; that imprisoning people, including Members of this House, without trial, for refusing to make these "Loans", is the ultimate interference with those liberties guaranteed by Magna Carta. When the loyal subject is deprived of his fundamental liberties, then as Sir Francis Seymour said, what need have we to give when the King's Ministers will take what they like regardless? The way to make this approach to the King is by a private Bill, to which he can assent.

Pym. The King has made it clear that he will not countenance any measure Parliament puts forward if it goes any further than Magna Carta. Yet we must have protection against forced loans, and the ravishing of our daughters by the soldiers billeted on the people.

Me. This has not been done by the King, under the pleasing shade of whose crown I hope we shall ever gather the fruits of justice, but by counsellors who have extended the prerogative of the King beyond the just symmetry which makes a harmony of the whole. *(I hear whispers of "he means the Duke")*. The sovereign and the subject, though both be innocent, both are injured and both need a cure. The Privy Council has taken from us all means of supplying the King.

A Member. It is the King we must control.

Me. Mr Speaker, by one and the same thing - bad advice - have King and people been hurt, and by good advice must they be cured. Let us trust in the goodness of the King and he shall not refuse us, with God's help.

A Member. God's help may be hard to come by when His Majesty will not even let us worship as we will.

Me. Mr Speaker, I speak not of worship and religion, but of the administration of the realm. The blame for current ills lies not with the King but with his administration. This remonstrance must concentrate on four crucial grievances. It must seek an end to imprisonment without trial, the means by which many of us were imprisoned recently; unparliamentary taxation, such as the Forced Loan, which is why we were imprisoned; forced billeting of troops in our homes, when the old law is clear, 'that no man shall be forced to accommodate soldiers, except inns, and the innkeeper shall be paid'; and impressment to fight abroad. Many of us know this was used instead of imprisonment to force payment of the loan, because we have seen our neighbours marched off to the army or navy because they would not pay. Let us hope that we shall carry their Lordships' House with us, so that His Majesty may see that the wisdom of both Houses is expressed without disadvantage to King or People.

Speaker. The member for Tavistock.

Pym. Honourable Members would do well, Mr Speaker, to heed the words of the member for Yorkshire. It is not seemly - indeed it is not sensible - to confront the King with yet more grievances on top of those which have already been addressed to him.

Me. True. It were better to concentrate on a limited number of substantial complaints than to offer His Majesty so many criticisms that for very weariness we shall tread the olive and lose the oil. Let us first satisfy the King with a competent sum of Revenue and then present our humble

request to him to consider our views. The greatness and power of His Majesty is our prop and ought to be dear to us.
A Member. As like as not he'll take the money and give nothing in return.
Me. This House has the sense to see that such an attitude confronts the King at the outset, leaving no escape for either side. The Bill I have proposed is a middle way with a better prospect of success. This motion should be put.
Denzil. I second the motion.
Coke. Mr Speaker, kindly put the motion.
Speaker. All those in favour say "Aye." (There is an overwhelming roar of *"Aye".)* All those against say "Nay." *(A very few mutter "Nay".)* The Ayes have it.

There is a loud chorus of, "A Bill of our Rights, yea, yea, forward with the Bill" and other shouts, which go on for some time. A number of us then carry the Bill up to the House of Lords, where it is passed after a short debate. The King gains little more support than he had in the House below.

Thomas. June 1628. Westminster

From Parliament the Bill of Rights was taken to the King, who received it graciously enough, considering he was aware that along with the Bill we should seek the dismissal of Buckingham. He gave our deputation his word as King that he would observe its provisions, but he declined to commit himself to any particular cure of our complaints. He said that should satisfy us 'without additions, paraphrases, or explanations'.

The House was not at all happy with this message. We

all wanted it in the form of a Bill, which when signed, would make it an Act of Parliament, with the force of law.

To sweeten this medicine we told him we would give him five generous subsidies if he agreed to this, a suggestion I had put before the Commons.

By June his military situation was so desperate that he seemed prepared to do as we asked, but then he suggested the words "The King wills that right be done according to the laws and customs of the realm." He tried tenaciously to hang on to his right to put us in prison without trial, saying the foundations of the Kingdom would crumble without it. In response to criticism of the Duke he tried to forbid us to lay any scandal or aspersion upon the State, the Government, or any of his ministers.

We were not prepared to accept his kingly word. Surely he did not think that we could accept a form of words which rested on the law as it already stood, on the customs of the land? According to him, that gave him the right to billet the troops, taxation without representation, imprisonment without trial, and so on; those phrases of his would not bind him, would change nothing.

As for allegations about Buckingham, the King got just what he did not want: another bitter attack on the favourite followed.

Does the King think we were all born yesterday? Perhaps that *is* what he thinks. He obviously doesn't think a lot about the rights of ordinary Englishmen. What he thinks about is his Divine Right, which means, in simple terms, he can do just as he likes. We knew what we wanted, and that was the old Norman French phrase for the assent to a private bill, namely *'soit droit fait comme est desire'* or 'let the law be as is desired'.

On top of all the abuses of our rights that are the subject of the Bill of Rights, and the money question, we are being plagued with religious abuses too; at least, that is what many members and their constituents allege. This is a topic I do not want to be drawn into, as it detracts from the more pressing arguments about billeting, press-gangs, and so on. Further, although the writing is on the wall that there will probably be increasing troubles about worship in the future, they are not already on our doorstep, as the Forced Loan has been.

The main sign of the worship troubles which may come is what has happened to poor old Archbishop Abbott, for whom I have great respect. His objection to the Forced Loan is well known, he is now unpopular with the Court for that, but his toleration of the more Puritan forms of service is his undoing.

A fat little red-faced bishop, the Bishop of Bath and Wells, is making a name for himself. Because of his desire for more ceremonial enrichment of church services, he has a growing reputation with the King and the Court. Strong as my faith in Christ is, I am not that concerned with how other people worship as long as I am allowed to worship in my own style. This Bishop, William Laud, is very firm in his desire that all should worship in a style which, although not Roman, requires rich vestments for the priests, gold crosses on altars, particular kinds of music, and orderly parades of priests and choirs in the aisles of the Churches. He wants 'the beauty of holiness' pleasing to the eye and ear, as well as being experienced spiritually; for him the three go together.

This sort of thing is anathema to the more Puritanical elements of society, and trouble is brewing. Some people are imprisoned for their views by the Church Courts. Where Archbishop Abbott was tolerant, not pursuing such matters with any vigour, Laud is implacable. As the King's views on worship are similar to Laud's, this Bishop is bound to come out on top, at any rate for a time. He started in a nasty way, by hounding Abbott, after it became known that Abbott had written a tract about the Forced Loan which said: "When I beheld that some were to be imprisoned, I thought this was a somewhat new world, but I swallowed my own spittle and spoke not of it to anyone."

The contrast is astonishingly clear, since Laud is not a man to keep quiet about anything to do with what he regards as 'his' Church. Having the ear of the King, and many of the clergy being of a similar mind and taste in worship, he has persuaded the monarch that Abbott should be prevented from exercising his office. The Archbishop is, in effect, suspended from duty now, partly on the issue of liturgy and ritual, but to a considerable extent for his denunciation of the Forced Loan, which aggravated Charles enormously. Another sign of the times is the appointment by the King, almost certainly on Laud's advice, of Dr Montagu to the See of Chichester. This rigidly austere cleric has published some books expressing views very similar to Laud's, which have been roundly condemned by Parliament. Passion about religious questions runs so swift, that I am determined to avoid them. I say not a word in Parliament about worship. Some of these 'faith' arguments are so trivial. One side says the altar should be at the eastern end of the Church; the other says it should be a Communion Table in the nave right in front of the choir, or at the top of the steps – if there are any – into the chancel. How can anyone get really furious about this? Does anyone know exactly where in the dining room above the tavern the Last Supper was actually served? Isn't the idea of the bread and the wine being the symbol of Christ's sacrifice the important thing?

Even so, I am Puritan enough to dislike too much pomp at Church. One priest told me that in Durham Cathedral "The Sacrament itself is turned very nearly into a theatrical performance, and the congregation is seduced with pleasant music, glittering pictures, and histrionic gestures".

Bearing in mind my speeches on the Bill of Rights, I dare say the King will look even less favourably on me than he has in the last year or so. He will be well aware of my role in opposing the Duke and the royal policies. He knows that in March, when Sir John Coke, Secretary of State, demanded arrogantly that the House should vote money before there was more discussion of our grievances, I spoke powerfully for a delay of two or three days. I told the House that unless we were sure of our liberties and privileges we could not grant subsidies; we needed these rights secured, confirmed, so that we could give in a happy spirit. I'm sure the King will have hated that.

Even when we were prepared to offer the King the five subsidies, I maintained forcibly that I should not agree to them unless our fundamental liberties were guaranteed by the Bill. That captured the mood of my colleagues. The King was furious, and sent a message on 12th April that we had broken faith with him after what had seemed an excellent start, and the nation could not afford to put one new fighting ship in the water without the money. A couple of days later he appeared in the Commons himself to tell us that he would observe the rights of his subjects, but would not sign the Bill, and thus make it an Act of Parliament.

I took the lead in the Lower House which debated this for another two weeks; we still gave the King no money. We hoped that delay would make the King see reason, or at any rate yield what we wanted. On the 28th Charles sent another promise to obey the law, but there was still no sign of his agreeing to our Bill.

I always try to express myself moderately, get the House to behave moderately too, but I did not want to weaken our stance by making it look as though we were about to yield. I told the House that the Bill contained all we wanted, but not to forget that while we want cast-iron assurances from the King on our liberties, we had no desire to alter the balance of power between the sovereign and his subjects. Again we refused him the subsidies he asked for, he replied that he would sign a Bill giving effect to Magna Carta and all the other old Acts about the freedoms of the people, but he would have nothing added to that.

Fortunately Sir Edward Coke came to the rescue by suggesting we put the Bill forward in the form of a Petition of Right. If the King accepted that, he would be shackled by it as if it were an Act of Parliament. Of course, I spoke in support of this, the House voted for it, and so did the Lords, but only for a while.

The King sent the Lords a letter promising there would be no imprisonment without trial, and the Lords were softened up by that, although it goes nowhere near far enough. The peers told the Commons that if we went any further we would interfere too much with the King's prerogative powers.

I could not put up with that; once again I addressed the House in firm terms. Later I penned a letter to George Radcliffe. After customary enquiries as to his health and his family's, I set out the text of my speech:

'We have put to one side the Bill which we debated for securing the just, fundamental, and vital liberties of the King's subjects. We are now reduced to a Petition of Right, which is as low as we can possibly go, yet retain the honour of this House, keeping faith with those trusts for which we are accountable to the people.

'Now, unless the Lords co-operate with us in this, the sinews which allow us to move will be severed, and the stamp of approval which validates our actions will be removed. If Lords and Commons join together, this Petition will make history, as the record will show. If Lords and Commons are separated, our labours are as useful as glass hammers.

'There are, therefore, two expedients we must use in this business. First, we must not weaken our Petition in any way, not by a tittle or a jot, either in whole or in part. Secondly, we must win the coalition of both Houses in this endeavour. If we fail in either of these objectives, we destroy our own efforts.

'Our minds and our intentions are made up; we desire no new liberty for the subject; we have no wish to diminish the just, the lawful prerogative power of the Crown; we do not seek to lessen His Majesty's power to punish the criminal; we desire only to protect the innocent, since

without fair trial, and with arbitrary imprisonment, there can be no peace for the innocent.

'Mr Speaker, with your leave I move the House that we may end this conference with good manners towards their Lordships, and persuade them not to vote further on these matters until we are nearer agreement with them. Let us again profess our equal care with them to carry this Petition whilst preserving the sacred rights of the Crown undiminished.'

When I had finished, Sir John Eliot was doubtful about dealing with the Lords in this way. He thought the strategy was good, but if we pandered thus to the Lords, we were just playing second fiddle to them. He seemed to imply that I was being hypocritical.

Someone else actually said as much. I was angered by that, since all I was trying to do was use moderate methods to bring both Houses and King together. If Lords and Commons cannot work together, we stand no chance with the King.
Dear George, I am your affectionate friend,
Thomas.

I was beside myself with joy when the Lords agreed with the Commons.

The Petition was taken to the King on 26th May, and the hot-heads were incensed when he tried to avoid dealing with it. As a result the King once again got just what he did not want: the allegations about Buckingham were revived. Even Sir Edward Coke, definitely not a hot-head, rose in the House and called the Duke 'the cause of all our miseries, and the grievance of grievances', and yet another bitter attack on the favourite followed.

The King was misguided if he still expected us to rely solely on his word. When he gave his assent to the words "*soit droit fait comme est desire*" on the Petition on 7th June the Commons immediately renewed the allegations against the Duke and the demands for his dismissal.

****

I have placed myself in a double bind. The King may think I was the foremost promoter of the Petition, which is true, and that I am also immoderate in my advocacy of it, which is untrue, and certainly not my intention. Conversely, many in the Commons (like Eliot) may see me as doing everything I can to preserve the King's prerogative, despite my working so hard to get the Petition endorsed by the Lords and accepted by the King. In some situations if you are not seen as on the lunatic fringe in favour of a policy, you are seen to be against it.

During the last three weeks of Parliament the House vented its fury on the fact that, the customs having never been voted to the King, and the customs rates never approved, the continued collection of these taxes by the Crown is illegal, and that the money taken should be refunded. Lumping that together with the attack on Villiers, and the attack on that silly sermon of a few weeks ago, preaching that we should simply pay up, it is hardly surprising Charles halted the sitting. I did not contribute to that debate.

Whilst that argument raged I had a totally unanticipated visit from Richard Weston, the Treasurer who succeeded my friend Cranfield, Earl of Middlesex. He saw me at my London home.

An exceedingly suave, subtle gentleman, I nevertheless felt there was something untrustworthy about him, though I cannot define it. "The King and I have been talking about you, Sir Thomas. I've been aware for a long time that you have, until the last couple of years, always supported the Crown, and most royal policies. The King's attention has been drawn to the fact that, for those two years, although you are in the front line of battle over the liberties of Englishmen, of Parliament in particular, you are never extreme, but combine your advocacy of the Petition of Right with attempts to get the Commons to supply the King's financial needs."

"My Lord Treasurer, if you have pointed out these slight virtues to the King, I am most grateful."

"Sir Thomas, I'm on your side, because you, like me, favour peace, not war with Spain. Even the Duke of Buckingham begins to see that if he wants to fight France, he needs peace with Spain. We can help each other. The King makes you an offer to join his ministry in due course, and I am here to summon you to an audience."

Arabella. 20th June, 1628. Westminster

I've been in London for a few weeks with Thomas. I left William and Anne in the care of their nanny at Wentworth Woodhouse. It has been marvellous. Thomas has been so energetic, not just in the House of Commons, but also in the bedroom. I think it is because he is rather excited by his part in the debates, the success he had over the Petition.

Yesterday capped it all. We had a visit from Richard Weston in the morning, and Thomas was closeted with him in his study for a long while. When they came out, I invited him to stay to luncheon, and he kindly did so. He seems extraordinarily pleasant for as important a being as the Treasurer, and as straightforward and honest as Thomas. I think they like each other well. They are of similar height and colouring, but Weston is not as powerful-looking as my husband. Conversation over the meal was friendly and general, about our children, the forthcoming hunting season, our homes and estates, his family; all that sort of thing. I picked up no sense of what the men had discussed, and as they did not drop any hints, I did not care to ask. If they wanted me to know, they would say so.

About half-past-three Weston left. As soon as the footman closed the door behind him, Thomas seized my hand and dragged me, laughing, up to the bedroom. He slammed the door behind us, grabbed me round the waist and kissed me until I was breathless. I was as excited as he was, but I was desperate to find out what lay behind this sudden passion, pushing him away a little – only a little.

"What is it Thomas? What has happened? What did Weston say?"

He kissed me again, and again I had to break off. "Tell me, my love, or that will be the last kiss."

Thomas laughed at that, and said: "Oh no it won't, lovely one. When you hear what he said you won't be able to stop kissing me!"

"Are you being a beastly tease, husband? Or are you going to tell me?"

"I am to have an audience with the King early next month. I am offered a position under the Crown. We are on our way, Arabella!"

I pushed my hands against his chest again. "Is this one of your silly jests, Thomas?"

"Far from it. He even gave me this note from the King."

He held it up for me to read, which I did, aloud. "'You are to come to the Palace of Whitehall on 17th July'. It's unbelievable." I threw my arms about his neck and kissed him voraciously. "So you are to be a friend of the King."

"Hardly that, my love. Apart from Villiers I think Charles has no friends. I fancy Villiers would not let anyone else get close enough to the King to become his friend. The Duke will have no rivals, actual or potential. Even the Queen is not allowed to get close to him."

"I cannot say you don't let me close to you, husband." I kissed him again, and with my left hand fondled him through the cloth of his breeches. He was as hard as a cudgel already. He returned the compliment by unlacing my dress as fast as he could, and kissing and nibbling my breasts and sucking and biting on my nipples.

I had just released his weapon from his clothes when he pushed me back on the bed, threw up my skirts and petticoat, and plunged himself into me. I was desperately ready for him, but this suddenness was a surprise as he is normally so tender and attentive to my wants. To my surprise I found I was as keen and eager to start with the main course as he was, but he was too rash, too out of control. Like a young man having his first maid, after no more than twenty powerful strokes and thrusts he came with a loud shout, leaving me gasping and unsatisfied on the brink of my own climax.

Even so, I was glad for him, knowing that he would not leave me like that. His lovemaking has been very strong these last few weeks. If it is not excitement, as I suggested just now, then it must be the rush of whatever humour it is fires men up for the battles they have on hand, whether of the soldier's violent, or the politician or lawyer's intellectual kind, especially when they have planned and won their battle, vote or case.

He did not leave me like that. Thrice he did not leave me like that.

****

How we found the strength to get dressed and go down to dinner later I do not know. Fortunately our romp went uninterrupted by the servants.

Naturally, as we ate we returned to the forthcoming audience with the King, and I raised a new thought. "Thomas, if the King is pleased with what you have been doing in his cause, even though you have also been working with Coke and Eliot and the others, won't they see your going over to the King as some sort of betrayal?"

It turned out not to have been a totally new thought to my husband; I might have expected that. "You're probably right; I've been thinking much the same myself. It's John Pym I shall have to look out for. He's a very wily parliamentarian."

Thomas. 20th June, 1628. Westminster

John Pym had supported me in the debate about the Bill of Rights and the Petition of Right. He is another fat little chap, and whilst he may be similar to Bishop Laud in many ways to look at, they are totally unlike in matters of faith and politics. First, he is a staunch Puritan; secondly, he holds the Royal Court in contempt. He has no time for the Crown and Buckingham, but that didn't stop him accepting the post of Receiver of Rents for Crown Lands in Hampshire, Wiltshire, and Gloucestershire earlier in his career.

He comes from a Somerset family, and his father, Alexander, seems to have been the first to establish any claim to fame (as opposed to infamy - one ancestor had been heavily fined by Henry VII for supporting the pretender Perkin Warbeck), by becoming a JP and a well- respected barrister of the Middle Temple. He - Alexander - had just been elected MP for Taunton when he died in 1585, when John was about one year old, so he's about eight or nine years my senior.

Unlike me, Pym went to Oxford, and like his father, he studied law in the Middle Temple. He first entered Parliament for Calne in 1621, later for Chippenham, then Tavistock in 1624, which is when I first came across him. Like me, he supported the supply of subsidies to the King then, but in his case that may have been a reflection of the fact that the collection of the King's rent for three counties was up to him. He is an extremely hard worker, very conscientious, completely convinced of the correctness of his own point of view, quite oblivious to anybody else's. He has no discernible sense of humour, cannot learn or remember his own speeches, whether in Parliament or in Court, but has to read them from his own unintelligible notes.

That makes it sound as though he would be a terrible and hopeless politician, but his mastery of parliamentary procedure gives him a huge advantage over many of his opponents, as anyone who falls foul of him quickly discovers.

He was passionate about religious questions in the Parliaments of 1625 and 1626, being extremely severe about the toleration of Catholics. Pym also savaged Richard Montague, Bishop of Chichester, for 'inclining and reconciling the people, as much as he can, to popery'. He was equally passionate and a prime mover in the impeachment of Buckingham, bringing up to date the knowledge and practice of this antiquated procedure.

Pym was also the man behind the attacks on Sibthorpe, the priest who had delivered a sermon in favour of the Forced Loan. I thought John Pym a frightful man to be anyone's nemesis.

Thomas. 26th June, 1628. Westminster

Debate about the dismissal of Buckingham raged for a while. Charles would not tolerate the attacks on his favourite; today he prorogued the sitting until the autumn. Fortunately for him, I had helped persuade the House to grant the subsidies just before he did so.

Nothing could illustrate more clearly how the King and Buckingham misconceive what passes for a foreign policy and what would please the people than the announcement of a new attempt to rescue the Protestants of La Rochelle. More wasted money? More dead soldiers? More military disgrace? Is that what the subsidies will be squandered on? Only ambitious officers of modest intellect hoping for pay, promotion, and plunder would fancy another such enterprise.

Charles I. 17th July, 1628. Whitehall Palace

The Queen and I are sitting in our private audience chamber. It is a relatively small room for a palace, particularly one built by Cardinal Wolsey for himself when he was Archbishop of York. In his day it was known as York Place. There are two modestly throne-like chairs on a small dais. Apart from some of my beloved pictures on the walls – I can see a Michelangelo, a Holbein, and a da Vinci opposite me – and some long, rich, velvet curtains at the large windows, there is no other furniture.

It is almost noon, and I am sitting back in my chair, legs crossed, and for me I am fairly relaxed. I prorogued Parliament three weeks ago, so at least those aggravating MPs are not causing me any anguish for a while, though I wish they had given me more money than those three niggardly subsidies.

Henrietta Maria is leaning forward in her seat to look at me earnestly as she speaks. She is a quite lovely, rather tiny woman, if truth be told, looking enticing in a burgundy velvet gown with a wide lace collar and a triple string of large pearls ending in a sapphire pendant. It is a shame I do not love her, but her jealousy of my great friend, George, is more than a little off-putting. Her English has improved enormously in the three years we have been wed, and I do rather care for her French accent. It is as attractive to hear as I find her face and figure to look at now that she is no longer a child, but I find it very annoying that she tries to advise me on what to do. That is what she is doing at the moment, and we have that man Wentworth arriving in a few minutes. I am beginning to wonder why I asked her to join me this morning.

Queen. Is this wise Charles? If what the Speaker tells us is to be believed this man - this Wentworth - he is a trouble-rouser. He says the most terrible things about what you are doing. He is causing trouble.

Me. My dear; first I think you mean he is a rabble-rouser, and second he does not say terrible things about me or what I have been doing, but about what is being done in my name.

Queen. So I hoping – sorry. So I hope. In France if he said anything against the King he would lose his head.

Me. But this is not France, and I am not Louis. In France, the Estates - what we call Parliament - are withering. The Kings call them less and less frequently. In England, Parliament grows stronger all the time. Henry VIII spent all the money his father had saved, and more besides. He didn't dissolve the monasteries just because he fell out with the Pope. He destroyed them so he could spend their money and sell their land. Queen Elizabeth and my Father had repeatedly to call Parliament to ask for money. I am too poor to do otherwise.

Queen. But a King should be able to do as he likes - it is his right.

Me. And so it is, my love, but a wise King wants to carry his people with him so that they see that he acts only in the commonweal.

Queen. Commonweal?

Me. He must act in the whole country's interests. He should listen to the people through the voice of Parliament, but he alone should decide what is done.

Queen. But Wentworth, he is telling everyone what you should be doing.

Me. That is exactly why I have commanded him to attend upon me! When he tells people what I should do, they listen. When he tells them what they should do about their grievances, they listen. But he is not disloyal to me. He's not disloyal to the throne. There is an old English saying: 'If you cannot beat them, join them'. Well, a King can't join the opposition, but he can invite its fighters to join him.

Queen. That is what you ask this Wentworth? To join you? Is a monstrous gamble. And if he will not serve? What if he wants to rule? What? You may live to regret it, Charles.

Me. *He* may live to regret it. He may die because of it. Think of all those who died for serving the Tudors. Wolsey, More, Cranmer, Cromwell *(I give a wry laugh)* - all Thomases - just like Wentworth. Even the best bloom of the flower of chivalry - Walter Raleigh - imprisoned and beheaded.

Queen. Men ought to be beheaded for treason.

Me. But was it treason? Wolsey knew no greater crime than failing to achieve a policy on which the King had staked his all in a game in which the Pope held all the Aces. Thomas More was beheaded because he couldn't hide his conscience from the King. Cranmer was burnt alive because he refused to hide his from Queen Mary.

Queen. But Raleigh - he was executed by your father, I think?

Me. He was, after many years in prison under Elizabeth, and a disastrous voyage to South America, when he fought the Spanish, and failed to fill my father's coffers.

Queen. So, if this Thomas Wentworth fails you will execute him?

Me. *(I chuckle at that)*. I doubt that I am the executing kind, Henrietta, but even if I were, the danger to my servants comes not only from me. Look at how the House of Commons seeks to destroy George Villiers.

Queen. *(Contemptuously)*. Buckingham! Yes, you love him, but you know, Charles, even though you are my husband and my King, that I cannot see him as you do. You love him, but you do not love me, and I am your *wife*.

Me. Enough, Henrietta! I have told you before not to speak to me like that. I am your husband. I am also your King, as you say, and obey me you shall.

Queen. I try, Charles, I try, but sometimes is very hard. I do not want to see you turn from me to love some Minister. And Villiers is not even clever at advising you - at least, that is what they are saying in the Commons - that is what this Wentworth is saying in the Commons.

Me. I am not choosing Wentworth for love - I am choosing him for fear of what he may do if I don't. He is a powerful speaker, and carries men with him, as he did over the Petition of Right. I need men like that working for me, not against me. In any case, you know that George wants to continue the war with France …

Queen. My motherland. That just shows how stupid he is!

Me. I shall ignore that. He wants to continue the war with France, but he thinks now that we should make peace with Spain.

Queen. Wentworth has been saying for years you should make peace with Spain. He doesn't want war with France either, because it costs you too much.

Me. How on earth do you know that?

Queen. You dismissed all my French servants and ladies in waiting, Charles. You replaced them with ladies chosen by you – or by Buckingham, is more like. These ladies are married to men who know, or are the daughters, of great lords. They talk. I listen. So, this Wentworth, he makes the Duke come up – you say up, or round?

Me. Round, probably.

Queen. The Duke is coming round to Wentworth's way of thinking?

Me. I doubt he'd admit that, but yes. So am I. I cannot afford to fight two of the world's most powerful nations at once. I can't really afford to fight one! Wentworth may have been right all along. I'm told he works very hard at any office he is given, as he has done on the Council of the North.

Queen. So there are three reasons to use him. He is eloquent and persuades people to agree with him, he is efficient, and on this point about war he persuades Buckingham. *Peut etre* he will not be so bad after all.

Me. Precisely, and on top of all that, he seems to be a pretty honest gentleman. I hope I may profit from his counsel.

Queen. And I may counsel you also?

Me. I'm not so sure about that. I'll have to think about it. What would people say if a woman busied herself with politics?

Queen. Have you forgotten the glory to which your Queen Elizabeth, a mere woman, raised this realm?

Me. You are right my dear. "A mere woman, but with the heart of a King" was what she said. Sometimes I forget that you have the blood of Kings of France and Holy Roman Emperors in your veins.

Queen. My mother ran France after my father was killed, until Louis was old enough to take the reins. *(A pause).* I am still not sure you should have this man, Charles.

There is a knock at the door and the Chamberlain steps inside the room when I answer. He bows and says: "Your Majesty - Sir Thomas Wentworth seeks admission."

"Then admit him."

The Chamberlain bows again, goes out, comes back, and announces Wentworth with another bow. I know I am King and am supposed to love all this flummery, but sometimes it just wastes time when I want to get on with the business of the country. Still, if I am to preserve the dignity of the monarchy – so diminished by my Father's vulgarity - I have to put up with it whether I like it or not.

Wentworth comes in. He is tall, and rather good-looking in a threatening way. He is dressed entirely in black, apart from a plain square white collar; I can see no jewellery. He does not seem at all abashed at appearing before me. He bows and kneels. "Your Majesty, you honour your humble servant beyond measure."

Henrietta gasps sarcastically, in what I take to be disbelief. I cover her hand with mine to stop her saying anything, and keep it there. For my part, I cannot think this arrogant looking man really thinks of himself as humble. Perhaps he is not quite as honest as I have been told. Perhaps I am unjust, though. There are very few courtiers who do not flatter me. I observe that he has a slight Yorkshire accent.

I wave my other hand in a gesture indicating that he should rise.

Me. Your speeches are provocative, Sir Thomas. Humble men do not customarily provoke.

Wentworth I seek your pardon, Sire, if aught I say offends. Your Majesty's Court is not often in Yorkshire and I haven't had much chance of learning Courtly Language, saying one thing and meaning something else. If my speeches give the impression that I -

Me. Do not trouble to explain your speeches to me, Sir Thomas. A dozen courtiers a day endeavour to do so, every day that Parliament sits. I think they will make me mad. Kings are by their very nature suspicious - they need no lessons in paranoia.

Wentworth Then Your Majesty will know that I am Your Majesty's loyal servant and -

Me. That you are critical of the manner and style of government, not of the fact that I am the governor? Yes, I know all that even if others do not.

Wentworth. Then, Sire……?

Me. Then Sir Thomas, will you turn your oratory to good effect in my cause? Will you advise and guide me, and present my policies to Parliament and the people so they see, so they learn, that they are my first care under God?

Wentworth. Why me, Your Majesty? There are other orators in the Commons.

Me. There are, but they are not moderate in their expression. Eliot is one of them, and I have a mind to lock him in the Tower for the way he speaks about the Duke, and our policies. Such men have never supported the idea that the King needs money to govern, as you have done. Many of them want war with Spain and France, but I cannot afford it; you know that, and you have always wanted peace with

Spain. Even the Duke is beginning to see that two wars are folly. Will you serve, Sir Thomas?
Wentworth. Your service shall be my constant and thorough study, Sire. I vow to devote all my care and diligence to the well-being of Your Majesty and your subjects. *(He kneels).* At your right hand, I would lay down my life in that service.
Me. I pray that you will not have to do so, Sir Thomas. It is not often that I have to ask a man twice to accept preferment. Do I have to ask twice if you will accept the title of Baron?
Wentworth. I doubt that you will ever again have to ask me twice to do or be anything in your service, Your Majesty. I am overwhelmed and more grateful than I can fairly say.
Me. I suspected you might say you felt humbled by it, Sir Thomas, but I dare say your ambition lies higher than a mere barony, and that there is no promotion you would consider too high for you. *(He smiles. Was that a nod I saw?)* Have you considered a title?
Wentworth. It would be false to pretend I have not thought of it. Sire. Would you find Baron Wentworth of Wentworth Woodhouse, Newmarch and Overly acceptable?
Me. If it is acceptable to you, it is to me. You will have to write it, and I shall not. If you don't find it cumbersome, why should I? That is all.
Wentworth. Your Majesty.

Correctly interpreting that as a dismissal, he bows, making a flourish with his broad-brimmed black hat, and backs out of the room. I find I am still holding Henrietta's hand, which is a fairly unusual occurrence.

Thomas. 1st August, 1628. Westminster

I'm at Parliament, about to enter a corridor between the Commons' and Lords' Chambers, when, before I open the door, I hear quite loud voices, and I stop to listen; I think one is John Pym, and the other Sir Harry Vane. He is MP for Thetford in Norfolk, though in the past he has normally represented Carlisle. Harry is a bright fellow, though I suspect he may be going deaf. He is very much on Pym's side in our struggles with the King and the Duke, but does not make this public as he has profitable offices under the King, some of them going back to James's time.

He is a big man, with a sportsman's florid face, a huge moustache above a small beard. There is something almost piratical about him. Unlike me, he dresses in the height of fashion. They are discussing the political problems.

Vane. The situation is getting serious, Pym. Bishop Laud's power increases all the time and the King espouses his doctrines for reform of the Church. We're getting nowhere so far as ridding ourselves of the Duke goes. And now there is talk of peace with Spain!

Pym. I'm tempted to say "Don't speak of Laud to me" and dismiss him with the contempt he deserves, but he's dangerous. A little, low, red-faced man of mean parentage he may be, but he's not without worldly wisdom. He has the King's ear, and the King listens. These religious questions concern me most, but Laud's efforts to inflict High Church Orderliness on England, and this talk of a new Prayer Book, may play into our hands.

Vane. True. Two nights ago, in a Tavern not a mile hence when I heard talk of it. One man said "The way Laud goes about his business is fit to cast himself and God as the worst tyrants in the world".

Pym. Yet King Charles is Laud's master so he should share the blame. And share it he must if the rumours are true.

Vane. Rumours?

Pym. Have you not heard? Not even in your tavern? But no, I suppose it has not yet percolated so far. Rumour has it that when the Archbishop of Canterbury is dead, the Bishop of London, our unlovable William Laud, will be the new Archbishop, our new Primate of all England.

Vane. Then God help those of us of a Puritan turn of mind. Laud is, as you say, dangerous, and rises too quickly for my liking in the councils of the King and the Church. He was Bishop of St David's for a few years, then Chaplain at the Chapel Royal, then Bishop of Bath and Wells for a year, and elevated to London last month. If he reaches the very pinnacle of the Church he'll make life impossible for Puritans.

Pym. We must count on it – and the help of God and the people's fear of Popery and High Church. The King fails to understand these matters. He can't govern the country forever without money from Parliament. He cannot expect the House of Commons to vote Taxes and Subsidies which they fear will be used against them and their religious consciences. If we - if I - can so manage the next Parliament as to keep those fears for their religion, unjust taxes, arbitrary imprisonment and so on in the forefront of their minds, then we shall make it impossible for the King to control Parliament. And in the end we may be able to control him.

Vane. Right now he's controlled by his advisors, including Laud.

Pym. 'Controlled' is too strong a word - the King knows his own mind. The difficulty is that he seems unable to take good advice, but to prefer the bad sort from those not fitted to give any, like Buckingham.

Vane. And to cap it all, the Queen is a Catholic. The talk in the Taverns is clear - the Catholic Queen is behind many of the causes of discontent.

Pym. Yes, but a change in the King's counsels may be coming. Have you heard that the King has raised Thomas Wentworth to the peerage?

Vane. Sorry, I missed that. What did you say?

Pym. The King has raised Wentworth to the House of Lords.

Vane. My God!

Pym. Yes. To the House of Lords, and what's more, to high office. He is soon to be appointed Lord President of the Council of the North. Some say he may be appointed Lord Treasurer, though I doubt that will happen. We must watch him closely.

Vane. That we must; he's a powerful speaker, an able administrator, and absolutely fearless.

Pym. Aye, fearless. That may yet be his undoing. He has principles, and he stands by them. I fancy we shall find him unyielding when what is politic conflicts with those principles. He can't afford to make too many enemies of the rich and powerful. The poor and powerless don't count. His policies may help the lower orders, but they command no majorities, and pay no armies.

Vane. His principles!! What have principles to do with politics?

(I open the door and enter the corridor. They are standing by it to my left),

Thomas. What have principles to do with politics Sir Harry? Much, I hope, for without the one the other is a short route to chaos.

Pym. Didn't Sir Thomas More say that any man who puts himself forward for public office is automatically unfitted for it?

Thomas. So he did Master Pym, yet the three of us have not been backward in putting ourselves forward, have we? But it is only by adopting some principles and sticking to them that we have any hope for the future. Promise of office should be a spur to better things, not a recipe for greed and corruption.

Pym. Are you without greed and corruption My Lord - what is it now - Baron Wentworth of Wentworth Woodhouse, Newmarch and Overly? And tomorrow, perchance, Lord President of the North? What other titles await you?

Thomas. Why, Mr Pym, if I didn't know you better I should say you were envious. I'm as fond of money as any man and I do not expect to go out of politics poorer than I came in, but my greatest ambition is to serve His Majesty and the people well, and to shelter the poor and innocent from the proud and insolent.

Vane. Much good may that do you if the proud and insolent are against you. Your persistent attacks on men in high places will embarrass the King, ultimately returning to haunt you.

Thomas. I attack only those whose corruption undermines the power of the King, or oppresses the poor. Having served in three Parliaments I can see it's far safer that the power of the King should increase than the people should gain advantage over the King. His power may prejudice a few particular people, but if they get power over him it ruins everything, like a schoolroom in which the pupils gain ascendancy over the Master, who can no longer teach, whilst the pupils can no longer learn.

Pym. Yes, My Lord, and so to get your own share of power you've gone to the House of Lords and left the Commons. You may leave us, but we shall never leave you whilst your head is still on your shoulders. *(Pym is really annoyed when I laugh at that).*

Thomas. I care naught for your threats, Master Pym. They are the essence of pride and insolence. Is the Commons so wonderful a place? I believe if I walked into a chamber full of Members of Parliament and shouted "Fly at once, the secret is out," many would be killed in the stampede for the door.

Vane. And what secret is that?

Thomas. Why, Sir Harry, they all have a secret - even you, I dare say. But I jest. I don't share the King's prejudice against Parliaments in general. I object only to the behaviour of certain Parliaments in particular. I do not forget that I was a member of the Lower House, and now I am a member of the Upper.

Pym. Have you rejected your old opinions, then, that it is better for King and Parliament to agree than for one to try to gain the supremacy over the other?

Thomas. I still hold that view. If the King had honoured the grievances of the Petition of Right, and if the Commons had granted him the Revenue he needed, we should not now be in this present ghastly pass.

Vane. But the King would not listen.

Pym. He must listen. Parliament is a vital organ of state and he should learn the needs of the country from it.

Thomas. I agree, but recent Parliaments have confused legitimate needs with unjust demands. They've thrown away the chance of offering sound advice to the King on the mood of the people.

Pym. Do you truly think you can help the King take more notice of the people, My Lord?

Thomas. If the King governs justly for a time, he'll gain the affections of the people, and the past will be forgotten. I tell you this, gentlemen, should the people think that if Parliament gains power over the King, Parliament will listen to the people, they shall be much mistaken. *(I turn smartly away and stride off down the corridor).*

Pym has not finished, however. "You must be happy for your friend on his elevation to the Lords, too."

I stop and turn. "Which friend is that, may I ask?"

"Why, My Lord, surely you have written to congratulate Sir John Savile on being created Baron of Pontefract."

I was truly shocked. "We pronounce it Pomfret in Yorkshire," which even I find a pretty feeble retort, and now it is Pym's turn to laugh.

Thomas. 24th August, 1628. London

Buckingham has breathed his last. News came by the fastest horsemen from Portsmouth to the King; Villiers was stabbed to death there yesterday. The news spread like a flood through the cities of London and Westminster. The King will be distraught, but Parliament is rid of one of its most serious problems, the people celebrating in a manner verging on the riotous. There are bonfires everywhere, the taverns and inns are full to overflowing, bells are even being rung in some churches, and not the death toll either. Such gaiety, such rejoicing has not been seen for many a year. I heard one old man say he's seen nothing like it since the Armada was driven off.

Apparently what happened was this.

Lieutenant John Felton was one of the Duke's officers during the invasion of the Ile De Re. He had had no pay, had been stood down, and thus deprived of his ambition, would get no plunder. Last year, when the army was retreating from St Martin to Loix, the commander of Felton's group of soldiers was shot dead, and he took command. As a result he expected to be promoted to his late superior's rank, but Buckingham passed him over. On returning to England he had no position and little money. What he saw as betrayal by Buckingham worked on his mind in depressing isolation.

He bought copies of the Parliamentary speeches which were aimed at the Duke. These inflamed his passion to revenge himself and the country on this 'cause of all the evils the kingdom suffers, and the enemy of the public', as one of the speeches called Buckingham, and as some sermons repeated. One such speech was found in Felton's hat. He said he put it there in case he was slain before he could explain himself.

Buckingham was being accommodated by a Captain, the reception rooms of whose Portsmouth house were swarming with people that morning because there was gossip (quite untrue, as it turned out) that La Rochelle had been relieved. Army and navy officers were worried that, if it were true, they might lose the chance of another campaign in France; refugee Huguenots who were convinced the story was just a rumour, were all there clamouring for Buckingham's attention.

Felton had no trouble insinuating himself into the clamorous crowd, stabbing the Duke straight through the heart as he moved from one room to another. None of us who had spoken against Buckingham, wishing to be rid of him, had foreseen this result of our efforts. I cannot say that any of us were sorry, but it was not the end we had expected.

I'm far from sure what is going to happen to me now. Will Buckingham's removal ease my path or make it more difficult? If I do not go up the ladder, who will? If it is someone else, will they tread on my fingers to make sure I do not get any higher? Not that I am really very high yet. I may be a Baron, but I have no important office. I am not a member of the Privy Council, so my opportunities of impressing the King with anything I may say or do are fairly remote. Still, I must stick to what I believe in. Much as I want power, riches, I do not want them at any price.

My philosophy of government is practical, and so, I hope, are my principles. I do not want war with the Austrians over the Palatinate and Bohemia. The country can't afford it; we can't win with the size of army we can raise; the

Emperor has a well-trained and experienced army already, even if they were given a mauling for a few years by the Swedes under Gustavus Adolphus. I despair of seeing what we could gain by victory anyway. Sorry as I feel for the French Protestants, fighting Louis XIII is a waste of money and men for the same reasons.

The war with Spain must be terminated as soon as possible. It harms our trade, and the nation will never be prosperous if we go on with it.

Our prosperity depends on stability at home, which in turn depends on the liberties of the subject, the peaceful ownership of our properties. Those are the things for which I fought so hard nursing the Petition of Right through Parliament, and having it accepted by the King. If we manage all these elements, we can put the economy of England on a sound footing. With stable finances we can have good government, and the King, the fount of all justice under God, can shelter the poor and innocent from the rich and insolent, as I have said before.

At the moment the King tries to govern the country, but Parliament tries to govern the King and the people; it just does not work to have two rival overlords. For me, the King has to be the ruler. The Crown has the power to appoint or dismiss ministers. The King has his Privy Council from which to seek advice. When it comes down to it, Parliament is little more than a debating chamber with no power to do anything except obstruct policy by withholding money. At least, that is what it usually does, rarely offering useful advice. I have to try to make King and Parliament function together, but if that is impossible, the King must be the ultimate authority.

I know people like Pym, Eliot, and even Denzil, think my view is naïve, but it is pragmatic. I may secure surer results by saying and doing what I mean than by making shady deals to agree to things I do not believe in so that I can get my own way on something else. I fail to see how that sort of compromise can be a matter of principle. It may be the way politics normally works, but that does not mean I have to like it.

Thomas. 5th December, 1628. London

It is three months and two weeks since Felton assassinated the Duke of Buckingham. I have wondered for much of that time what would happen to the murderer in the end. I recorded earlier that when news of the Duke's death spread there was great rejoicing all over the country, except in the King's private world. A neighbour, Sir John Hippisley, told me that it was he who whispered the news of Buckingham's murder to the King who was praying in the Royal Chapel. The King showed no emotion, but at the end of the service retired to his bed where he was distraught with grief for days on end. How the pealing of bells, the people's gaiety, must have clashed with, increased his tears and sobs!! Will he ever get over it?

The people's joy did not quickly vanish as so many public demonstrations of feeling do. Wrong as Felton's crime was, there was an almost heroic aspect to it, since he rid the nation of an incubus that no other method had succeeded in doing. Immediately after the killing he appeared before the crowd in which he had been concealed, publicly acknowledging that he was the perpetrator. It seems he believed he would be praised for his actions, but he was arrested at once, hauled before the magistrates, sent to London for questioning.

Did he act alone? Were there accomplices? The Privy Council was very anxious to know these things.

Felton was fortunate that the Petition of Right had been accepted by the King, since it forced the prosecution (backed by the Privy Council) to apply to the Courts for permission to rack, to torture him for details of the accomplices he was suspected of having. The Judges stood firm, denying the request, stating that torture was contrary to the laws of England. It pleased many - me, Sir Edward Coke, Eliot, and others - that our Petition should have borne fruit so very soon, we were biased, for Felton had done what we lacked the courage to do.

In the meanwhile public joy at Villiers' death continued. A priestly Oxford scholar wrote that Felton had saved England and the King from Buckingham's corruption. An unknown hand penned some doggerel the first couplet of which recited:

'The Duke is dead, and we are rid of strife
By Felton's hand that took his life'.

Felton was tried two weeks ago. Curly haired, rather handsome, and surprisingly gentle-looking, he was hanged a week ago today, on 29th November. He was fortunate not to have been drawn and quartered as well. This was not the end of the extreme vexation the King suffered from the aftermath of his favourite's death. The murderer's corpse, taken from Tyburn to Portsmouth to hang in chains as a warning to other malefactors, has become instead an object of the veneration normally reserved for the relics of a saint.

I have been luckier than I anticipated. I am shortly to be appointed President of the Council of the North, and because of that, I am to be a Viscount, a step up from a Baron: Viscount Wentworth of Wentworth Woodhouse, Newmarch, and Oversley. (The King was right; that is a ridiculously long name, but it would look very silly to try to change it now). I've only been a Baron for five months and now I'm a Viscount, so how high can I go, and how quickly?

I came by this promotion to President and this elevation to another rank of the peerage due to my having dealt, at last, with Savile of Pontefract. For some time I had been approached, as a member of the Northern Council, with tales, in some cases with evidence, of Savile's taking bribes, indulging in other dubious conduct. I had been able to do little about these matters during Buckingham's lifetime and his patronage of my old enemy, but once he was gone, I sent all I had against Savile to the Privy Council. The complaints were upheld, and he was removed from the office of Vice-President. The President, Lord Scrope, in the pockets of Savile and the Duke, was finished too without them.

The vacancy had to be filled, and I was the King's choice. Has all this happened in five months? I can hardly believe it; I have waited so long.

I shall have a salary of 2000 pounds a year. I am buying more land than I am selling, spending more than I receive, but increasing the amount of property I own as a result. In due course rents will balance the books.

Arabella. 30th December, 1628. York

I am the wife of a Viscount. I am the wife of the President of the North. I'm a very contented woman. I have a handsome, clever, powerful, rich husband, and two adorable children, William, and Anne (we call her Nan). I love Thomas very much. He tells me I make him happier than he has ever been, but if I am honest with myself, our being Viscount and Viscountess Wentworth, and he President of the Council, play a great part in his happiness.

We are trying hard to make another baby, a past-time I have no objection to at all. Indeed, the fact that success is eluding us for the time being is not a worry for me since without being pregnant we can go on trying for so much longer, and that is a pleasure and anything but a worry. Should a lady enjoy it quite so much? Perhaps I am no lady.

Today I have been enjoying Thomas in a quite different fashion. I went with him to hear his speech opening the Council of the North as its new Lord President. Old Scrope has gone. He was tired and almost past it, and Savile's stooge into the bargain. In his place the North now has a President who is young, dynamic, ambitious, and beholden to no-one except the King – and me, he would say!

As best as I can recall, this is what he said:

"I come before you all today as the most grateful man in the world. I think you can see that for yourselves. The great trusts you have placed in me are their own testimonial. Even when I was treated by others like a deadly disease you dared to clasp me to your bosoms again. What greater confidence or warmer affection could be placed in the scales to weigh my good fortune?

"In the other scale let us put the free bounties I have received from my gracious Master, His Majesty the King. Let us weigh what has happened to me in the space of a year. Then I was like a bird cast out of the nest, and put in prison. Now I am back on my own Yorkshire soil, amongst the companions of my youth, my house honoured, and I entrusted with the rich endowment of this office, a barony, and the title of Viscount.

"Am I not a lucky man? Can you show me so sudden, so strange a variation in private fortune? Tell me, was anyone ever so extravagantly rewarded? Was such credit ever given to so great a debtor? Thus I am faced with an obstacle before I begin, from owing more, both to King and people, than I shall ever be able to repay.

"Yet in an effort to make good my indebtedness to you all, and to the King, I swear that throughout my ministry in this office I shall devote all my care and diligence to the well-being and joint interests of sovereign and subject.

"I am well aware that of late some ill-disposed persons have tried hard to separate those interests. They try to represent the interests of the King and his people as though they were opposed to each other, with different objectives. That is a wicked and corrupt concept, a monstrous suggestion. We cannot all be the head of the family, or all its limbs. Princes should be kind fathers nurturing their subjects like children, protecting their freedoms; the sober and respectable rights of the people should be precious in the eyes of the King. The King's government should shelter and shade the people that they may live in comfort and peace.

"The King's subjects, on the other hand, should be solicitous to protect the prerogatives of the Crown, for it is the authority of the King which is the keystone of the arch of government. Without it the whole structure falls apart, into a heap of broken walls, foundations, and battlements. The strength and beauty of our system of government would be lost.

"This system of love and protection descending from monarch to people, and of obedience and loyalty ascending from them to him is what should always pass between a King and his people. The faithful servants of King and people, the ministers, the Members of Parliament, and the Lords, should weave these elements together, labour and study hard to maintain the rights and duties of both without enlarging or diminishing either, and, by observing the old traditions and customs, strangle any chance of dispute at birth.

"Anyone who tries to separate the interests of King and people shall never be able to restore them to their former glory and good order.

"Let us work together to maintain that sense of order. Gentlemen, I call upon you to support me in the efforts I shall make to serve both you and the King. I ask you to put your private interests to one side, to join hands and hearts with me and with each other, so that we may go on cheerfully as one man in the service of the public. My own life I dedicate to that end, I do assure you. Here and now, before you, I offer myself as an instrument for good for the use of every man. He that uses me most has the greater part of my heart, even though he be the least significant man in the Council's jurisdiction.

"Having said which, His Majesty has instructed me to say this: he will no longer tolerate numerous applications to the Courts in London designed to take away the right of this Court to deal with local matters. That procedure has led to endless strife between the Council of the Welsh Marches and the Chancery Court on the one hand, and the Court of King's Bench on the other. It is a procedure open only to the rich who can afford lawyers to argue endlessly in one Court after another, and so deny the more humble subject any justice anywhere. Neither the King nor I have any quarrel with the jurisdiction of the Common Law Courts, but we shall not let those Courts take away the powers of the Courts set up by the Monarch for specific purposes in different areas of the country.

"The King is the fount of all justice in the Kingdom, and he has endowed this Council of the North with all his power. The Court of this Council is a shelter for the poor and innocent from the rich and insolent.

"It is my greatest ambition above any earthly thing, to serve His Majesty and you acceptably and fruitfully. I challenge you to give me your help as best you can; indeed, I demand it of you. You will not as friends, you may not as Christians, you cannot as lovers of your country, deny me this."

When he sat down there was a stunned silence for a moment. Then loud applause and cheers echoed around the room. I was so proud of him, but I wondered about the wisdom of using his saying about 'poor and innocent and proud and insolent' so publicly. Many of the Lords and 'gentlemen' on the Council, and many of those in the galleries, are amongst the proudest and most insolent you could wish to meet. They are very far from wanting the poor and innocent whom they victimise to be protected or sheltered by anybody.

But then that is Thomas all over. He says exactly what he thinks and means what he says, regardless of the consequences. He had enemies enough in the last two Parliaments when he was opposed to the Court and to Buckingham and his policies. Is he going to start making enemies on the other side now he is working for the King? He has enough trouble with the Saviles; I dare say most of the gentry there today realised Thomas's reference to being treated like a deadly disease and a bird cast out of the nest was aimed at them.

I shouldn't be surprised if he's bound to be a pretty aggressive and demanding bird in the nest when we get to bed tonight, he's so pumped up and full of himself. So he should be; I think he's wonderful.

Christopher Wandesford. 20th January, 1629. York

Tom has lost no time. He wants a Council he can control. Who better to help him do that than George and I? He has made some other appointments to make sure his policies are followed. Since Presidents of this Council have always appointed their friends and supporters to sit on it, one might be forgiven for thinking that nepotism was rife in the North. In fact one would usually be right, but in Thomas's case, he picks men who have ability: they are noticeably not "Yes men," either. I can hear someone say, "Well, Kit, as one of them you're bound to approve of his choice".

I suppose so, but no-one can question that George's ability is proven. He has a very successful practice in London and up here. He's been Tom's right hand legal man for years now, and for other members of the Wentworth family. I had a letter from Denzil the other week saying his Father, Earl Clare, has now taken to getting his solicitor to brief George. You don't get that kind of work if you're no use in Court.

Even his spell in prison in the Marshalsea and Dartford with Tom eighteen months ago did his career no harm at all. It may even have done him some good on both sides of the political divide, since no-one could deny that he was a man who stuck to his principles, and it gained him a lot of publicity. He was lucky there, though, in a strange way; if he had been imprisoned after trial and found guilty, his Inn would probably have had to disbar him. Barristers with criminal records are not permitted to appear in Court.

Not only has Tom put us both on the Council; he persuaded the King to appoint George as his Attorney-General in York, so he is the Council's lawyer. A better one the King would be hard put to it to find, but what will old enemies like Savile think?

Being friends with Tom has certainly been advantageous to me, and to George. He assisted me to be chosen as MP for the town of Richmond, Yorkshire in 1625 and again in 1626 for Thirsk, when I helped Eliot with the attack on Buckingham. Tom thinks the impeachment was unwise; I have come to agree with him that what the Commons needed was patience and courage to find a proper cure for all the wrangling between King and Parliament. Concentrating on the wrongs done to individuals should not blind us to the necessity to save the ship of state first, and then go after the captain who ran it on the rocks.

That was the attitude I adopted when I sat for Thirsk in the 1628 Parliament. Tom is right. We have to work with the King, not against him. Yet sometimes I have to wonder at Tom's methods. Recently George told me that "Tom loves justice for its own sake." Yet something happened last week that makes you wonder whether what he really enjoys is discomforting 'the proud and insolent', as he calls them.

The Court of the Council had assembled, and was waiting for Tom, as Lord President, to enter. In he came, preceded by certain officers and the Sheriff bearing the Council's mace. Everyone stood and doffed their caps, and bowed. These formalities are not so much to honour the President as to acknowledge that he is the King's representative and the personification of justice on the King's behalf. The Presidential party, in ceremonial regalia, proceeded down the middle of the Court, between the benches on either side, crowded as they were with bowing, hatless men. One man stood tall, his scarlet hat jauntily perched on his head, right by the centre aisle, not two feet from Tom. This arrogant young fellow was Henry Bellasis. Some say he was prompted to this display of discourtesy by Tom's own disdainful and autocratic manner, and that Tom's affronted reaction was a personal one.

I do not see it like that. I believe Tom was affronted on the King's behalf, but I thought what he did was inappropriate. He stopped, took Bellasis by the forearm, and commanded him to bow and remove his cap on the instant. Bellasis smiled, and did nothing. Tom immediately called the constables and had him arrested, taken to the jail, and then sent forthwith to the Star Chamber in London to answer for his behaviour.

Whilst I accept that what young Henry did was extremely offensive, I fancy that I should have dealt with him rather differently. I should have snatched off his cap, thrown it on the ground, stood on it, told him I believed his Father had raised him better than that, and walked on. I expect that would have raised a laugh at his expense, and that would have been the end of that. As it is, Tom has definitely established himself as a President not to be trifled with, but he has also made an enemy or two. Henry will not enjoy being held in custody until his case is heard, nor will he and his Father, Lord Fauconberg, welcome the fine or other penalty his foolish conduct merits.

These two are well-known, well-connected, and quite well liked in the North. They have been friendly with Tom in the past. Indeed, when Tom got me my Parliamentary seat at Thirsk, he did so by using his influence with Fauconberg, in whose gift that town is. That influence with the Bellasis family will be lost now; and any influence they may have elsewhere will be used against Tom, not for him.

Of course, Tom has shown, without any shadow of a doubt, that he fears no-one, on the Council or outside it. May be that is due to his wealth and his enormous sway as a mighty landowner, but in my view he would probably be the same in any event as Lord President even if he were relatively poor. He is arrogant, but determined to do the right thing.

He has established a commission to look into the operation of the Poor Laws here in the North. That will not be too popular, to put it mildly, bearing in mind that the rates to help the poor and build work-houses and so on, come from the rich. He has also laid out policies to keep an eye on the performance of the Justices of the Peace. That is part of his plan to make sure that justice is available for all. That will not please those landowners who use their position on the bench to oppress those whose lands they have taken, wish to take, or have taken advantage of in other ways.

We shall have some exciting times, I can see.

Arabella. 10th February, 1629. York

Thomas and the children and I are still up North, and I have just come in from the town. I go straight to the library, where I find Thomas working with Christopher and George Radcliffe. Thomas looks up.

"Thomas, I must tell you!"

"Where have you been, my love?"

"I've been to the dressmakers and the furriers. I thought I told you where I was going."

"So you did, but I forgot."

Radcliffe smiles at me. "I thought you usually send for these people to attend you here."

"I do, but it's so cold I thought a walk would brace me up a bit, and I went to see if some new, warm clothes I ordered were ready for a fitting. Then I went to select some fur for a new coat. But I have something I must tell you."

"The snow is still thick on the ground, and it's been there four weeks now. No sign of a thaw. You'll need the furs, dear." Thomas comes from behind the desk and places a chair for me before the fire. "What sort of fur did you ...."

"Never mind that, Thomas. I picked up the most amazing piece of news in the dressmakers. I met the Dean's wife. The Bishop told her husband that he has heard from the Bishop of London that it's all over the City."

Kit laughs. "What is all over the City?"

"About Frederick and his boy."

"Frederick? You mean the Elector Palatine?"

"Yes, Thomas, that Frederick. He was on a boat sailing from somewhere near Haarlem to another town when the boat sank. He was badly injured, and they say he might die."

"And the boy? What's his name?" Thomas asks. All three men are standing in front of me now.

George speaks before I can. "I think he's a Frederick too. Or was, if he didn't recover."

Thomas nods. "That's it. Frederick Henry. I think he's about fifteen. The King will be sad if he has lost a nephew." Thomas is quite stern. "But it's a good thing Frederick and Elizabeth have two more boys; Charles Louis and Rupert. Otherwise they'd have no heir; not that they've got much to inherit now Frederick has lost Bohemia and the Palatinate."

I am intrigued by what has just been said. "What about an heir to the English throne? Elizabeth could be our Queen if Charles has no children."

That stops all three of them, until George chimes in. "And her eldest son could be our King, if something happened to her."

Thomas's mood changes. "No more talk of that. Next you'll be imagining the death of the King, and it's treason even to speak of it. But until the King and Henrietta have some children, and preferably some boys, Elizabeth is next in line."

"Then we must pray that they beget some soon, husband, or a new Queen Elizabeth would have us fighting in Europe for Charles Louis' lands and titles."

The men all mutter at once. "God forbid."

Denzil Holles. 20th April, 1629. King's Bench Prison

I had a visit from Thomas today. He is, of course, in the House of Lords now, so we are not working together in the Lower House, and I cannot work even there until I get out of here. In fact, I am fairly certain that we shall be working together in no sense at all soon. He is more and more part of the Court faction, and I am still part of the opposition. Our ships are drifting further and further apart.

This may be a prison, but my room is dry, I have reasonable furniture (mine, of course), some books, and as I have money I am treated well. There is even a fair sized barred window, so I have some daylight, but I must have an oil-lamp alight. The damp squalor in the cells occupied by the poor is dreadful.

Thomas was well aware of the fracas – almost an affray – in the Commons on 2nd March, but anxious to hear the details from me, principal actor in the drama as I was.

"Parliament had only been sitting for a few weeks, and the main Commons debates were about religion and money. There's so much strong feeling about all this church ceremonial – what some are calling Arminianism – and the House is largely against it."

"It's the doctrine Laud favours."

"Yes, Thomas, and it's odd that you favour him. His friendship will do you no good."

"I hardly know the man, but from what I've read of his sermons and pamphlets, he has very similar views to mine on the role of the Monarch, and of the Church and Monarch in supporting each other. Remember what King James said when the Scots and Puritans wanted to get rid of the Bishops? No? Perhaps you are too young."

That annoyed me. "I'm not that much younger than you, Thomas, but tell me anyway."

"What he said, Denzil, was 'No Bishop, no King!' He knew the one depended on the other. The gossip is that Laud will soon be Archbishop of Canterbury. So why do you believe that being friends with him will do me no good?"

"Because it makes you look pro-Catholic. Soon after the King opened Parliament a member called Rouse told the House 'an Arminian is the spawn of a Papist, and if you look closely, you will see an Arminian reaching out a hand to a Papist, and a Papist to a Jesuit, while the Jesuit gives one hand to the Pope and the other to the King of Spain'. You can't afford to throw in your lot with the Catholics."

Thomas was majestic: "If the House thinks that's what Laud is doing they are much mistaken. He and I have little time for the Pope and his flock, and my desire for peace with Spain is due, not to a love of Rome, but of saving us from the expensive disasters Buckingham was wont to inflict upon us. Heaven knows, the Commons doesn't trip over its own feet in the rush to fill Charles's war chest, does it?"

That stopped me a bit; Thomas had, as usual, exposed the hypocrisy of the Commons for what it is. "The point is that Laud is going up the Church ladder much too fast for our liking. There'll be no stopping him until he has homes in Canterbury and Lambeth Palace. I doubt the people will put up with it, even if the King – and you – might like it."

"I cannot say I like it, but I prefer to have him as an ally in supporting the Crown than on the other side, Denzil."

"You mean on my side, then. Be careful how many enemies you make, Thomas. If Laud is your ally, then so are Bishops like Montague at Chichester. They take this idea of the Divine Right of Kings too far. I always thought your idea was that the King and Parliament should work together, but if Montague is right, the King doesn't need Parliament at all. He can just do exactly as he likes."

"I don't think that, Denzil, and well you know it. What worries me though is that the way the Commons – and you – behaved in March will make the King think he should never deal with a Parliament again."

I began to get angry. "That wasn't about religion. Anyway, what do you expect. It was about money."

Thomas was calm. "I know that. When I was in the Commons last year we were going to grant the King his Tunnage and Poundage in the customary way at last, but when the King prorogued Parliament to stop the attack on Villiers the chance was lost. That was what the main debate was about at the beginning of March and …"

"You hardly need to remind me what it was about. I was there; you weren't."

"So tell me." Thomas spoke as if cross-examining me.

I restrained myself. "Very well. Money and religious matters are tied up to some extent. Sir John Eliot told the House we should not vote the King his Tunnage and Poundage, nor let him set the rates himself unless he has a religious policy that suits us. There was a great deal of sympathy for that. The next day the Speaker read out a message from the King ordering us to keep to subjects we understood. Well, bloody hell, you can ...."

"No need to swear, Denzil. You know I care not for it."

I laughed at that. "*You* don't like it? Arabella doesn't like it, you might say. And you can – what? - imagine how the members reacted to that? Yes, indeed you can." I continued: "They were furious, and insulted. Fancy suggesting that they didn't understand their own religion or the practice of it! Many of them read the Bible every day, and most are regular Church-goers, even if they don't all go to the same type of Church. Some shouted angrily that telling us what we could and could not discuss was another infringement of freedom of speech in the House, and the Petition of Right wasn't a year old yet. There was chaos."

Thomas was thoughtful. "It was certainly not a wise message. I wonder who advised the King to send it."

"Who cares; it was probably his own idea. Anyway, the next day, 2nd March, the Speaker had another message from him, telling him to prorogue the House again. Speaker Finch tried to rise from his chair, to adjourn the House, but I ran across the chamber with Ben Valentine and William Strode, and we grabbed his arms and forced him back down and a couple of us sat on his lap. If the Speaker rises ...."

"Debate has to stop."

"Finch was in tears."

"I'm not surprised. And then you put those motions before the House?"

I laughed. "We were almost robbed of them by Eliot, yet he had drafted them. He was so mad with rage at Finch telling the House to adjourn, that he tore up his notes and threw them in the fire, saying that the King was stopping us debating them."

Thomas said: "So how were they put forward?"

"I had them off by heart, and recited them, and the clerks wrote them down. First, no-one should make innovations in religion, or encourage Popery or Arminianism; secondly, no-one should advise or help the King on the collection of Tunnage and Poundage without Parliamentary sanction, and thirdly, no-one should pay it; and anyone who did any of these things was a capital enemy of the Kingdom and Commonwealth."

"So Parliament could have them executed, Denzil?" Thomas was mocking.

"Exactly."

"And then what happened?"

"Your friend Christopher Wandesford was one of those who voted against the motion, but we had a majority. A week later the King dissolved Parliament, and ..."

"What did you expect?"

"... and his guards came to the House and arrested me, Eliot, Valentine, and Strode, and a few others. We were taken before the Court. Eliot refused to make any defence or apology, and told the Judges that 'being but a private man, I will not trouble myself to remember what I may have said or done as a public man' and they sent him to the Tower. We say what the Judges did was illegal."

Thomas nods. "But laying hands on Finch like that to hold him in his chair was an assault. Not just that, but an assault on the Speaker! Assault is a crime, Denzil. If a peasant had done it he would have been hanged, flogged, or branded. Didn't any of you apologise?"

"Of course not! We didn't regret what we'd done. We had nothing to be ashamed of; in fact we were rather proud of it."

"And here you are." Thomas swept my cell with a searching expression.

"Yes Thomas, here I am. All of us were fined, and some were sent to prison. A few were allowed out on bail as long as they behave themselves, but I told the Judges that I would rather be the subject of His Majesty's mercy than of his power. One of them asked me: 'Don't you mean you'd rather be the subject of his mercy than of justice?' And I said: 'I say of His Majesty's power, My Lord. His justice and his mercy should be the same thing.'"

Thomas laughed at that. "Very noble. In fact almost what More is supposed to have said to Thomas Cromwell. Cromwell told him that if he would not acknowledge Henry as Head of the Church, he was threatened with justice, and More is said to have replied: 'Then I am not threatened.'"

"So here I am, in prison."

"What will you do?"

"I shall try to make peace with the King. I may need your help."

"We shall see. I must go. Arabella sends her love."

"She's a good sister. I hope she is well. Give her mine."

Thomas nodded. "By the way, did you hear the sad news about the Queen?"

"No; what has happened to her?"

"Fortunately nothing happened to her, but she was pregnant. It proves that it is true, and not just Court gossip, that the King and Queen are actually in love with each other now. She had a baby son, and unfortunately he died an hour later."

"But we still have no heir to the throne. Charles has no brother, and his sister is tied up in Europe fighting the Emperor and Spain. If she becomes Queen it'll cost the country a fortune."

"Then Charles and Henrietta will just have to keep on trying, won't they, Denzil."

Thomas. November, 1629. York

The King has made me a Privy Councillor! Now I can really serve, advise, achieve much for him, the country, and let us make no mistake, for me too. I'm a Viscount, a Privy Councillor, and President of the Council of the North. Can I go yet higher? (I always seem to be asking that question). I think so. I want to be the King's right-hand man as Buckingham was, but I'll be better than the Duke. I know I have my own interests, but I can put the King and the country's needs before mine, and that is how I shall rise, too.

Many men in my position use the money they collect for the Crown on their own business. They 'borrow' it. They often deliberately fail to pay it into the Exchequer when it is due. They rip off more than the percentage they are entitled to for collecting it, and some do not even keep accurate records of what they do collect, so they can keep a huge chunk secretly, and still take their legal slice of what they must hand over to the King!

That of course is what Sir Arthur Ingram used to do (or perhaps still does). I do not do this and have no intention of starting. Certainly I borrow the money and use it to buy property, invest in the alum industry, and things of that sort, but I pay it over in full when it is due. I do not take more than I am entitled to, but I must admit that when I took over collection of the recusancy fines I arranged to double what I was entitled to as my cut, because I was doing it so efficiently. I made no secret of it, and the King's revenue increased sharply. Money is coming my way, and money is power.

Power may be coming to me, but that old bastard - no swearing, Thomas - Savile still manages to annoy me when he can, such as the business of draining Hatfield Chase. It's a marsh where many local people live and work. They like it, even if I would not, and they know how to make a living out of it, unpleasant as that might seem. Savile and a gang of speculators wanted to drain the marsh, reclaim the land, and evict the people. They would then let some of the people return, divide the rest of the land between themselves, and keep it.

They had the backing of the King. I dare say this was the idea of one of his advisers, or perhaps Savile got the idea from a Dutchman, Cornelius Vermuyden, and sold it to His Majesty. Be that as it may, the King wanted the scheme to go ahead because he had three manors covering a vast area there, and some hunting grounds too. If the land could be improved he'd be able to sell some off, and make better use of what's left.

I'm all in favour of improvement and better finances, but ignoring the rights of the poor is just the sort of behaviour I cannot abide. I don't suppose anyone told the King that the poor will be badly affected. Jesus was right; the rich should help the poor, not victimise them. These speculators had hired Vermuyden to do the work for them. He is a famous engineer from Holland, building dykes and canals to keep the sea out, so he knew what he was doing; no doubt about that. He did some work for the King at Windsor a while ago.

But this marsh is common land, and he had no right to do the work, and his paymasters had no right to ask him to do it. The rights to these commons rest with the locals. They were up in arms about it, sometimes literally, Vermuyden said. Perhaps, but it was one of the local fenmen who was killed in a violent encounter, not a developer. What made matters worse, and helped provoke the riots, was that Vermuyden wasn't even employing local labour to dig the channels and ditches, and build the embankments. He brought over a hundred or more of his compatriots from Holland, which just rubbed the locals' noses in it; not only would their common land and the living they make from it be lost, but they were not even earning anything out of the work.

No-one in Yorkshire was ignorant of the rivalry between me and Savile; they knew it was a far from friendly affair, so these fenmen came to see me, asking for my help. I thought the law was on their side, so I agreed. Could I pretend the fact that I could spike Savile's guns at the same time was not a factor? Hardly.

For me there was another bonus. Three of the men had been with the fenman who had been killed in the fight. They told me that the local people had been marching to the place where a channel was being dug when they were set on by a group of Dutch workers. The fenmen fought back, but were outnumbered and disorganised. The Dutch, however, had a leader who shouted some orders, and they could hear he was English.

They said he was dressed and spoke 'like a gent'. One of the men followed this 'gent' home to see where he went. When he told me it was to the manor house in Wroot, I knew it was my old bully from school, Chesworth. It made sense for him to have become an acolyte of a cad like Savile. I could not investigate this myself, but accompanied the men to see a local magistrate, to help them interest this Justice of the Peace in their story. One of my lowly companions told the magistrate that he had seen Chesworth strike the fatal blow which killed their friend. The others were unable to say that was so.

The crime was investigated, eventually Chesworth was charged with leading an affray, and with murder of the fenman. I could not resist sending Christopher to watch the trial and report to me. Chesworth's feelings at seeing the victim of his schoolboy bullying rejoicing in his downfall would be worth knowing. The judge directed the jury that they could not convict Chesworth of murder on the evidence of one man, with no corroboration, so he was acquitted on that count, but the jury upheld the evidence of the fenmen on the affray charge. Chesworth was found guilty and sentenced to three years in prison. It was not a happy time for him.

That's all been going on for some while. A few weeks ago I took the fenmen's case to the Council; now I'm its President. If the case comes before me, should I hear it? Probably not, but I don't think I'll be able to resist the chance to put Savile's nose right out of joint.

The difficulty is the King's interest in the drainage project, and the fact that some of the Privy Council support him. I shall have to be very careful.

Arabella. 31st May, 1630. York

There is great rejoicing throughout the nation. Two days ago the Queen was delivered of a healthy baby boy. Let us pray he lives. Thomas says he'd better, or we'll be fighting in Europe, repeating what I said a while ago, about The British Isles having no heir to the throne, unless it's Charles's sister Elizabeth. If that's what happened, would her husband Frederick become King? Or their eldest son? Well, it doesn't matter now Henrietta Maria has done her duty.

We have various bits of business news from Sir Arthur Ingram today, which is why Thomas keeps in touch with him. He writes that my brother is now out of prison. Denzil paid his fine of a thousand marks, and sent the King a petition – a very grovelling one, by the sound of it – asking to be set free, and he was.

I'm surprised Denzil didn't write to tell me about this himself, but relations between him and Thomas seem to be getting slightly strained. I know he did not care for Thomas going over to the King's side, and leaving the Commons, and then there's been that strange business with my Father.

Someone produced a document planning some sort of coup against Parliament by the Monarchy, and my husband sent it to the Secretary of State, Sir John Coke. My Papa had a copy of it, and he got into trouble over it, but it turned out be an old thing someone had written back in King James's time, and he'd thought it ridiculous. Papa was not at all pleased, and Denzil blames Thomas.

Thomas said it was all a bit silly; an army would be needed to keep control of the people for the plot to work, and the King just doesn't have one. He's hardly got any soldiers at all. In any case, I think it's a daft idea. Armies have officers, and officers have families too; they don't want them locked up for what they think or say. The ordinary soldiers are the same. They don't want to use a musket on their own Mothers and Fathers for having ideas. They may start off shooting other folks' parents, but when it gets nearer home, I'm sure they'd lack enthusiasm for it.

Denzil thinks Thomas should have thought about the effect on my family, especially on my Father. Lord Clare is not likely to be well received at Court now. But how could Thomas have known my Father had a copy of the document? Denzil is wrong about that. Come to think of it, how did Coke find out Father had a copy?

After Thomas was appointed to the Privy Council last November, he advised the King that as the Huguenots have been defeated by King Louis, there's no need to fight France any longer. There have not been any real hostilities between us and the Spanish for some years, so peace can be made with both countries. Thomas told the King he can't afford any more wars if he doesn't have any Parliaments, and Charles now sees the force of that.

I don't think Thomas is under any illusion the King likes him much, though. Clearly, the King is grateful for his advice and the efficient way he's running the North of the Country, and getting good revenue out of the fines on the Catholics, but there is nothing very friendly in their dealings.

It seems to me the King just sees him as a higher type of servant. It wasn't like that with Charles and the Duke of Buckingham; they were like David and Jonathan.

Perhaps it makes Thomas a bit sad, though he doesn't say so. He talks a lot about his plans for making the King financially independent, and making the country work properly, not just for the rich, but for the benefit of the poor, too. He wants to make the Poor Laws work thoroughly; he doesn't like the way a lot of the rich avoid paying their contribution to the rates and the upkeep of the housing and the creation of jobs for poor people.

I say 'thoroughly' because that is what he and this Bishop Laud write to each other about. They call their policies 'Thorough'. Thomas wants to make the state and its servants thorough, and Laud wants to do the same with the Church. What worries me is that many Puritans will hate Laud for all his incense and candles and robes and decorated churches, and there are many men who think the King should call Parliament so they can make a fuss about their 'grievances', as they call them. Will these people turn on the King one day and on Laud and Thomas for helping him? God alone knows what might happen then.

Christopher Wandesford. 16th February, 1631. London

I'm staying with Tom in the city. Yesterday he came back from a Privy Council meeting and told me there have been reports of food riots in Rutland. The Council resolved to take care of this sort of thing by making sure the market was well supplied with corn and bread to be sold to the poor at fair prices.

This morning Tom had me draft a letter for him to Richard Marris, his steward at Wentworth. The letter was about the price of wheat, and for once it made me question some of Tom's motives. The background to the riot in Rutland and the draft letter is the shortage of wheat throughout much of the country due to the very poor harvest last year.

The Privy Council was really worried that there might be a famine, so it fixed the price of all cereal crops. The sale of corn to foreign countries was banned; the amount of grain that could be used for brewing beer and other drinks was restricted. To avoid a black market in flour and bread, the magistrates were ordered to investigate anyone suspected of hoarding basic foods-stuffs, or the grain from which they could be made. The Council went even further. It passed laws ensuring that the grain discovered was to be distributed and sold to the poor at the fixed price before anyone else could buy or sell it.

Of course, Tom is on the Privy Council, he's President of the Council of the North, and is very much in favour of this sort of law. He worked very hard on the Commission looking into excessive fees charged by officials for doing their jobs. He not only argued that the superior officers should not charge excessively for their services on top of their official salaries; he also proposed that they should be held to account for the fees their minions charged, too. That was a pretty revolutionary idea, and not the sort to make him very popular. Neither was his work on the Poor Law Commission, bearing in mind that you can't really help the poor unless you take cash from the rich. Even if they go to Church every Sunday, one thing the rich do not care for is parting with their money to help the lower classes. Heaven knows what they think the parable about the rich man and Lazarus at his gate meant.

Anyway, it is that background, and that benevolent aspect of Tom's policies, which worries me a bit. This is what the letter to Richard says:

Dear Richard,

Thank you for your last report. I am glad that all rents are up-to-date, and that there seems to be plenty of food about in Yorkshire. It is, unhappily, not the same down here. The price of wheat is astronomical. I am told that is because shipments of corn from the Irish harvest last autumn have not been delivered yet.

I want you to go around the county buying up all the spare wheat you can, get it to Hull or other ports as fast as possible, and shipped down here.

The price you pay should be much less than it will fetch in the London markets, and we can see a healthy profit, even if we sell cheaply.

Let me know how you get on.
Wentworth.

I gave the draft to Tom, and he approved and signed it, as he always does. With not a little trepidation I said: "I'm not sure you should do this. You're on the Council down here, and up there, and it's your duty to see that the Order in Council stopping people making money out of the corn shortage is obeyed."

Tom looked up from copying the letter. "Is that what it looks like, Kit?"

"I'd say so. If that isn't the way it looks, why don't you explain it in the letter?"

I got one of his arrogant looks in response, but not his temper, thank the Lord. "Richard is my agent, Kit, my servant. I owe him no explanations."

"Perhaps, but what worries me is not what Richard thinks, but what others may say. They are sure to work it out."

Tom was unmoved. "I do not propose to defend myself against accusations which have yet to be made. It seems to me that if I ship a lot of wheat down here, and we put it on the market, that will itself lower the price, there will be more flour and bread for the Londoners, and I shall still make some money. Is that wrong?"

"But the price is supposed to be fixed!"

"Will anyone complain if the price goes down?"

He and I are friends, but it was chancing my arm to argue with him too much over that, so all I said was; "I just don't think it looks right, that's all."

He thanked me for the warning, but I am still very unhappy about this episode. Tom is implacable with people who profit from flouting the law. If he had caught Savile doing this, he would have chased him up-hill and down-dale to recover the money from him. Calling Tom a hypocrite is more than I dare do, but it is what I am close to thinking.

Thomas. 13th April, 1631. London

Today is my 38th birthday. I have a letter from Richard Marris who is at Wentworth.
10th April.

My Lord,

I have sent off the second of three shipments of corn today. I was pleased to hear that the first arrived safely last week from Whitby. Today's cargo left from Hull. The third will go from Hull, too, probably in about three weeks.

Buying the wheat and other grains is becoming increasingly difficult. Your fellow Councillors here are diligent in looking for evidence of black-market activity, so I have been using others to act as my agents – well, yours really – in secret so that your identity as the buyer is not known.

Not only are the magistrates and the Council to be feared. The people are very stirred up, and threats of violence, indeed of lynchings, are uttered against cheats and black-marketeers. Am I to go on buying?
I am your obedient servant, My Lord,
Richard Marris.

I show it to Christopher. "What do you think?"

"I don't think you should get Richard to buy any more. It's dangerous."

"Did I tell him to buy in secret through undisclosed agents?" Kit mumbles "No".

"Has the price gone up in Yorkshire?"

"Not that I know of."

"Did the price go down in London when our shipments were sold?"

"A bit." Christopher looks like a startled rabbit.

I try to sound a little less aggressive. "So we have not harmed our fellow Yorkshireman and we've made life a bit easier for Londoners. Is that it?"

He is reluctant. "I suppose so."

"And I have made some money, and you and Richard have had a bonus. Is that so bad?" Kit just looks at the floor. I continue: "And when the next two shipments arrive the price in London may go down further, and we shall not be so profitable on those."

"Maybe."

"You see Kit, the reason for the order in Council was that we wanted to stop real profiteers from cornering the market in their own area and then selling the goods to the local people when they had forced the price up. I haven't been forcing the price up anywhere. I've just been getting Richard to buy what is available, and send it down here so that London can eat. How would you feel living down here with hundreds, if not thousands, of starving people from the east side of the city rampaging through the streets looking for food?"

"Rather scared."

"Yes, rather scared. So would I. Anyway, with luck the Irish corn shipments will arrive in London soon, and there will have been no food riots."

Thomas. 30th May, 1631. York

I returned from London two weeks ago. Just before I left the Irish wheat boats arrived, and the price of bread came down sharply. I wrote to Marris at Wentworth telling him this and saying: "The shortage in London is over. God be praised; gains there will be none." Of course, I had made some gains, but there would be no more.

The plague is running round the country like an affliction of rats. People are dying in large numbers, labourers are hard at work digging pits, burying the diseased corpses in them. There is no time to make any attempt to distinguish one body from another, many families having no idea where their dead have gone. I set up a committee to try to isolate the sick from the general public, and check the spread of the disease. It is very hard work.

It's difficult to know whether we are succeeding, as some people do not succumb to this dreadful scourge, some villages escape almost completely, and no-one understands it. Even doctors and physicians blunder about in the dark. I'm not aware of a single person who can be said to have been cured by any medicine or any of the strange and sometimes bizarre remedies these barbarous barber surgeons dream up. One of the worst is supposed to eliminate what the doctors call 'an evil humour' which they say causes the plague. To suck this humour out they heat up glass vessels – jars or stout glasses – over a lamp or fire until they are almost red hot, and then place the open end of the vessel upside-down on the patient's body. They are already in acute distress from thirst, and the pain of the 'bubes' growing in their groins and armpits, and sometimes their knee and elbow joints. As the hot glass cools it sucks a great lump of their flesh up inside it. The glass cools down more, and falls off. The patient is left with a nasty burn and a blister, and then dies anyway. Gruesome.

Despite travelling about the northern counties quite a bit to see for myself how the measures we are taking have progressed, I have not contracted this plague, and I thank God it has not stolen Arabella and the children from me. We have done as much as we can to help the poor, who always suffer more from this sort of thing than the rich, like me.

After all, they have so little to start with, and the burden on a young widow with four or five small children, whose husband is newly in the ground, is overpowering. She has neither money, nor leisure in which to go out to earn any. Does she go on the streets to beg, or worse? We have to help these people.

Doing so is tiring and extremely worrying, but today is a good day, with very different work. I'm presiding over a Court in the case of Vermuyden's drainage scheme at Hatfield Chase. Circumstances have changed significantly in the last few months. I've used my position on the Privy Council to petition it and the King to support the local people against Savile, this Dutchman and his backers. I persuaded a lot of the country folk affected by the scheme to write to the King and Council with their complaints. I've even had George and Kit penning letters for the farmers and others who could not write.

It has taken a year or so, but it has worked and the King has set up a Court of Sewers for Hatfield Chase. It is a sort of Commission to enquire into the problem; he has appointed me to be its chairman.

Several farmers and others who live and work these fens appear before us. The Council Chamber is a large square, with dark oak panelling in a linen-fold pattern, heavy brass sconces in the walls for candles, and two huge crystal chandeliers at either end of the room hanging from the ornately plastered, very lofty ceiling. I cannot help wondering whether these working people have ever been in a room like this in their lives. Are they frightened? One in particular impresses me. He is a tall, strong and, for a peasant, extremely eloquent man, even if he cannot read and write. He tells us his name is Arthur Fenn – quite appropriate – and that he lives in Low Eggborough, a small village near the border with Lincolnshire. Our clerk administers the oath, reading out the words which Mr Fenn repeats.

I invite him to tell us his story.

"My Lord, I farms fifty acres just outside the village, and I lives on the farm. Corneloos Verminden and Lord Savile called a meeting about eighteen months ago. I went. They wan'ed to talk about a scheme to drain all the fens round about Hatfield Chase. At first I were in favour of it. I thought it'd make more of the land useful, if it was drier."

"What changed your mind?"

"Some of my neighbours, people in Eggborough and other villages, was gettin' very alarmed and unhappy. They'd been told as how this scheme'd be good for them, as I'd been, but as the work went on they found that Lord Savile and his friends, and Mr Verminden, was taking over a lot of the common land where they used to graze their cattle and pigs and sheep, where they could forage for firewood, and blackberries, and such like."

"Is it important to them to be able to do that?"

"Very important, My Lord. A lot of them are poor and without them things they can pick up on the common, and keeping a few animals on it, many o' them'd starve, or die o' cold in winter. And – well – I hope you don't think me impertinent, but there's som'at else."

"Yes, Mr Fenn. What might that be?"

"Well, like I say My Lord, it may be impertinent, me being what I am and you being a great Lord and lawyer and President an' all, but ain't it the law that a man's rights can't just be took off him, like, in England?"

I cannot help smiling at that. "Certainly, Mr Fenn."

"Well then, My Lord, if that's so, and a man has a right to go on the common, like, and put his animals there, who can take it away, if yuh knows what I mean?"

"That is the point exactly. That is what this commission is looking into, and we shall be asking Sir Cornelius and his friends how they deal with your argument."

Fenn is anguished: "My Lord, don't take agin me like that. I ain't arguin' with nobody; leastways, not with you."

"Of course not, Mr Fenn. You are not arguing with me. What I mean is, I want to see how the other side deal with what you've been saying. Have no fear. You are in no trouble." Fenn thanks me and calms down. "Was there any other point you wanted to tell me?"

"Yes, My Lord, I thank'ee." He draws a big breath and himself up to his full height. "It's the floods, My Lord."

This is what I have been hoping for. "Are you talking about the floods at harvest last year?"

"That's it My Lord. It was like this. All round the Chase and Hatfield Moors – the whole of the Isle of Axholme, y' might say - we had good crops, and we was gettin' in the harvest. Well, there's many streams - like the Went and the Aire - what flows through these parts into the Don and the Trent. Normally they don't cause no trouble; well, not in September, like. They can flood a bit in winter sometimes, but it don't matter too much then."

Mr Fenn seems to have lost himself somewhat. "So what happened last September?"

"Well, My Lord, lots of them streams got flooded right high, and people was driven out o' their houses in Fishlake and Sykehouse, and Snaith, and their fields was washed out, and their crops was lost."

"How did you find out about this? Was your farm affected?"

"A couple of my fields on the edge of the farm was drowned, like, and a couple of cows with 'em, but we was lucky, My Lord."

"But how did you find out about the other villages?"

"I mean, we all knows about 'em now, don't we My Lord, because everyone was prayin' in all the churches for them as suffered back September, and you and your Council was goin' round givin' money and food to the poor folks. But how I knows it then was the people. All these poor mites come off the highway into Eggborough, 'cause Your Lordship knows it runs past my village. They come off the main road seein' as how it was flooded, and they was trying to get to Knottingley or Pomfret."

"Thank you, Mr Fenn. Do go on. What were these poor people doing?"

"They was looking for places to sleep, and a bite. Loads of 'em was just women with little brats, like; some o' the menfolk had stayed behind tryin' to save what they could. They was all wet through, and the kids was cryin'. Some of the women, too."

"What happened to them?"

"My wife's a good woman, My Lord, and she can't watch nobody in trouble like that without she's got to do som'at. So she tells me to lay a lot of clean hay and straw in our barn, so's they can sleep there, and she sends our young Arthur off to the neighbours what hadn't been flooded too, and gets them to do the same. Sal, she …"

"Sal, Mr Fenn?"

"That's the wife, My Lord, Sally Fenn. Well, she goes out to these poor folks and tells 'em to go to the barn, and she sends others off to the neighbours – except old Wainwright, o' course – he's too mean. And then all the women got together and makes this big cauldron of broth, and we feeds 'em, and they sleeps in the barn"

"Tell me, Mr Fenn, what caused this problem, this terrible flood?"

"First, I only knew about it 'cause the women in the barn told me about it, and I could see from my own two fields that there was some problem somewhere. But next day, when the water had gone down a bit, I got a little boat I keep to row down the stream to the river for a bit o' fishin', like, and I goes up-stream towards them villages. An' that's when I see it."

I am beginning to get rather impatient; he talks as though he's repeating a tale in his corner by the fire in the tavern, but I restrain myself. "And what was it you saw?"

He turns and points across the Court rather dramatically at Vermuyden and Savile. Vermuyden is short, but clearly muscular, almost as though he digs his ditches and canals personally. His hair is flaxen, and hangs down straight around his head as though cut under a bowl. "I sees them men, and some others, My Lord. They was standing by the side of the stream – well – more like a lake it was, at that point – and beside them, running into the stream was this big channel what they'd dug. Full of water, it was, rushing out of the ground and into the stream. It ain't a big stream, normal like, so it couldn't cope with all this extra water, and that was what flooded it all."

"How do you know these men dug the channel?"

"A few weeks before I was on my way to Doncaster market. I were riding my old cob along the byways, across the country, when I sees this big channel being dug by lots of men, and looking over it all was these same two gen'lemen. So I goes up to 'em and takes off my hat, and asks 'em what's going on. Then I recognised 'em from the meetin' when they was setting up this drainage thing in the first place.

"Very well, Mr Fenn, and what did they tell you?"

"Lord Savile, he don't talk much to the likes of me, but the one with the foreign voice, Mr Verminden, he knows me from afore, and tells me it's a canal – I thinks that's the word he used – to drain the Chase and the marshes, and it'll be good for everyone."

"Did you believe him?"

"Looked all pretty neat to me, My Lord, then, 'cos there weren't no rain or nothin'. There wasn't no reason to think it would all go wrong."

I have to tread carefully here. I do not want to be seen to be getting into the ring myself. I am the judge and should seem to be impartial. "Are you saying that no-one was ever worried about these drainage canals before the floods?"

Mr Fenn is alarmed again. "No, My Lord, I didn't say nothin' like that. No. There was lots of folks real worried about it as soon as they heard about the scheme. There's even some in Eggborough, people what live or 'ave land on the low-lying bit where the two streams joins up; they was sayin' that the canal would flood the streams and their 'ouses. Then there was others what makes a living in other villages getting fish and reeds and peat and stuff out o' the marshes and bogs."

"Thank you Mr Fenn. Is that all?"

"Ain't that enough My Lord?"

Even Savile laughs at that, and so do I. I turn to Savile and Vermuyden. "Have you any questions for Mr Fenn, gentlemen?"

Savile rises, arrogant in his bottle-green finery and delicate lace cuffs. He sneers at Fenn. "You lost two cows, Fenn. Anything else?"

"Just a bit of wheat, like."

"My Lord, to you, Fenn. And this gentleman is Sir Cornelius Vermuyden, not Mister Verminden. Don't forget it. I dare say you are going to sue for your two cows and your bit of wheat, aren't you? Isn't that why you have come here, to bolster your claim?"

"I can't afford no lawyers, My Lord. I ain't never sued no-one, and I ain't goin' to start now."

"Your evidence is nothing but what you have been told by other people, isn't it?"

Fenn turns to me. "That ain't fair, My Lord, I told you that I seen all them things with my own eyes one time or 'nother."

I cannot help glancing at Savile with a warning look, as I say to the witness: "So you did, Mr Fenn. And it is up to me to decide whom to believe when I have heard all the evidence."

Savile is, of course, not abashed. "You made the rest up, didn't you, Fenn?"

"No I never, and you can get that gentleman – Sir Corneloos - to tell His Lordship that I seed you both by the river them two times, and what happened."

Vermuyden tugs at Savile's cloak and when he stoops to him, I can tell from Vermuyden's expression he will not lie. He has a reputation as a strict Lutheran; I doubt he has ever lied deliberately in his life. He is an expert in his drainage profession, and I suspect he just made a big mistake here. He's not had as big a task as this one in England before.

Savile does not stop. "Now this whole area is known as the Isle of Axholme and the Hatfield Chase or Marshes, is it not?"

"Aye, it is." He adds after a pause: "My Lord."

"That's because it's boggy, isn't it?"

"Yes, My Lord."

"And it's boggy and marshy because it floods, isn't it?"

"It does that, My Lord."

"It has always flooded, hasn't it?"

"It has, My Lord."

"So nothing has changed, has it?"

"Oh yes it has." Fenn turns to me. "Yuh see, My Lord, it flooded every couple o' year or so, but only on the low bits, like. I know I ain't as bright as that Lordship over there, like, but we ain't all stupid neither. We don't build our homes and barns and villages on the low bits what flood. We builds on the higher ground what the water don't hardly ever reach. Well, this time nearly all the buildin's went under, an' yer knows what it was." Fenn points straight at Savile. "It was all that water rushin' down 'is canal, what I seed with me own eyes. We ain't never had the canal before, an' we ain't never had all them houses flooded out before neither."

Savile looks down at Vermuyden, who registers no reaction at all. Savile looks up again, and I ask him: "Have you any more questions for Mr Fenn, My Lord?"

"No, My Lord Wentworth, I do not."

"Or any witnesses as to the flood, and what caused it, or anything else?"

"No My Lord, I do not. Despite our history I did not expect Your Lordship to accept the evidence of … of … peasants like these against me and Sir Cornelius. It is a betrayal of our class." Savile sits. I am surprised by that last remark. Savile is himself disdainful of foreigners, and would have no reason to suppose I should favour a Dutchman who had only been knighted six years ago, and for what? Digging ditches?

I do not need to retire to consider my decision, but I need to confer with my colleagues. We adjourn to my adjoining chambers and I ask if we are agreed that the evidence of Fenn and the others should be held to be true. They all agree. In fairness, I believe some of them would not dare disagree with me in any circumstances. I outline the form of order I have in mind. They agree that too. We return to the Court within ten minutes.

"I shall give judgment at once. The commission finds the evidence conclusive that the flood did considerable damage to the villages of Fishlake, Sykehouse, and Snaith, and to the inhabitants of those villages, and their crops and cattle. The flood is due to the defendants' negligent design. We have also heard evidence that those undertaking this project to drain Hatfield Chase and its marshes have taken considerably more of the reclaimed land than the area originally sanctioned by His Majesty as their reward for undertaking the work. We have found that evidence to be true.

"I therefore order that, first, the undertakers will forthwith cut a new channel to divert the drains away from the affected villages; secondly they will submit plans to the Court showing that the new works will not adversely affect any other village or hamlet; thirdly, they will surrender all those parts of the land they have taken which are shown coloured red on the plan drawn up and put in evidence by the Court surveyor. That land will be shared amongst the villages, and will remain common land. The Court will rise."

As my colleagues and I leave the Court I hear Savile say, in a very loud voice:

"Wentworth will not get away with this, Vermuyden. We shall do all we can to delay and frustrate this judgment."

George Radcliffe. 5th October, 1631. York.

My Lady Arabella Wentworth died yesterday in the President's fine house in this city. Aside from my own wife, she was the best of women, kind, considerate, loving, and caring. The servants and local people, to whom she ministered like an angel throughout her marriage to Thomas, are very much cast down. Thomas is in a dreadful state. I am afraid to go home and leave him. I fear to contemplate what he may do if left to himself. I shall have to stay by him until his crisis is over and he begins to be himself again.

For such an apparently hard man he weeps without shame, and trying to cheer him up seems a Herculean task at present. If anything he is in a worse pass than when Margaret died. He finds no comfort just now in the three living children she bore him, but that is understandable, because their youngest son, never a strong boy, died a few months ago, and if Arabella had not been pregnant when she fell, she might not have been carried off by the miscarriage which the fall induced.

It is a strange story. The weather had been fine, and a few days ago it was warm and sunny, and the Viscount was walking in the garden, talking to me and some other guests. Arabella called to him from the open door of her sitting room which looks out into the garden. Why she called we shall never know.

He hurried to her as he always does, and I heard her say: "Thomas, you have a wasp on your coat," and I could see her step forward to brush it off, but suddenly she stepped away again - I know not why – slipped, screamed, fell across a small table, and rolled off that to the floor.

I ran to the door as Thomas knelt beside her, and we lifted her to a couch.

"What's happened?"

"She brushed an insect off my coat, and it flew at her. She tried to get out of its way, tripped over that table and fell on the floor".

Arabella groaned in pain. She was conscious. "My pains have started. I think my waters have broken." I looked down, and saw that her skirts were wet. Without any urging I ran to the hall and shouted for a servant to hasten to the doctor.

When I went back, Thomas asked me to send for a surgeon. "I have done so. He should be here soon. He is unlikely to keep you and the Lady Arabella waiting." There are definite advantages in wealth and power, though they do not stop this sort of thing occurring.

The doctor could do little except help the tiny dead morsel, which should have been a baby, leave its mother, and he did what he could to ease Arabella's suffering. She faded away over three days, dying on the 4th. The doctor offered Thomas a sleeping draught, but he is not one to indulge what he sees as 'that sort of weakness', even though I can see that in the next few days or weeks, some sound sleep is exactly what he will need.

In fact I am in much the same need myself, but at least I have not suffered the loss of my wife to add to my cares and woes. What has been causing me and Thomas a lot of concern, if not anguish, has been the number of serious attempts that are being made to undermine the authority of the Council, Thomas's role as President, and mine as the King's Attorney in the North. These matters come in addition to the normal run of ordinary cases, and the other duties that devolve upon us in trying to carry out the King's wishes and policies. We shall have to watch carefully how they develop, and with Arabella dead, Thomas is in no condition to watch out for anything. That is almost the worst woe of all.

Thomas. 9th December, 1631. Wentworth Woodhouse

I have hardly been able to think for the last six or seven weeks. Arabella gone? I can still hardly believe it! She was such a fine woman, such a fine wife in every way: intelligent and quick like the rest of her family; an excellent mother who had presented me with my treasured son and heir and two gorgeous daughters, Nan and Arabella, of whom I am equally proud and fond.

Oh, Arabella! If you had not been trying to bear me another son, you might still be with me! God's mysterious ways are impossible to comprehend. I cannot write more. Ink is likely to be blotted by tears if I go on. I loved you, my darling Arabella.

Thomas. 17th January, 1632. Wentworth Woodhouse

To my amazement in the middle of last year the King offered me the appointment of Deputy Lord Lieutenant of Ireland. I asked for clarification.

Yesterday I received a letter from the King.

12th January, 1632.

My Dear Wentworth,

I have been giving serious consideration to the request you made for certain assurances about the way in which you might be allowed to govern Ireland in my name. I have discussed them with the Treasurer, Weston, and my Chancellor of the Exchequer, Cottington, and with Bishop Laud. Weston and Cottington were rather amused that, as Weston put it, you sought to impose terms and conditions upon me as though we were merchants engaged in commerce in silks and spices from India, but Laud took a different line.

He pointed out that almost ten years ago my dear Father, King James, sent a commission to Ireland to enquire into the loss of Crown and Church lands and income there. It reported that both King and Church had been defrauded by the very people he had appointed to look after these things for him. Those people were, as you may be aware, almost exclusively Protestant settlers of the last fifty years or so. That was unfortunate because at the time we were at war with Spain, and could not risk upsetting those men when we needed them to keep the lid on the Catholic pot, and prevent Spain being given a foothold to invade Ireland. Consequently we could not act on the commission's recommendations.

As we are now at peace with Spain and France those considerations no longer apply. Those were Laud's arguments, and the other two could not refute them. He proposed, and I accepted, that it is time to take a new broom to Ireland, and recover Crown and Church lands and income. Weston and Cottington had perforce to acquiesce. You are the new broom.

The assurances you asked for, to which I agree, are:

1) You may leave Ireland to attend my Court and the Privy Council as often as you feel the need; this was the term my two money men had the most difficulty with; I felt they wanted you exiled to Dublin and forbidden to return, as though they do not want you near me. That is a trifle odd when they recommended you for the post in the first place, unless securing your departure was why they suggested you. The Bishop, on the other hand, was entirely behind your having this right; he mumbled something about it being essential if all is to be thorough.

2) You may deal direct with Lord Treasurer Weston on matters concerning Irish finance.

3) I shall not make any grant of lands or estates in Ireland without consulting you first, and you may give or withhold your consent as you see fit.

4) *I shall not entertain any petition which would enable the petitioner to avoid your Irish Courts, nor shall I allow any appeal against any decision of yours unless you are clearly guilty of unreasonable conduct or an obvious injustice.*

5) You may keep the Presidency of the Council of the North. I trust you are satisfied that your Vice-President, Osborne, is up to the task. You must appoint a suitable man to be your Deputy if he is not.

Your final request was that I should confer an Earldom upon you to reinforce your authority and place you on a level with men like Ormonde, Cork, and Clanricarde. I do not see the necessity to do that at this juncture. The fact that I have appointed you, and you have my unconditional backing must, in their eyes, I warrant, give you all the authority you need.

I shall be obliged if you can adjust your affairs in England as soon as possible, and take up your post in Ireland, in which I wish you every success. May God Bless your endeavours.
Charles R.

I am mortified about the Earldom, but content with the rest, writing immediately with my grateful acceptance in unequivocal terms.

Thomas. 21st February, 1632. Wentworth Woodhouse

Over the last month or so I have been obtaining reports and information about the state of the accommodation I am likely to have when I arrive in Dublin. It seems that the

Deputy is supposed to live in the Castle, although I am told that it has been neglected for so long that my last couple of predecessors have lived in houses they built or rented. I'm not at all sure I want to acquire property in Ireland. I have no idea how long my appointment might last, or whether I might be called back to London for some even more significant post - or mayhap something less pleasing.

I must give directions for repairs to be carried out, and dispatch an order for work to start immediately.

Thomas. May, 1632. Whitehall

I've met a most interesting man from Ireland. He's one of the New English Protestants, and is Vice-Treasurer of that kingdom. Francis Annesley, Lord Mountnorris, seems a clever chap, and being so recognises (although he is not blunt enough to say as much) that if I am to be Deputy Lord Lieutenant there, I am worth cultivating. It is hardly surprising that I feel the same way about him. I can only be of use to him in the future if I choose, whereas he can be of enormous help to me now, if I can recruit him.

It shouldn't be difficult. He tells me: "I'm over here in London trying to clear my name of allegations that I've been misusing my public office and the administration for my own purposes".

"What do these allegations involve, then?"

"Oh! I don't think we need to look into them. They are false." Annesley smiles. He's almost fifty, I should say, fairly slim, with grey hair, which he wears longish, to the bottom of his neck, and a pointed grey beard and moustache, not unlike mine. "The thing is, I'm not a member of the clique of powerful Protestant nobles that runs Ireland behind the scenes, and you need to know about that. I've acted against them on the King's behalf."

"Well, I suppose if that's true, it explains why you might be the victim of trumped up charges."

"That's it! I'm outside the charmed circle because I report to the King against the Irish Council."

There is something sly about this chap; I'm not sure how far I can trust him, but he must hoard a lot of dirt on these people. It would be worth a great deal to me to be familiar with all this dirty washing.

I must find out all I can about the Irish nobility, the way the administration, the government works, the army, the Irish Treasury. Then I can make policies, plans to implement them. I shall try to make Annesley my ally. William Laud tells me that Annesley's alleged crimes involve helping himself, from the monies he collects on behalf of the King, to 'commissions' to which he has no legal entitlement.

If true, this proves that he will be well-acquainted with the seamier side of Dublin life, and, if guilty, that he is someone on whom I should keep a close eye. I do not want my Irish Court to be renowned for its corruption, as those of so many of my predecessors have been.

Something else has been brought to my attention about this man. He has a foppish air. He went to live in Ireland in 1606, when Sir Arthur Chichester was Lord Deputy there. He joined Sir Arthur's household, living with him in circumstances of curiously close intimacy. He was rewarded with a small number of offices of state in Ireland, and – when he was only 22 – a pension! What did he do to earn these perks? It reminds me of King James and his affection for

Carr and Villiers. The mind boggles at what some men will do, indeed appear to enjoy, for money, for advancement.

Despite that, I do not suggest there is any mere pretence of pleasure at perverse relations with other men about Mountnorris; that seemed to me to be his natural bent when I met him. I'm glad to say I was spared any of his advances. Close, loving friends I may be with Christopher and George, but I've never had any interest in or desire for other than verbal intercourse with my own sex.

Perverse tastes or not, Lord Mountnorris did not balk at marriage to Dorothea eight years ago, nor at what it takes to beget two sons, with, he tells me, another child on the way. Laud has also told me that Annesley became the owner of the Mountnorris estate in 1612 because King James had been so impressed with Chichester's reports on 'this fine young man'. The estate includes a castle with its surrounding lands.

By that time Chichester was long gone, the new Deputy being Lord Falkland, who had been in office six years. Annesley at that time enjoyed the salary of the paymaster of the Armies and Garrisons of Ireland, with the chances of embezzlement and other perks which such posts carry. This caused him to fall out with Falkland, who tried to sail a more or less honest ship; Annesley did all he could to stir up storms and contrary winds for the Deputy. So bad a voyage was Falkland having that in 1625 the English Privy Council was told by the Secretary of State that some of the Irish Privy Council, 'amongst whom Sir Francis Annesley is not the least violent and impertinent', were making Falkland's attempts to govern almost impossible.

Far from getting Annesley punished or reprimanded, the result, somehow, was that he was promoted to Vice-

Treasurer of Ireland, which simply increased his opportunities for stealing from the King. I can only imagine how Falkland felt about that; much as if a stiletto had been thrust between his ribs from the rear. In 1628 Charles made Annesley an Irish peer as Baron Mountnorris.

But that was just the start, and it would get worse. The cause was an Irish family, the Byrnes, who from time immemorial had owned land in Wicklow, which had been the subject of legal disputes. The results had been unfavourable to the Byrnes, and they accused Falkland of being unjust towards them. The Irish Privy Council set up a committee to investigate, and Annesley was on the committee. False witnesses were called and Annesley used his position as a committee member to ensure that all findings went against Falkland. In August 1929 Charles recalled his Deputy to London.

That was what gave rise to my being offered the government of Ireland last year, but in the intervening years, Mountnorris and Richard Boyle, Lord Cork, ran the country for Charles as Lords Justice. This story of Mountnorris's campaign against Falkland made me determined that, much as I might make use of him now in learning the wrinkles of political survival in Ireland, in setting up a skeleton administration there before I sailed for Dublin, I should never give him the chance to best me or take money from my – I should say the King's – Irish coffers.

I learned something else from Mountnorris: just how careful one must be about the religious divide between Catholic and Protestant. He told me that this was another cause of Falkland's dismissal. The Old English and the small but sturdy middle class – lawyers, merchants and so on –

still own most of Ireland. They were content with law and order which came with English rule, were, as a result, loyal. The difficulty was that they were, almost entirely, Roman Catholics. The Protestants resented any favours or privileges extended to the idolaters, as they saw them. They wanted to take over their lands, rob them of any power. That's what they still want.

The Catholics can sit in Parliament and practise law, but the Protestants take every opportunity to denounce these rights. Falkland tried to steer a middle course hoping to get peace for all. He offered to be lenient with the Old English Catholics in return for some generous subsidies. The 'rights' he wanted to sell them for their money are called "the Graces." If they could prove sixty years' title to their land they could keep it. They could hold public office. They could practise their religion.

The New English, or Protestants, were appalled. Guaranteed land rights for Catholics would stop them stealing Catholic lands; they certainly didn't want 'Papal spawn' holding office under the Crown. Some of the richest, most powerful New English were members of the Irish Privy Council. They had no intention of letting Lord Deputy Falkland guide this sensible subsidy raising measure through the Council. This was another reason, Annesley proudly told me, why Falkland's return to ignominy in England was engineered.

In spite of the fact that Falkland lost his job while the Catholics have not had the benefit of his side of the bargain - to get the Graces legislated - I am told they are still paying the subsidies into the Treasury regularly. How can that sort of loyalty be sacrificed?

Perhaps he thinks I'm grateful to him for getting rid of Falkland, showing how Catholics should be dealt with. I am grateful, but not for that; I'm pleased he has shown me just how vital it is to prevent either side – Protestant or Catholic – from becoming more dominant than the Deputy. I shall have to work out a policy.

Annesley is not my only new contact who will be of use to me when I am in Ireland. William Railton is Clerk of the Privy Seal and Keeper of the Privy Council Chamber here in London. He agrees to be my messenger and agent, to help with business both public and private, to keep me informed. There is a gulf between him and Annesley: I trust Railton; I cannot say the same of Annesley.

Thomas. June, 1632. Great Houghton, Yorkshire

It is early summer, the weather glorious. I must confess that news of my promotion to Deputy in Ireland lifted my gloom to a considerable extent. And gloomy I have been since Arabella's death. She was such an angel. She made me feel so young, and I had to be young in outlook to keep up with our four children – well, four until Thomas died not long before she did. The other three, William, Ann, and little Arabella, miss her dreadfully. Dearest Arabella is only two, and by way of further confession I have to admit that I have so much business with the Council of the North, the Privy Council, all my own interests, I hardly know her. More importantly, she hardly knows me.

This means I cannot be much comfort to her, must seem like a stranger some of the time. I've been making an effort – not always successful – to be at home more, get home earlier so that I see them all before little Arabella's governess and the Nanny put them to bed. I find it dreadfully upsetting when Arabella rejects me, as she is so like her dear Mother. I want to love, be loved, more by all the children now my lovely wife is no longer here. Once or twice I've found myself on the verge of losing my temper with her, but have kept it at bay. Thank goodness I have, since I should only terrify her, making things infinitely worse. So I cuddle her when she lets me, we are beginning to play little games, and when William and Ann join in, she finds it much more fun. Six year old William and five year old Ann have a much better idea of what amuses a two year old than I do. I lack the spontaneity.

Unfortunately this attempt at domestic fatherhood cannot go on. I am commanded by the King to go to Ireland. Refusal of so great an honour is just impossible, even if that were my inclination. And it is not; far from it. There is hardly a greater honour in any of Charles's three kingdoms. He has plenty of loyal Dukes and other nobles in Scotland who would not welcome interference from an Englishman. The only higher position I can think of in England is to be one of the Secretaries of State, or Treasurer. Even so, in some ways the Deputy Lord Lieutenant of Ireland is the more important, as he is almost a King in his own realm. London is too far away, with the dangers of a sea to cross, for there to be much risk of detailed instructions from Whitehall Palace or Windsor Castle arriving on a regular basis. If I agree policies with the King, and follow them, I dare say I shall be left to my own devices in implementing them.

I shall have the Irish Treasury, the collection of customs duties and taxes under my control. I shall be commander of the Irish Army. I shall have every opportunity to advance the development of agriculture and industry there.

I cannot wait to get started, but I have been working to put my own affairs in order here in England, arranging a deputy to run the Council of the North for me. I must test Sir Edward Osborne, my Vice-President, a bit more; I have found him very loyal, reliable so far. Perhaps I can leave the Council to him.

Fortunately Christopher and George, who are available to accompany me to Dublin, will do whatever I ask. At last I shall have the chance to see they are properly rewarded for all they have done for me hitherto. But they are not the answer to my family problem, which is, put simply: how do I care sufficiently for the children? I have no intention of leaving them in Yorkshire. I could not bear to be without them. And there is something else. After ten years of happy marriage to Margaret, and seven years of an idyllic existence with Arabella, I am thoroughly miserable with no woman in my bed, no lady to grace my table, adding that undefinable magic a good wife brings to a happy home, rearing happy children. It was a challenge to find a replacement for either of my previous goddesses, but I think I have succeeded.

Today I am courting the very lovely daughter of Sir Godfrey Rodes. They are almost neighbours, living at Great Houghton, not very far from Wentworth. Her name is Elizabeth, she is twenty-five. I took the precaution of speaking to Sir Godfrey before embarking on what I hope might be a successful flirtation. I wanted him to know in advance that my intentions were honourable. In any case, the

Rodes family are fairly strict Puritans of very respectable repute; should I have made any advances to his daughter without his permission, he would very likely have refused consent to her marrying me on principle.

Let's be honest, though. I may be some years her senior, forty years old next year, but I am a Viscount, wealthy, and likely to be more so. I have powerful posts under the Crown, and about to take up another, even greater, in Ireland, which leaves the ones I already enjoy in the shade. I suspect Sir Godfrey sees a dynastic tie with the Wentworths as valuable, a feather in his cap, as well as a sure foundation for Elizabeth's security, if not her happiness. As to that, it will be up to me to make her happy, and I shall do my best. I have never had an unhappy home, having no intention of starting one now.

I was received graciously at lunch by Sir Edward and Lady Rodes, having spoken to him for an hour or two beforehand. He left me in the library for a while, went to ask his wife what she thought about having me for a son-in-law, which I thought rather unusual, but showed a lot of care for Elizabeth, that he reposed a lot of trust in her Mother. When he returned he was smiling, shook my hand, wished me luck in my suit.

So now Elizabeth and I are walking in the garden. She holds a pretty pink parasol as the sun is strong today, and she is rather fair. The top of her head comes up to my shoulder. She wears a pink striped dress to match the parasol. I have my hands clasped behind my back to avoid any risk that I may hold her arm or hand or do anything else untoward before I am as sure as I can be that it would be welcome. That is hard, as she really is rather pretty. We have passed the usual pleasantries at the table, but there has been rather a silence since we came out into this walk between tall, immaculately trimmed yew hedges.

Elizabeth breaks the ice. "And your children, My Lord, how are they?" as though continuing a subject of conversation, when in fact we had not touched on it.

Me. Well, thank you Madam, and I hope playing happily at home. But may we dispense with this formality? Did your father tell you why I have come? *(How could I make such a churlish start? Do I want to frighten her to death? Surely there are some occasions when I could abandon my blunt, plain speaking approach?)*

Elizabeth. *(Who is unabashed).* Yes My Lord; to ask for my hand in marriage.

Me. Your father has been kind enough to say he will consent to my suit if it - perhaps I should say if I - please you. That you please me is clear, for were it otherwise I should not be here. And this isn't my first visit.

Elizabeth. No, My Lord, we've been honoured to receive you here many times in the last few months, but I fear our modest household may not be what you are used to. As Lord President of the North you must be accustomed to the finest of everything, and far more than my parents can offer.

Me. They don't need to offer me anything but their warm family hospitality.

Elizabeth. My Lord, I know….

Me. Come, let us end this stately dancing. I'm a man and my name is Thomas; I want to marry you, and I want to call you Elizabeth. I want you to call me Thomas.

Elizabeth. Very well, I shall try to remember to call you Thomas, My Lord.

Me. *(I chuckle).* You need more practice, Elizabeth, but if you become my wife, practice you shall have.

Elizabeth. Yes My Lord - I mean Thomas. Here in Great Houghton - here in my father's house - we don't have many lords as guests. I'm a country-woman, with no real experience of Society.

Me. But in Ireland, as my wife, the wife of the Lord Deputy, you'll have much experience of Society. That is, if you would like it.

Elizabeth. I'm not sure that I should like it, Thomas. I fancy I'm not suited to pageantry and the bustle and swirl of a busy Court. We are puritans. My pleasure is more likely to be found in tending a quiet home, and doing what I can to see that my husband is keen on returning to it - and to me - as often as he can.

Me. Then you are an unusual young lady, my dear. Most of the women at Court cannot bear to be parted from it for an evening, unless that evening be spent in the arms of their latest lover. *(I wish I had not said that. She may be shocked. But she takes it in her stride and I admire her the more for that).*

Elizabeth. I have no taste for lovers, My Lo…, Thomas. And if I am to take on your children, and God willing, have some of my own, I shall be busy enough, and happy enough, running your household. I think you have three children; is it so?

Me. It is so. You've been making enquiry about me, Elizabeth? I'm flattered. Did you find out their names?

Elizabeth. *(She is embarrassed)*. My Lord, I….. In truth, you are a celebrity here in Yorkshire now, and our neighbours are anxious to talk. Your visits here have been the subject of much gossip. But it didn't concern your children, and I do not know their names.

Me. My son, William, is named after my father. The girls are Anne - we call her Nan - and Arabella. I see them less than I like. Carving a career in politics, perhaps in anything, is strange, Elizabeth. We say we are doing it for our children, for posterity, yet we venture forth in the name of fame and fortune and leave behind our little ones just at the time they need us most. It's a paradox. *(I pause a little)*. And for my children, whose mother is dead, it's doubly hard. My dear, I need a wife, but it would be wrong of me not to acknowledge that my children's need for a loving step-mother is a weighty factor in this courtship.

Elizabeth. I know Thomas, I know. If I can make the children happy, I shall. And if they are happy you will be too. Your happiness shall be my first concern, and if my happiness should be yours, what need would I have of lovers?

Me. My happiness shall be your first concern, Elizabeth? Does that mean that we are to be married?

Elizabeth. If you will be my lord, Thomas, then I shall be your lady.

Me. Then I am a fortunate man, and you, My Lady, need have no fears about the Lord Deputy's Court. You need never go there unless you want to; if domestic bliss is the happiness you seek, you will have it aplenty.

Elizabeth. I am content Thomas, and shall strive to make you so.

Me. Content? Dearest Elizabeth, you've done so much already. If only you knew how the thought of going alone to Ireland has been weighing on my mind! But now, with you, the prospect is an altogether sunnier one. Do you think you can bring some sunshine to Dublin?
Elizabeth. *(She laughs).* I shall try.
Me. Your smile will be sunshine enough. We'll have need of it. I'm told there's an Irish Bishop who constantly prays for rain. Who knows? Perhaps he spends too much time in his Cathedral to see what Irish weather is like. Perhaps he never goes out. But you and I, my darling, must go in, and I must tell your father of my good fortune.
Elizabeth. I shall not bring you a fortune, Thomas. My father is not rich, and neither his purse nor my taste will stomach an expensive wedding. I should prefer a modest family ceremony.
Me. As befits a modest lady, though in my eyes you have little to be modest about, and much to be proud of. As for money, I have more than enough, and if a large dowry were what I wanted, your father's house is not the place I should have come looking for it. You were - are - what I wanted, Elizabeth, and I shall ensure that you want for nothing.

We go into the house. As we do so, Elizabeth takes my arm, and smiles at me. The parents are delighted, it is clear that Lady Rodes is excited that Elizabeth has made a good match. Sir Godfrey makes it plain that Elizabeth will get a dowry of 1,000 pounds (more than I expected) and an annual allowance of a hundred pounds a year. She will also get her quiet wedding; in fact he wants it to be more or less a secret wedding. He is concerned that many will criticise me for marrying so soon after becoming a widower. He thinks she should remain out of the public eye until we are in Ireland, and I can see his point. Earl Clare and the rest of the Holles family have hardened their attitude towards me, being among those who say I killed Arabella. Preposterous, but I can do without scandal, and I'm sure Elizabeth would have no idea how to handle it.

Christopher Wandesford. September, 1632. York

Almost a year ago I was writing of attacks on Tom's efforts to reinforce the authority of the Crown and the Council in the North. Some really serious matters have been and still are affecting his efforts. First there is the Scot, Sir David Foulis. The second is Sir Thomas Leighton, who is Foulis's son-in-law. The third is Sir Thomas Gower.

Foulis, an important local landowner, used to have a position at Court, but quite what it was, I know not. Whatever it was it must have involved the handling of Royal Revenue, because some time ago he apparently managed to embezzle nearly 6,000 pounds, and bought an estate with it in Yorkshire, to which he retired. When his misconduct came to light, it seems he was afraid that Tom would pursue him with his customary vigour on behalf of the Crown. Foulis embarked on an attempt to create a smoke-screen round himself by alleging that Tom, too, was helping himself to the King's cash.

Tom had been commanded by the King to enforce the very old rules under which any man owning land yielding rents of forty pounds a year or more had to pay fees to the King instead of providing armed retainers, or make a bargain with the King by paying one large sum to cancel out that feudal duty, known as Knight-Service. Crazily, Foulis started telling his acquaintances that Tom was pocketing the money, and that the receipts they were given for the lump sums had no effect on their liability to go on paying the fees each year. There were many willing ears as the gentry did not care to have to make these payments.

Sir David's surname invites the quip that he was 'Foulis' to make these allegations, since he knew the business of collecting Royal revenues, even if he had found ways of avoiding the paperwork so that he could keep the money himself. He also badly misjudged Tom, who was scrupulous about such things as the law and the records. Indeed, one of my tasks was the supervision of the clerks who held the cash and entered up the books.

We reported the figures to Richard Weston, the Treasurer, on a regular basis, and Tom and I would have been as stupid as Sir David if we had tried to mislead him over their accuracy. After all, prior to Tom's appointment as President, the tally from these sources was pathetically small, and after his appointment, it rose dramatically. Why should Tom tell the Treasurer lies about his success if he did not hand over the money? Why should I cooperate in such a fraud knowing that if Tom fell, he would take me with him?

It was at this point that Sir David's son-in-law, Sir Thomas Leighton, became involved. He is the Sheriff of the county. One of his minions told him that some of the wealthy had not paid their knight-service dues. Tied in with what Sir David was saying, this fuelled the idea that Tom was stealing the money, because in fact the men in question had paid. These payments were recorded in my books.

Tom was angry. He summoned Leighton to appear before the Council, and he refused to come, on the advice of – hardly surprising, this – Sir David. Foulis told a crowd, including Leighton, at a banquet, that the Council of the North had no jurisdiction to command a Sheriff to appear before it. Tom was absolutely furious. His aim was, in accordance with the King's commands, to assert the power of the Council as a reflection of Royal authority, and the actions of Sir David and Leighton were a direct attack on that aim and, therefore, on the King.

Fortunately for Tom and Leighton something happened almost immediately that saved the situation for them to some extent, but not for Foulis. Leighton, as Sheriff, was ordered by the law courts to recover possession of a fortified manor house. The previous owner had sold it off to pay his debts, and then refused to leave. Leighton was forced to eat humble pie before the Council and seek Tom's help in evicting this man, who was so entrenched in his old home that the Sheriff had, with Tom's consent, to borrow the Council's cannon and troops to blast him out. Thus peace seems to have been restored between Tom and Sir David's son-in-law, if not with Sir David.

Foulis fled to Whitehall, and endeavoured to persuade the King that he was of such importance in the North that the King would do better to side with him than with his President. I helped Tom with a letter to the Monarch setting out his case.

Your Majesty,
I have been informed of the charges Sir David Foulis is levelling against me, and I deny them robustly. I have taken not a penny of what is due to you; the records make that

plain, and I have faithfully reported all monies received as knight service fees or settlements to the Treasurer, Sir Richard Weston.

If I may be so bold, Sire, I should point out that your authority will not be enhanced by taking back into your service one such as Sir David, who is well-known to have served your Treasury so falsely in the past. Rather than that, you should make him an example of your justice, by bringing him before the Law Courts. It is the only way to deal with the presumptuousness which is common these days, that every man is as good as the King, and entitled to challenge his power. I cannot abide this attitude.

It matters not if forty or more Foulises or Wentworths are swept away as long as Royal authority remains unblemished.

King Charles took no notice of Foulis. He was not taken in by this nasty, tiny 'gentleman'. He left it to Thomas to sue him for defamation in the Star Chamber.

The third attack on the Council started a few days ago. It was aimed at George Radcliffe.

Thomas. 25th October, 1632. Great Houghton

Today I married Elizabeth Rodes. We are staying at the house of her Father, Sir Godfrey, for a few days. The wedding was a very small, quiet affair, in accordance with his and Elizabeth's wishes. It was a happy day, but the start of what should have been happy matrimonial experiences in the bedroom did not materialise. Elizabeth seems to have some fear of love-making, and I did not find a way to release what I am sure is a passionate nature. I cannot bring myself to deal with that here at present. Perhaps I shall do so another time.

Even now I cannot go to Ireland yet. I still have details to settle at the Privy Council, the Council of the North, the arrangements for my own properties and business interests to finalise with Peter Man and Richard Marris. On top of that I cannot possibly leave with the Foulis and Gower cases unfinished.

George Radcliffe. 10th December, 1632. Wentworth Woodhouse

It is rather odd, in a way, that Thomas has become so friendly with William Laud. They do not quite see eye to eye about Church services, since William is very High Church (some say almost Catholic), and Thomas comes from a less theatrical religious tradition, although he is not exactly Low Church either. However, they have met a number of times at Privy Council meetings, and found that they have very similar views about supporting the authority of the King.

This has resulted in their corresponding a great deal about their policies for the country and the Church, and they seem to agree about almost everything. As I help Thomas with his business of all kinds, including Council and government matters, and write some letters for him, I get to see quite a lot of this correspondence. They call their policies "Thorough".

We have been working in his study on some of these letters today, but Thomas is in a strange mood. We heard this morning that Sir John Eliot died of consumption on 27th November in the Tower. He'd been sent there arbitrarily (illegally, some say) after a farce of a trial for the part he played when the Speaker was held in his chair in the Commons in 1629. The King hated him for his leading role in the failed attempt to impeach his friend Buckingham. His cell was as horribly damp as the one Thomas More ended up in before they removed his head. Receiving this news, Thomas laughed, saying: 'Thank God one obstacle's out of the King's way. And mine."

Then he became quiet and thoughtful for quite a while, and eventually said to me: "I'm rather ashamed of what I said just now. Eliot was a noble character, and stood up for what he believed in, even if it wasn't always what I believed in. For a long time we were on the same side. He was too hot-headed, even if he was a fantastic orator."

"Being in the Tower for three years must have cooled him off a bit."

"Well, he's dead cold now alright. He never did apologise to the King, which is what the Judges ordered him to do."

"There was a lot of ill feeling about his imprisonment, Thomas, and now he's dead it'll get worse."

"You may well be right." Thomas glances at the letter we had had from London, and looks back at me: "His family asked the King to move him to a better, drier, cell, and Charles refused. He wouldn't even let them have the body back to bury it!! He's supposed to have said: 'Let Sir John Eliot be buried in the church of the parish where he died'. So he was interred in the churchyard of the Tower. That does seem so mean, so petty, George."

"Yes, because it wasn't his wife or children who needed to be punished. People say the King has no heart."

"Some of the others who were arrested at the same time …"

I interrupt: "Like Denzil Holles?"

"No, George, I didn't mean him – he made an apology, paid his fine and was released. I meant others such as Strode and Valentine, who were involved in that assault on Speaker Finch three years ago. They are still in prison, and likely to be there for several years yet. It won't do the King any good at all."

"Speaking up about it won't do you any good, either, Thomas. You work for the King now."

Thomas smiles. "Then this talk must remain a secret between us, mustn't it? We live in dangerous times for public men." He pauses. "When he was young Eliot was very friendly with Buckingham. They travelled abroad and about the country together, and Buckingham made him Vice-Admiral of Devon."

Again I interrupt. "But it was as Vice-Admiral that he became disenchanted with his friend Villiers for the disasters at Cadiz and the Ile de Re, wasn't it?"

"Yes, George, quite right. Eliot has been in prison more than once. About ten years ago, as the Navy's top man in Devon, he made a plan to catch a notorious pirate called John Nutt …"

"Yes, I've heard of him. He plundered the South Coast for years and robbed merchant ships – even English ships – in the channel."

Thomas nods. "Well, Sir John caught Nutt, but he was a friend of George Calvert, who as you know was a friend of mine. Calvert persuaded King James to pardon Nutt, and for his pains poor old Eliot – well, not old; he was only about thirty then – went to prison for a few weeks on some trumped up charges. He was in the Marshalsea, where you and I were four years ago."

"As you say, Thomas, these are dangerous times for public men, and no-one is more public than you are becoming. Take care, because......"

There is a knock at the door, and Lady Wentworth comes in at once. As she shuts the door behind her I bow and say "Lady Wentworth." She begins to drop me a curtsey but Thomas rises from the desk, and puts a hand on each of our arms before she can speak. "Careful, George. Remember, this is not Lady Wentworth yet. That's why she knocks at the door." He winks. "This is the children's governess on probation to see if she is fit to come to Ireland with us. I asked you before to call her Elizabeth, and you, Elizabeth must, for the time being, call him Sir George."

"I'm sorry, Thomas, I forgot. It won't happen again." George actually blushes.

Elizabeth is amused. "And when the world knows I am Lady Wentworth, you must still call me Elizabeth, Sir."

"And you can forget the 'Sir' then, too. But forgive me, what did you want?"

"To give you both some important news. A messenger just came. He gave the message to me as he has to visit others in York, Halifax and Leeds as soon as he can."

"And the message, my dearest?"

"Frederick is dead; the husband of our King's sister Elizabeth is dead. He died, I gather, of a terrible fever on 29th November."

"And he had been so ill after that boating accident two or three years ago, when his son died. The King will be grieving for this loss." Thomas is thoughtful. "I must write to him expressing our sorrow. Charles Louis is now the claimant to the Palatinate, and he's still only a boy."

Thomas. 12th December, 1632. Wentworth Woodhouse

I am President of the Council of the North, and Deputy Lord Lieutenant of Ireland too. I keep repeating it, wondering if it is actually true. The latter is a post which has been the death knell of many a political career. I have to consider carefully how I should exercise the power this exalted post gives me, what I want to achieve.

It is a strange situation. I do not share Charles's contempt for Parliaments. Having been in both Houses in England, seeing the advantage of a well-managed legislature, that is what I intend to have in Ireland. The King has no idea how to manage the Lords and Commons. Like his Father before him, he thinks all he needs to do is tell them what he wants, it is their duty to give it to him, and he will get what he wants. I know that isn't how it works.

Even so, when he dissolved Parliament in 1629 I thought it a great opportunity to get things done if we could steer clear of war, as there would be no interference from politicians. With all power resting in the King, emanating from him, we could make England rich, prosperous. The King's service could become very efficient; the more efficient it was the more revenue could be collected; with more money more could be done for the people, for the administration of the country.

I do not know that my colleagues on the Privy Council see it like that. Except, perhaps, for William Laud, they just seem to be happy to make policy almost on a day-to-day basis, without any long-term plan, with no real care for the masses. William always knows where he is headed, and we are going in the same direction. For us the King and the Church stand or fall together; that was the paramount fact on which we worked - still is. It is the same in the King's mind, I am sure, but he sees no necessity to work towards that. He thinks that he embodies all of it, so that's the end of the matter.

Other Privy Councillors, like Weston the Treasurer, Francis Cottington, the Chancellor of the Exchequer, are very clever men, but the day-to-day routine, and making sure they keep their jobs, are enough for them, especially when they are getting richer. And they are. So am I, but money is not everything. I want power too, because it gives me the chance to do good.

We can't rely on the way things have been done before. We need to make the King's government live up to the power it enjoys but has for so long seemed unable to exercise successfully. Whilst the King has silenced Parliament, he has not silenced its members. Putting Eliot in the Tower might have shut some people up, but discontent continues to rumble throughout the land. If the actions the King takes are just and fair, aim at pleasing the people rather than negligently alienating them, a few years of going alone without Parliament could set the country on a safe course.

I don't fool myself that we could run the country for more than a few years without summoning the representatives of the people to Westminster. That would have to be done once the King's authority has been shown to work, and work well. If we could do that the people would put all the mistakes of the Buckingham era behind them. Most people live for today, do not seek revenge or harbour vendettas for what has gone wrong in the past. Memories are short. Once Parliament is called again, it would have to be managed. I manage the Council of the North; I know it could be done with the whole country. With God's help it will work.

Properly managed, Parliament could do what it was always intended to do: inform the King of the people's problems, offer solutions for him to consider, and put up the money to make the policies work. I would have to make sure that the two Houses did not make war on the King by withholding taxes to try to force him to do what they want. The King would have to listen, to correct all just complaints. What happened in 1628 was stupid. I did not go along with the Forced Loan, but I was against the sort of brawl with the King which took place then. There's a world of difference between freedom to think and say what you like whilst acting in a conscientious manner, and unrestricted licence to behave just as you please, ending up destroying everything that is worth preserving.

What do others think about this? Truly, I do not care. I'm sufficiently sure of my philosophy to pay little heed to their opinions of me. If they are rich, powerful, and opposed to my ideas for taking care of the greater part of the people, I should find ways to bring them into line, or bring them down.

To do all this I should need – the King needs – a loyal band of servants to implement our policies. He has nothing like enough, and too many are only interested in their own pockets. I think that my fellows in the Lords, as well as the gentlemen who are the backbone of the judiciary as Justices of the Peace, with all the functions the law and government impose upon them, will happily enforce the King's laws when they are seen to be fair, lead to stability, prosperity. I believe they will work as hard as I do. I believe that if the King's officials had adequate salaries so that bribery and corruption could be reduced, government would be more efficient, stronger.

In addition to all that, I should like nothing better than to be the King's friend as well as one of his ministers.

William Laud, Bishop of London. 18th January, 1633. Fulham Palace

To Thomas Wentworth, Viscount Newmarch.
My Lord,

I trust you are well, and had a good journey back to Yorkshire from our last Privy Council Meeting. I do not intend to make this a long epistle. To come immediately to the point, I have the unpalatable task of warning you that a rumour is circulating in the cities of London and Westminster that you have installed a pretty young woman at Wentworth, and that she accompanies you on some of your circuits in the North, sometimes at the Lord President's House in York, and on other occasions elsewhere.

You must not think that I tell you this in any prurient spirit of criticism or condemnation. I know not the truth of it, but as you are now not only President of the North, but must shortly take up your position in Ireland, it would ill become you to have any scandal the basis of which were true going the rounds. Of course, if this matter were true, you would appreciate that I, as a cleric, cannot approve.

Perhaps you would be good enough to let me know whether this gossip is true or false, so that I can defend you should the need arise. As you are aware the King is fairly straight laced, and might well not feel able to maintain you in office in the event of scandal.

I am your constant friend, and pray for you daily, as I do for the King and the rest of the Council.
William + Londiniensis.

Thomas. 2nd February, 1633. Wentworth

This letter is quite alarming. How these rumours germinate is quite beyond me. Or is it? One may well say "Not in front of the servants," but you do not actually have to do anything in front of them. They are not stupid. Elizabeth has not been living at Wentworth continually, but has spent several periods of two weeks or so at her parents. I have been telling anybody who enquires that she is visiting with a view to seeing whether she would be suitable as a governess for the children, should they like her. She has accompanied me on some of my duties, but only when we have taken the children. We go to bed and wake up in separate rooms, though we do not always spend all night in those rooms.

In the main this is due to our desire to follow her Father's wishes, keeping the marriage secret until we are in Dublin. However, it is partly due to the unfortunate, unhappy fact that we have been unable, so far, to establish a satisfactory conjugal relationship in bed. I think it will come, but at present I have to be patient, and am rather afraid of her attitude, as I have described earlier.

Now I shall send Laud this rather misleading but partially accurate tale of a young woman who is and is likely to be a companion to the children, and tell him the truth of it in private when I see him at the next Privy Council meeting. I sit at my desk penning a letter to him at once.

In the meanwhile, for her sake as well as mine, I have to send her away to avoid scandal growing out of control. I resolve to send her over to Dublin as soon as possible with the children, to await my arrival in a few months. That should reinforce the tale that she is governess to my children. We shall resume married life when I get there, making the marriage public.

I wish I could go too, but with all the litigation arising out of the Foulis and Gower cases on top of my political and business affairs, and the need to find people to take charge of them whilst I am in Ireland, I am simply not ready to do so. There's been that idiot Sheriff, Leighton, to deal with and the Gower case will probably go on for a year. Besides, I'm still advising the King as a member of his Privy Council; the advice of which he seems to take most notice comes from me, Laud, Weston the Treasurer, and Cottington, the Chancellor of the Exchequer.

Interestingly, I had always thought of Weston and Cottington as my friends, and I am sure it was through their influence with the King that I have the post of Deputy in Ireland, for which I am grateful. My gratitude was tarnished, rather, when Laud told me that he had reason to think that those two were wary of my relations with the King, jealous of the sudden rise in my fortunes at Court, putting my name forward for Ireland as a means of getting me out of the way, so that my influence with the King might be reduced. That is what the King wrote, too. Not for the first time I have been told that this post sentenced my predecessors, Grandison and Falkland, to oblivion. That, however, has not discouraged me.

Elizabeth. 3rd March, 1633. Dublin

It is miserable here, cold and damp, and no Thomas! Dublin may be the capital city of Ireland but it is a poor place compared with York. I arrived from England a few days ago. The journey from Wentworth to Chester wasn't bad, but the Irish Sea crossing was rough.

I'm in quite a nice house, but I think the Deputy and his family are expected to live in the Castle. Yesterday I went there with my new Irish maid, Kathleen, who is very pleasant indeed. She had been there before, which was useful. We were shown round by the Constable, a big beefy man with black hair and moustache. He was very attentive and seemed apologetic for the state of the place.

He pointed out that the East Wall, where there are no buildings, had not been repaired for so long it had partially fallen down. The main entrance to the Castle is on the North side with a draw-bridge, and there is a moat. He said part of it is the River Poddle. The walls would form a rectangle if they were all still standing, with a tower in each corner. The Deputy's House is against the South Wall and in its shadow, which is a shame as the sun shines – when and if it does –

from that side so the house never sees it. No wonder it is cold and damp.

I'm sure Thomas will be disturbed by the squalor all this creates. I must write and warn him of it. He's rather fastidious and likes everything to be in order, as it is at home. He will be furious that the repairs he ordered are so slow in being carried out.

Charles I. 14th March, 1633. Windsor

A week ago I promulgated a new Commission for the Council of the North. I have been impressed with the manner in which Wentworth has restored its power and authority, and felt it only right to give the Council some firm guidance on how it should proceed from now on, freeing it from interference from the Courts in London. There is little point in having a body in the North charged with looking after that region on my behalf, and then having every important decision it takes challenged in King's Bench or some other Court by an Earl or Baron who thinks the law doesn't apply to him. I know how King John must have felt.

Those whom Wentworth calls "the proud and insolent" love the law to control others, but have no desire to be under any sort of control themselves.

Despite such problems, my four years or so of non-parliamentary government seem to have been rather successful, if I say so myself, even if I cannot claim all the credit. I have made peace with Spain and France. Peace with Spain has brought an ingenious trade agreement engineered at the Exchequer by Cottington, my Chancellor. I shall have to give him some sort of title soon, I dare say. And Weston, the Treasurer too, I suppose. This trade agreement brings in a great deal of Spanish gold and silver so that the mint is churning out coins at a great rate.

Somehow this facilitates commerce, but I do not pretend to understand how. It suffices for me to know my Kingdom and my people are getting richer, since I benefit too. How is that? Well, on every pound of bullion that is minted the Treasury gets a percentage. With the extra income from that and no wars to bleed the coffers dry, I am just able to make ends meet, and run the country at least as well as if Parliament were paying the paltry amounts it used to allow me. I use the word 'allow' advisedly since that is how it always seemed to me; just like a poor widow going to the Poor Law Magistrates to ask for a pittance for food or clothes.

My sister Elizabeth is a fairly poor widow herself now. Frederick, her husband, was a victim of the plague some months ago, so I send her and her children what I can afford, but there is no question of my going to war with the Emperor or anyone else for her sake. I simply do not have the money, I still have no army, and the people would not pay to support an army in Europe even if I did. It is the old story; they say they want to fight to put Elizabeth and my nephews back on the thrones of the Palatinate and Bohemia, but they do not want it to cost them anything.

Things looked much brighter for Frederick and Elizabeth eighteen months ago when the King of Sweden, Gustavus Adolphus, was winning battle after battle on the Protestant side, but then he was killed in combat last year. Now Spain and Austria are doing all the winning again.

The fact that England is not in this fray is excellent for trade, I am told, and that increases my income from Tunnage and Poundage. We are neutral, in effect, English merchants trading with both sides. I recall that Wentworth was always against war, particularly with Spain. Perhaps I should have listened to his counsel – and Weston's – earlier. I cannot forgive his part in hounding Buckingham, but I should be foolish not to recognise that George's desire to fight Spain and France did no end of harm to my relations with Parliament, let alone the Crown's finances.

However, I must also thank God that I am His instrument for the government of England, Scotland, Wales, and Ireland, that He has blessed these Kingdoms with peace, and prosperity, and the North with better administration, a more cultured and less tribal approach to life. I am fortunate that Wentworth plays his part in all this, and that I have had the sense to employ him.

Nevertheless, he is a man of such energy and ability he worries me. These great virtues might make a King more afraid than ashamed to employ him in the mighty affairs of state.

Thomas. 20th March, 1633. London

I'm at Westminster for the Privy Council. Elizabeth is not with me. She is in Dublin now. I sent her there with the children and my young brother George. I could not have brought her here anyway, as I still seek to keep our union secret for the time being, but I have told William Laud the truth of it. He was mightily relieved. He is not one of those clerics who tells his flock to be moral but whose private life is more like a follower of Satan. He works hard at his Christianity, but is intolerant of denominations other than his own brand of Church of England. That is his major fault. Happily I have a letter from Bess which came today.

Dearest Thomas,

Thank you for your lovely letter. It cheered me up.

I miss you terribly, and the Castle is horrid; so cold at this time of year, and damp. You told me you had ordered repairs to be carried out a year ago, but even I can see so much needed to be done the builders have hardly scraped the surface of it. Some of the Castle walls have actually fallen down, and have not yet been rebuilt. At least the Hall and other more official parts of the place are functional now, and are being decorated.

Fortunately a Mr Hall came to see me. He said he was your agent for getting the repairs done, and you had told him to prepare accommodation for me in a house at Killmaignham. It's much more comfortable there. I think it will be some time before the Castle is fit to live in. The Manor at Wentworth and my Father's house are not too large, and feel like homes. I'm not sure Dublin Castle will ever feel like that.

It was not a good journey here, for William and I were sea-sick, but luckily Nan and Arabella were not. I'm very busy settling in and getting used to the servants. I shall write again as soon as I have time.

I love you, my dear Thomas, and long to see you again. Bess.

Today I am shown that the King does truly appreciate what I am doing in the North. He has issued a new

Commission with a set of instructions for the Council of the North; these make it clear that my Council – well, his really – is every bit as important and powerful as the Star Chamber. I regret that I shall not be in York to enjoy directly these new powers, but I can rely on Osborne to use them wisely, to write to me for guidance where he needs it. He is very loyal, reliable, and clever.

This new Commission is not something unusual. When a new President is appointed a new Commission is issued for his guidance. What is unusual here is the extension of the powers of the Council.

Thomas. 30th March, 1633. Westminster

Dear Bess,

I was so relieved to get your letter saying that you had arrived safely in Dublin, despite a bad crossing. I'm sorry you were sick. I was also pleased that my letter was waiting for you. I wrote it a couple of days after you left. This will be a rather short one as I have to pen some letters to Christopher and brother George giving them directions about some of the things I want them to attend to. I hope they are looking after you, and that you are not having any trouble with the servants who are so new to you. The fact that the work on the Castle is not yet complete, that in consequence you were uncomfortable, is distressing to me. I shall take steps to expedite the repairs as soon as I am with you.

How are you getting on with the children, and how are they?

I'm both glad and sad that you miss me. I miss you too. I am glad because you would not miss me if you cared little, and I'm sad to think that you may not be as happy as you usually seem. Marriage is many things, but companionship and fellowship are in the end the most important. Marriage ought to carry with it more of love and equality than anything else that there might be to worry about. I desire that it may ever be thus between us, nor shall it ever break of my part. Having said which, I must again apologise for having had to 'break' us apart by sending you away so soon after we were married. You may rest content that I shall never do that again if it is in my power to stop it.

Last night I was at dinner with Henry and Frances Clifford. Some of the ladies were very lovely and scandalously dressed - but not Frances. I should very much like to see you dressed in such a way, but only for my eyes, and in utter seclusion. I hope to be doing so in two or three months. Waiting is hard work.
Your loving,
Thomas.

Elizabeth. 10th April, 1633. Dublin Castle

My Dear Thomas,

Your sweet letter was delivered this morning. It was dated 30th March, so it has taken almost two weeks to get here. I know I say it in all my letters but I do love you and miss you. Having your letters and your news always cheers me up. The fact that they start "Dear Bess" is cheering in itself. Do you remember how, before we were married, you used to start your letters to me "Dear Madam"? I have *never told you before how that used to make me laugh; I know most men think women are silly, but I was not blind to the possibility that you might be coming to our house with a view to courtship. I thought it an odd way to address someone with a view to affection!!*

Talking of affection, and as you ask about the children, I am pleased to say they seem to be quite fond of me now. I think the fact they are young helps. William is a bit shy with me but he is very good, and does what I tell him nearly all the time. Anne is a bit more difficult, but she is old enough to remember Arabella and finds it a bit more difficult to adapt to me. Little Arabella hardly recalls her mother at all, so she is the easiest. She calls me Mummy or Mother, so the other two are starting to do so. She is also quite a strong character and can be a bit naughty at times.

When she is I find it hard to play the wicked step-mother and smack her; as governess I should have no qualms about that. Fortunately I am just a pretend governess, but if the children all call me 'Mummy', soon it will be hard to keep up that pretence. It is very wet here so the children cannot go out to play, but they are all very well.

I hope we shall have one or two of our own one day. As you are in Yorkshire or London and I am over here that is more than a bit difficult at the moment! You never complain, but I think that you feel there is something missing in our lovemaking. I do hope that it will be better when you are here. It made me so happy to read that you hope to be here in the next two or three months.

I was amused by what you told me about the ladies at Henry and Frances Clifford's dinner. As a good puritan girl I suppose I should be shocked, and even jealous, but you wrote so wittily that I knew you could not be serious about any of them (I hope). Happily I do not think there are many ladies here to take your fancy, though my handsome husband may take theirs. If there any beauties, I have yet to see them, but then, as you know, I do not go out much.

Please come to Dublin in two months, or even one, and certainly not in three. But that is selfish, since I know you have so much to do.

I must go and put the children to bed, or at any rate Arabella. I send them up at one hour intervals. I don't think it fair to put them all to bed at the same time. If I do, either William goes to bed too soon, or Arabella is up too late. What do you think?

You poke fun at me as I didn't sign my last letter to you. I shall not forget this time.
Your loving Bess.

Thomas. 17th April, 1633. London

I am still in town. For the last year or more, I've been trying to learn all I can about government in Ireland, about its finances. Both clearly need a great deal of reform. Mountnorris has given me a lot of help. One of the main money problems is the Irish customs farm. No; this is not an agricultural project for growing cash. It is a method of farming the collection of the customs and taxes out to a group of wealthy men who pay a lump sum to the King every year for the privilege of gathering in the revenue. On top of the lump sum, they have to pay the costs of collection. They pay the King half of the extra they collect over and above those sums, and they keep the other half. This saves the King the expense of employing people to do the work for him, and those people would not work so hard at it as the ones who aim to make a profit.

Even so, the system is hopelessly inefficient. In 1618, when George Villiers had established himself as King James's blue-eyed boy, the whole Irish customs farm was given to him - having been taken from a group which included Arthur Ingram - for 6,000 per annum, plus half the profits. Buckingham was to have it until 1628, but the King extended it so he got it until 1635 and, would you believe it, with no provision to increase the lump sum.

Then Buckingham was assassinated in 1628, and the farm went to his widow. She went on paying the King (now Charles) 6000 plus half the profits. Like her husband, the late Duke, the Duchess used agents in Ireland to do the work for her.

I was appointed Deputy Lord Lieutenant of Ireland in mid-1631, and shortly after that a new Book of Rates for the customs was brought out, which raised the amount of revenue which could be collected. The same thing had been done in England a few years earlier. I do not claim that the Book was my work. At the same time the men who worked for the Duchess were got rid of, a new group took over, including, as you might expect, Sir Arthur again, with a man called Cogan, and also George Radcliffe and Mountnorris.

Even though I was not yet in Ireland I strove to ensure that the customs were properly collected and accounted for. The new men had to pay the King 8,000 pounds to take up the farm, and 15,000 pounds a year plus half the profits. The farmers had to pay the Duchess a pension, but they still made a profit for themselves of about 5,000 this last year. The

King got his 15,000 plus his half of the extra, another 11,000. Everyone did very nicely, thank you.

Elizabeth. Dublin Castle. 3rd May 1633

Dearest Thomas,

I must tell you something quite extraordinary. As you know, we usually go to Divine Service here in the Castle Chapel, but this morning I went with the Wandesfords to St Patrick's Cathedral.

Behind the altar is one of the ugliest things I have ever seen. It is like an extremely crude Roman frieze, not beautifully carved, as they are, but as if it had been moulded out of clay or something. It also bore the most appalling colours, mainly reds and browns. After the service we asked the verger or sacristan what it might be. He said it is a monumental tomb for the late Countess of Cork.

It dominates the place so much it is difficult to remember that if we focus on anything it should be Jesus and the cross on the altar, not a memorial to a lady, even if she had been great and good. When you are here, I do hope you will be able to do something about it. I should not take it kindly if you had such a 'tribute' to me erected in such a place.

Please come to me soon. All my love, and the children send theirs.
Elizabeth.

Thomas. 3rd July, 1633. Wentworth Woodhouse

Your Majesty,

Strafford

Once again I must express my humble thanks for the honour and great opportunity you have granted me in sending me as your Deputy to Ireland.

I desire above all else to make Ireland a good source of revenue for the Crown, and the only way to do so is by fostering commerce, and introducing more manufacturing. By doing so I hope to leave your Irish subjects happier than I expect to find them, but I shall do nothing to prejudice those in England.

I plan to take advantage of the Spanish navy's need for a place to stop for supplies of food and water. It is a lucrative trade. There are other schemes of which I shall make a trial, informing you as they come to pass.

However none of this can work and revenue cannot be increased without your Royal authority being enhanced by a stable administration. There are many powerful nobles there whose only interest is in their own private ends. They don't give a fig for the public good. I intend to call them to heel by very firm government and by bringing unbiased justice to all, rich or poor.

If I fail to make you, Sire, a more absolute master of your Irish Kingdom than any of your forbears, it will not be for want of trying. In this I must endeavour to knit the differing sections of this strange society into a quieter unity. If I succeed in these aims – and I do not intend to fail – the opportunity, the means to supply your wants are there. I know you will not begrudge your humble servant some profit he may gain. However, unlike some, I shall not place my own interests above yours.
I am, Sire, your loyal and grateful Deputy,
Wentworth.

Francis Bacon wrote: "All rising to Great Place is by a Winding Stair". Indeed; but have I reached the top of mine? I leave for Ireland on the morrow. What will transpire when I reach Dublin?

Acknowledgements

The portrait used for the cover of this book shows "Thomas, Viscount Wentworth, later 1st Earl of Strafford, and his Hound," by Sir Anthony Van Dyck. For its use I am indebted to the Trustees of the Rt. Hon Olive, Countess Fitzwilliam's Chattels Settlement, by Permission of the late Lady Juliet Tadgell.

At Sir Walter St John's Grammar School, Battersea, England, I had one particularly good history teacher, Johnny Walker. Under him I studied 17th Century history. I was entranced by Strafford. At that time (1958-1961) he had usually been written up as a hero and a martyr as did C.V.Wedgwood, which I read. In 1961 C.V.Wedgwood revised her original biography of Wentworth following H.F.Kearney's book, "Strafford in Ireland," and J.P.Cooper's study "The Fortune of Thomas Wentworth Earl of Strafford." I am greatly indebted to those works. I also read Miss Wedgwood's books, "The King's Peace," "The King's War" and "The Thirty Years War."

I also used: Trevor-Roper's "Archbishop Laud", Upton's :Sir Arthur Ingram", McElwee's "England's Precedence," Watson's "The Life and Times of Charles I," and Mackie's "A History of Scotland," a copy of the transcript of the trial of Strafford from the British Library, copies of original documents from Sheffield City Library, and Wikipedia with regard to many of the characters. I obtained a copy of an old memoir about Sir John Reresby, and of what is believed to be Wentworth's own account of the 1621 Parliament in which he sat.

This novel started life in the first place as a play; James Hogan of Oberon Books gave me some help with dialogue, as did Peter Matheson, the Australian dramaturge.

The staff of the Wingham Library, New South Wales, Australia, and their colleagues in the Taree branch, tracked down all sorts of books and articles for me, including Rushworth's very full account of the trial published in 1700. I had help from Jennifer Allison, Town Guide of Northallerton, Yorks, the Staffordshire Record Office, The National Gallery of Ireland, William Derham at Dublin Castle, Liz Street at The National Gallery of Ireland, and Tim Kneble at Sheffield City Library.

I cannot claim that this work is totally accurate, because many of the authorities on which I relied do not make it plain when some events occurred, and without the help I have had, the errors would have been legion. Even great historians leave out dates, and divide their story into separate topics, making piecing together the sequence of events almost impossible. In any case, this book is fiction. Further, in Strafford's time an old calendar was used which started the year on 1st April, rather than 1st January. I have used today's calendar.

I thank my son Tim and my daughter Katherine, my friends Peter and Philippa Cocks, Joe Shevlin, Eric Blyth, Jean Burden, Phil Hewitt, journalist and author, and my cousin Loretta for all their help with the first drafts when this was published as a one volume tome of enormous weight. Its title was 'Deliver me from Evil'.

The guide staff of Wentworth Woodhouse gave my wife and me a truly entrancing tour in 2017 before the Trust which now runs it had started on the magnificent restoration.

My readers would find a visit to this magnificent stately home very rewarding. Being able to see part of the original late Tudor part of the building in which Thomas grew up and still lived in when he was 'at home' was, for me, rather exciting. In the late 17th and early 18th centuries it was completely swallowed up by the enormous but extremely beautiful structure built by the Watson-Wentworth family, which is the structure one sees today.

Michael Davies of the Mickie Dalton Foundation edited, formatted, and published the original book and this trilogy with great skill, and incredible expedition. His help was and is invaluable.

Finally, I thank my wife, Christine, for her patience during the hours I have spent researching and writing, and for reading and helping me correct the book.

I dedicate the book to her.

Terry Stanton.
Port Macquarie, Australia.
October, 2025.

www.ingramcontent.com/pod-product-compliance
Lightning Source LLC
Chambersburg PA
CBHW071950070526
44583CB00015B/1137